INVENTING
THE CHILD

Culture, Ideology, and the Story of Childhood

Children's Literature and Culture

Jack Zipes, *Series Editor*

Children's Literature
Comes of Age
Toward a New Aesthetic
by Maria Nikolajeva

Rediscoveries in
Children's Literature
by Suzanne Rahn

Regendering the
School Story
*Sassy Sissies and
Tattling Tomboys*
by Beverly Lyon Clark

White Supremacy in
Children's Literature
*Characterizations of African
Americans, 1830–1900*
by Donnarae MacCann

Retelling Stories,
Framing Culture
*Traditional Story
and Metanarratives
in Children's Literature*
by John Stephens and
Robyn McCallum

The Case of Peter Rabbit
*Changing Conditions
of Literature for Children*
by Margaret Mackey

Voices of the Other
*Children's Literature and the
Postcolonial Context*
edited by Roderick McGillis

Empire's Children
*Empire and Imperialism in
Classic British Children's Books*
by M. Daphne Kutzer

A Necessary Fantasy?
*The Heroic Figure in
Children's Popular Culture*
edited by Dudley Jones and
Tony Watkins

Little Women and
the Feminist Imagination
*Criticism, Controversy,
Personal Essays*
edited by Janice M. Alberghene
and Beverly Lyon Clark

Ideologies of Identity
in Adolescent Fiction
by Robyn McCallum

Narrating Africa
*George Henty and
the Fiction of Empire*
by Mawuena Kossi Logan

Transcending Boundaries
*Writing for a Dual Audience of
Children and Adults*
edited by Sandra L. Beckett

Children's Films
History, Ideology, Pedagogy, Theory
by Ian Wojcik-Andrews

Russell Hoban/Forty Years
*Essays on His Writings for
Children*
by Alida Allison

Translating for Children
by Riitta Oittinen

The Presence of the Past
*Memory, Heritage, and Childhood in
Postwar Britain*
by Valerie Krips

Inventing the Child
*Culture, Ideology, and the Story
of Childhood*
by Joseph L. Zornado

INVENTING THE CHILD

Culture, Ideology, and the Story of Childhood

Joseph L. Zornado

Routledge
Taylor & Francis Group
New York   London

Routledge is an imprint of the
Taylor & Francis Group, an informa business

First paperback edition published in 2006 by Routledge.

Published in 2006 by
Routledge
Taylor & Francis Group
270 Madison Avenue
New York, NY 10016

Published in Great Britain by
Routledge
Taylor & Francis Group
2 Park Square
Milton Park, Abingdon
Oxon OX14 4RN

Printed in the United States of America on acid-free paper
10 9 8 7 6 5 4 3 2 1

International Standard Book Number-10: 0-415-97966-8 (Softcover) 0-8153-3524-5 (Hardcover)
International Standard Book Number-13: 978-0-415-97966-5 (Softcover) 978-0-8153-3524-5 (Hardcover)
Library of Congress Card Number 00-039338

Library of Congress Cataloging-in-Publication Data

Zornado, Joseph L.
    Inventing the child : culture, ideology, and the story of childhood by Joseph L. Zornado.
        p. cm. -- (Garland reference library of the humanities ; v. 2185. Children's literature and culture ; v. 17)
    Includes bibliographical references and index.
    ISBN 0-8153-3524-5 (alk. paper) ISBN 0-415-97966-8 (softcover)
    1. Children--Social conditions. 2. Children and adults. 3. Parent and child. I. Title. II. Garland reference library of the humanities ; vol. 2185. III. Garland reference library of the humanities. Children's literature and culture ; v. 17.

HQ767.9.Z67 2000
305.23--dc21   00-039338

Taylor & Francis Group
is the Academic Division of Informa plc.

Visit the Taylor & Francis Web site at
http://www.taylorandfrancis.com

and the Routledge Web site at
http://www.routledge-ny.com

To Emily, Clara, and Jack

Contents

Series Editor's Foreword   ix
Acknowledgments   xi
Introduction   xiii

CHAPTER 1   History as Human Relationship   1

CHAPTER 2   Freud, Shakespeare, and *Hamlet* as Children's Literature   33

CHAPTER 3   The Brothers Grimm, the Black Pedagogy, and the Roots of Fascist Culture   71

CHAPTER 4   Victorian Imperialism and the Golden Age of Children's Literature   101

CHAPTER 5   Walt Disney, Ideological Transposition, and the Child   135

CHAPTER 6   Maurice Sendak and the Detachment Child   171

CHAPTER 7   Conclusion: The Etiology of Consumerism   201

Bibliography   223
Index   231

Series Editor's Foreword

Dedicated to furthering original research in children's literature and culture, the Children's Literature and Culture series includes monographs on individual authors and illustrators, historical examinations of different periods, literary analyses of genres, and comparative studies on literature and the mass media. The series is international in scope and is intended to encourage innovative research in children's literature with a focus on interdisciplinary methodology.

Children's literature and culture are understood in the broadest sense of the term children to encompass the period of childhood up through adolescence. Owing to the fact that the notion of childhood has changed so much since the origination of children's literature, this Garland series is particularly concerned with transformations in children's culture and how they have affected the representation and socialization of children. While the emphasis of the series is on children's literature, all types of studies that deal with children's radio, film, television, and art are included in an endeavor to grasp the aesthetics and values of children's culture. Not only have there been momentous changes in children's culture in the last fifty years, but there have been radical shifts in the scholarship that deals with these changes. In this regard, the goal of the Children's Literature and Culture series is to enhance research in this field and, at the same time, point to new directions that bring together the best scholarly work throughout the world.

Jack Zipes

Acknowledgments

I am indebted to teachers, students, and friends who have taught me. You are too numerous to name. I owe a special thank you to those who said just the right thing at just the right time, especially A. John Roche, Maurice Sendak, Jack Zipes, Daniel Quinn, Russell Potter, Richard Feldstein, David Wasser, Jon Hauss, and Jerry Griswold. Thanks go as well to Hannah Barr, Kathryn Kalinak, and Bennet Peji for carrying some of the load. Thank you to my parents, Robert and Josephine Zornado, without whose support this work could not have been completed. A loud and uproarious thank you to dear friends Jason Mauro and Jonathan Wagner, who listened to endless versions of this story and helped me find the one I wanted to tell, and thank you to Walter Van Sambeck for teaching so much with so few words. Finally to Lori Zornado, wife, partner, and muse, my thank you must say more than it can. Her gracious support and kind patience fill my story.

Introduction

*Feelings that are not repressed, that are instead
consciously experienced, never kill anyone.*

—ALICE MILLER, *The Drama of the Gifted Child*

When Eric Harris and Dylan Klebold shot thirty-six of their Columbine High
School classmates, they killed thirteen and wounded twenty-three. The killers
finished their brief reign of terror by shooting themselves. For a moment an
entire culture was silenced. Almost everyone gasped in horror and wanted to
know how such explosive violence could happen among adolescents. Struggling with the relational significance of the massacre, the dominant culture
made quasi-celebrities of the victims' parents, siblings, and friends, martyrs
of the dead, and monsters of the killers.

Yet, even as the media descended on Littleton, Colorado, in April 1999,
the story of Columbine had already been written long before. The enraged,
murderous actions of Eric Harris and Dylan Klebold manifested clearly the
story sold to children every single day. The lived relationship between the
adult and the child—and so between siblings as well—is the story of hierarchy, buried rage, domination, subjugation, violence, and an all-consuming
drive for power, even if it means the destruction of self and other. When cast
in this light, Columbine appears as a microcosm of American Cold War policy that promised the "American way" to all on the tip of a nuclear warhead.
The question remains, however: How does something so broad and
ephemeral as foreign policy or a culture's ideology inform the actual lived
relationships between individuals? It is the question that informs this book.

We came face-to-face with ourselves in Littleton and witnessed, as if for
the first time, the fruits of the dominant ideology in the behavior of two
teenage murderers. Part of the trauma for observers was the fact that as

shocking and insensible an event as Columbine seemed to be, we knew, or at least we had the opportunity to recognize, that the killers, the wounded, and the dead were our children. None are monsters, or if some are, then we *all* are. This is a difficult pill to swallow, so we allow and even participate in the media's making monsters of two young boys, themselves victims, who took their victimization out on the "other" wherever and whenever they found it on April 20, 1999—and they found the other everywhere they looked.

In this book I offer a way of seeing Columbine as well as countless other ordinary expressions of violence as a symptom of an adult culture long gone blind to the child and the child's most basic biological and emotional needs. The consequences, I argue, are profound and far-reaching. Each chapter in this book offers stories of childhood, history, and family and familiar children's stories that combine to tell a larger cultural story of violence and the misuse of power that proceeds virtually unchecked in spite of the dominant ideology's celebration of progress and technology. For some it may come as a monolithic story that defies the current sensibilities of an age dedicated to fragmentation and postmodern multiplicity. Yet even the postmodern intellectual perspective remains caught up in an ideology of obfuscation that blinds even the brightest scholar to the most obvious truth: there remains a master narrative to the story of childhood that continues to play out in and through the dominant culture, through the stories the culture tells about itself to itself and through the lived relations that result between the adult and the child.

To foreground the latent story of childhood—and I have managed only to sketch its basic outline in the following chapters—I use terms such as *ideology*, *culture*, and the *unconscious* along with various interpretive strategies that attempt a thick description of history, culture, ideology, and literary production. My method of interpretation makes no distinctions among received histories, children's stories, and the literary expressions of child-rearing traditions. All are texts and as texts they are cultural manifestations that, more than anything else, tell a story that directly and indirectly speaks to the nature and nurture of human relationships at the time of literary production. The author, in other words, learns the unconscious, ambient ideology of his or her era first and foremost at the hands of the adult world and the relationships the child is forced to participate in. The adult's physical and emotional domination of the child—often justified by a belief in the child's congenital need for reform—characterizes the childhood experience of Western culture. At the center of this study is not child abuse per se but rather the psychodynamic affects of ordinary and ambient child-rearing ideology as a mechanism for the reproduction of the dominant culture. The historical frame of reference of this study begins in 1564 and ends in 1999, even though the story of adult domination and child subjugation is age-old.

I chose the authors and texts I discuss in this book for their familiarity, to demonstrate the way in which a dominant ideology is unconsciously transmitted generationally through the most ordinary child-rearing practices. Stories of childhood, stories of human relationship, and stories of power thus become difficult to distinguish one from another, except as the dominant culture defines one—say, the picture book—as "innocent" and for the child and the other—such as *Hamlet*—"serious" and for the adult. Nevertheless, the picture book, or a Disney movie, draws on the same psychodynamic process by which mind and culture inform one another, and the literary text, whether for children or no, is an expression of this meeting and a reproduction of both. This is my point in reading Hamlet as a family psychodrama and a kind of children's literature, for although it has been argued that childhood did not exist in Shakespeare's England, relations of power and violence between the adult and the child certainly did. The *political* text, in other words, is always already a personal story of family and, as such, an indirect and latent story of the child's relationship to the adult. If there is a difference between say, *Hamlet* and *The Lion King* it is the awareness the authors invite their audience into. Shakespeare serves the status quo even as he questions it. Disney, on the other hand, reproduces the status quo as a reactionary gesture coded as "kid stuff" and movie fun. This is not to say that so-called adult literature always invites the reader's awareness; this is obviously not true. So too, for most children's stories. The vast majority of children's stories invite the child to identify with the adult's idea of what the child should be, leaving unquestioned the authority structure of adult and child always implied in the text and by the adult's reading the story to the child. Children's stories, in other words, are more often than not adult propaganda that serves to confirm for the child the hierarchical relationship between the adult and the child. They, in effect, reproduce the dominant culture's ideological status quo by confirming the macrostructure of the dominant culture's relationship to itself and to others in the mircostructure of the relationship between the adult and the child. Hierarchies of superiority and inferiority are implicit between the adult and the child, and the dominant ideology offers unconscious justifications that then justify the conscious use of subtle and chronic displays of power and violence often coded as the adult's love for the child. I take up all of this in some detail in the following chapters.

I draw on Louis Althusser, Antonio Gramsci, Raymond Williams, Theodor Adorno, Max Horkheimer, Terry Eagleton, Sacvan Bercovitch, Daniel Quinn, Jean Liedloff, Alice Miller, Louise Kaplan, and Fredric Jameson, among others, to explore how ideology invents the cognitive tools we use to contact our surroundings and so invents the surroundings even as we contact them. Our surroundings make sense only in and through ideology. Or, rather, when I explore what I take to be reality, I am in fact exploring the ideological nature of my own mind; I find there an oppressor and an oppressed, and so when I seek contact with the "external" world I find there the same dualistic structure of oppressor and oppressed. In short, when I explore the nature of my mind, I explore the nature of my *nurture*. Because I project my mind and its structure onto the world, it is not an absolute necessity that I project and so create a predatory hierarchy in the "external" world. Rather, the predatory hierarchy between races and genders, and between the adult and the child, is a symptom of our ideologically determined condition.

The terms *dominant ideology* and *dominant culture* should be explained, because I use them throughout, and though I am indebted to other scholars for my understanding, I use the terms in particular ways. For me the dominant ideology is the shared, unconscious experience of the obviousness and givenness of the individual's relationship to herself and to others. Though ideology may determine the nature of the lived relations that manifest ideology, the dominant ideology reproduces the specific structure of the relationship between the child and the adult along fairly predictable lines—so predictable, in fact, that the child's often unruly behavior within the adult's relational structure is frequently mistaken for the consequences of human nature rather than the effects of human nurture. I use the term *dominant ideology* to signify that although ideology is a broad, all-inclusive concept, the notion of a dominant ideology suggests that there is a particular ideology that reproduces the relational domination of the child by the adult and, by extension, the unconscious, shared mind of a culture.

For example, the dominant ideology from the child's perspective is always already defined by the ambient nature of the adult world. As an exquisitely aware being, the infant comes into the world and is almost always greeted by an institutional hierarchy that immediately represents to the infant the nature of the lived relationship as an event of power and control and so lays the ideological and pedagogical foundation for his psychodynamic development. The dominant ideology, then, is a particular story about human relationships that is unconscious and so remains largely unavailable to the adult even as it informs the adult's relational pedagogy. The dominant ideology is intimately related to the dominant culture, and the way in which I understand the two concepts to interact should be explained briefly. Consider the seldom-questioned conventions of hospital births, bottle feeding, baby cribs, and day care as ideologically driven cultural practices that have a decided—though often unrecognized—impact on the child's sense of well-being. The dominant culture enacts its unconscious ideology in the form of child-rearing pedagogy that makes manifest the dominant story of the relationship between the adult and the child as it is lived out in relationships. The dominant culture, then, is adhered to by the most powerful and influential people through whom a culture's values and beliefs about itself are reproduced, for example, its public schools and entertainment media. It should be noted that though the dominant culture may be consciously resisted by some, the ideology that informs the resistance to the status quo is nevertheless itself informed and even determined by the nature of the lived relations among a majority of people.

In this way, the rich and the poor, the weak and the strong, and the powerful and the marginalized unconsciously share and participate in the dominant ideology. How can this be? Because regardless of race, class, or gender, each individual was first a child in the dominant culture, and though the child may grow into an adult who resists the dominant culture, the adult's developing self was structured according to the dominant child-rearing pedagogy of adult culture. In other words, though we might not all share and practice the same manifest culture, we almost always share the same latent ideology in the form of an unconscious mind structured by the dominant ideology via child-rearing practices.

The logical irrationality that the dominant culture has lived with since World War II is, ultimately, a demonstrably false proposition when we consider that other human cultures have lived out other cultural practices and have not deemed it necessary to practice genocide, develop weapons of mass destruction, or inflict institutions of mass indoctrination on their community. Yet the technology that provides for weapons of mass destruction is, according to the dominant ideology, a sign of our progress as a civilization. Columbine High School interrupts the dream we have been dreaming even as it reminds us that our dreams of power and violence can kill.

The dominant culture remains addicted to the notion of a benevolent and idealized childhood in spite of the mounting violence that defines it. Violence on a wide scale cannot happen without rage, a felt sense of powerlessness, and a desperate emotional need that informs the hopelessness that justifies violence. Alice Miller describes it this way, and her perspective informs my own. She writes, "It is only the suppression of justified rage in childhood that makes a person violent and blind. Nothing else." In other words, video games do not make young adults violent. Relationships of violence and power reproduce individuals who participate spontaneously in violent relationships. Video games simply reproduce the nature of the relationships the child is already involved in. The evidence for this seemingly controversial thesis lies all around us and yet we refuse—or are unable—to see it. The practice of violence between individuals in real terms—as at Columbine High School—or idealized forms, as in video games or Hollywood movies, is a *symptom* of the dominant culture's child-rearing practices. Yet the buzzing confusion that surrounds ever-intensifying acts of violence has become so overwhelming that it has drowned out the far more significant forms of violence that occur every day between the child and the adult as an obvious matter of child-rearing principle.

I have no doubt that parents love their children. What concerns me is the way in which the dominant ideology structures the expression of that love. For the child that love is often a lonely, violent, painful, humiliating experience that has more to do with the adult's exercise of power and authority than with the adult's exercise of compassion and understanding. Why? Because the adult's love for the child and the adult's felt need to exercise control over the child are usually synonymous unconscious impulses. Contrary to popular opinion, love is an ideologically determined psychodynamic event in which the adult projects her unconscious mind as an enacted relational pedagogy. Adult relational pedagogy is always loaded with the repressed fear, anger, sadness, and need from the adult's childhood. The adult's unconscious projection in and through relational pedagogy represents a key psychodynamic mechanism by which the adult's love ideologically invents the child.

The story of childhood, then, is a story of the process of literary production as a cultural, ideological and psychodynamic event. It is a personal process, and a political one, a public as well as private event. The story of childhood is found in children's literature, its rise, and its ongoing popularity as a consumer product and as a central part of elementary school curriculum. Though my argument focuses on texts produced by adults with children in mind, I hope to make clear that the story of childhood is a story that transcends children's literature, for in a way, all adult literary production is influenced by the relational practices experienced by the child at the hands of the adult. It is a premise in my argument that adults invent history not so much from what really happened to them as children as from what they wished would have happened when they were children. Paradoxically, adult nostalgia for childhood more often than not carries a latent relational narrative between adult and child that justifies adult domination—often violent and terrifying domination—over the child, following the questionable premise that the adult can "make" the child a good person.

Children's literature is a part of a montage of adult cultural practices that, along with child-rearing pedagogies, speaks to the cultural context that gives to adult authors and children's texts and so to a reproduction of unconscious relational practices bent on exercising and justifying adult power over the child. The authors of children's texts often sweeten by degrees the exercise of adult power through conscious or unconscious appeals to nostalgia and longing in no way mitigates the effects of relationships based on the exercise of power. Rather, the adult's domination over the child appears so complete and so seamless—so a part of the obviousness of childhood—that for some even raising the issue of the child's subjugation seems ridiculous. After all, parents love their children. End of story. This, however, is not the end of my story; it is just the beginning.

This thing of darkness I acknowledge mine.

—SHAKESPEARE, *The Tempest*

Only when we are sick of our sickness
Shall we cease to be sick.

—LAO TZU, *Tao Te Ching*

INVENTING THE CHILD

CHAPTER 1

History as Human Relationship

*No universal history leads from savagery to humanitari-
anism, but there is one leading from the slingshot to the
megaton bomb.*

—Theodor Adorno, *Negative Dialects*

A STARTING POINT

The story of Western culture is, according to conventional wisdom, a story of
progress, growth, and development. Western culture it is said, has been a
grand experiment, wildly successful in its ability to transform the natural
resources of a continent—and a globe—into the finished material an
advanced civilization requires, such as automobiles, computers, military
hardware, medical technology, and common consumer goods. Not long after
the first European settlers established themselves on the American continent,
the story of the American experiment began to circulate *as story*. We told it to
ourselves while at church, at home, at work, and at rest, and of course, we
told it to our children. Words and ideas such as God, destiny, freedom, fron-
tier, enlightened self-interest, and technological progress—along with many
others—were invoked in order to justify and extend the story of Western culture as a process that would, ultimately, engulf the "new" world. First the
Bible and later science became supported and defended by what appeared to
be the American's "God-given" right to dominate and subjugate.

That all would share in what became known as the "American dream"
was part and parcel of the American mythos and as a result, helped to justify
the exportation of the American ideology from coast to coast. Whatever
human exploitation or habitat destruction that resulted—or results—in the

exportation of American ideology was—and still is—according to conventional wisdom, acceptable and even, if the truth be known, inevitable. The destruction of the rain forests, for instance, is the price we all must pay for progress, civilization, and inexpensive fast food, or so the story goes.

The exploitation of workers—often children—in places like Indonesia, China, and India is, according to the American ideology, the necessary price the dominant culture must pay in order to keep its economic house in order, for cheap labor overseas keeps American inflation low and the Western consumer shopping. Moreover, as the story goes, cheap labor is good for first-world economies and, in the long run, for developing nations as well, for in sewing our shirts and making our children's toys, developing nations participate in the "global economy" from the ground up. The ostensible logic is that soon the developing nations will become full partners in a global culture in which all players see eye to eye, in which all players have equal opportunity. Almost four hundred years have passed since the Pilgrims colonized America, and yet the story remains remarkably familiar: the American state, be it theocratic or economic, will lead by example and represent the leading edge of what an enlightened community can become.

Yet the self-same story that placed the Pilgrims and Puritans at the epicenter of their universe placed the Native American—among others—at its outer edge, casting the indigenous native as the perennial other and, as such, God's tool to deepen His people's commitment to their faith. God made the "savage" particularly susceptible to alcohol and smallpox *for a reason*. It seemed obvious to men such as John Winthrop, William Bradford, and even Benjamin Franklin that domination and subjugation were a part of God's—or Nature's—appointed way in the "new" world, just as it had been in the "old."

The nature of the relationship between the colonists and the Native Americans—as well as between so-called first- and third-world cultures today—actively prohibits the growth and development of the "other" culture, except along the lines of the more "civilized" culture. For example, developing nations today struggle to become like the West in two ways: they desire economic power and, more often than not, weapons of mass destruction. If not the first, then the second path offers a way for developing nations to establish credibility defined as it is by the dominant ideology of Western culture. Both paths, however, spell doom for the human species and for the global habitat. If peace is contingent upon economic parity, that is, of "raising" developing nations to the standard of living Americans have grown used to, then peace may prove to be too expensive for Western culture to support. As populations rise around the world—even as Western populations are projected to remain largely flat—the twenty-first century will witness more and more people demanding their share of the progress and comfort enjoyed by the West, and rightly so, given the exportation of American ideology and the "superior" way of life it implicitly and explicitly celebrates.[1]

Sharing the wealth has never been a part of the American experiment. What has been a part of the dominant ideology of Western culture is the belief in the rugged individual who makes for himself the world he desires. If this belief is put into practice by India, China, and other growing populations— and it is in practice in many ways already—the resources of the global habitat will be stretched beyond its ability to sustain itself. Admittedly, no one knows how many human beings can fit on the head of this pin called earth. Even so, at six billion and counting, most signs point to high probability of another doubling of the global population sometime in the twenty-first century.

As natural resources continue to become strained with continuing global population growth, political tensions will naturally rise, in which case economic parity as a path to political credibility will give way to what may prove to be a shorter, cheaper path to global credibility, a path celebrated by American culture from its very beginnings: military technology, especially in the form of weapons of mass destruction. In 1998 India and Pakistan revealed their own nuclear capabilities, demonstrating yet again that the ability to destroy entire continents—and perhaps the entire global habitat—with a handful of nuclear bombs continues to be a temptation that developing nations have a hard time resisting.

As if it weren't enough to ask the reader to take this doomsaying seriously, I want to complicate things even further by arguing that the predilection we have for ever-intensifying expressions of destruction is not the product of human nature but rather a predictable consequence of a style of human culture produced and reproduced in an ever-more-intensifying way over the past four hundred years, with roots dating back to the Agricultural Revolution some ten thousand years ago.[2] The way in which the adult invents the child—and so reproduces the dominant culture—is key to understanding the history that leads from the slingshot to the megaton bomb, for the production and reproduction of our style of human culture occur first and foremost in our style of human relationships, which is first experienced by the child at the hands of the adult. The adult invents the child and constructs the world.

The stories we tell our children—and tell ourselves about the child—are my primary concern in this book, for in these stories a culture confirms itself and so reproduces itself. These are no innocent things, these children's stories; rather, their innocence is an ideological projection by which we ignore their implications, their meanings, and the larger story they tell, for adults write the children's books. The child is always already faced with an adult reification of the world presented as "neutral" and "obvious." Children's stories speak directly to the nature of the human relationship that produced them. If we want to understand the way in which a culture envisions itself, we might look no further than the stories adults tell and retell to their children. With this in mind, this study explores only those children's stories that were unquestionably popular: from the *New England Primer* to the fairy tales of the Brothers

Grimm's, from *Alice in Wonderland* to Walt Disney's *Pinocchio,* from Maurice Sendak's *Where the Wild Things Are* to the PBS show *Barney,* understanding the way in which a culture reproduces itself through its children requires that the texts by adults for children actually reach a wide audience.

Seeing children's stories as a cultural reproduction of the relationship between the adult and the child—determined as it is by the unconscious ideology harbored by the adult—offers a way of seeing diverse forms of children's literature, human relationships, the story of Western culture, and the production and reproduction of the dominant ideology of Western culture as diverse expressions of the same story.

According to Louis Althusser, a culture's ideology is the determining psychodynamic phenomenon by which human beings become "social subjects." It follows that the rules by which social subjects interact produce lived relations—that is, relationships governed by an ideology that manifests itself in the practice, or the pedagogical expression, of those ideological assumptions, many of which are unconscious and invisible, even to the participants themselves. This is nowhere more true than when the adult interacts with the child. According to Althusser, social subjects are connected to the dominant relations of production—the material expression of a culture, its jobs, its economic base, its state institutions, and so on—and so, social subjects inadvertently reproduce the dominant culture as a result of the lived relations determined by the structure imposed on them by "the dominant relations of production."

Understanding ideology as an affective process does not deny ideology its cognitive content, but rather shifts the focus from the individual's intellectual development to the individual's lived practices in human relations, practices that are, quite frequently, determined solely by the adult. Where the individual first learns his or her way of practicing human relations, then, becomes of primary concern to an affective theory of ideology. Further, the development of an affective theory of ideology requires an understanding of how affective and cognitive experiences impact on the biological system, and how this impact leads to the reproduction of the dominant culture in and through the individual's conscious and unconscious mind, for it is the expression of and through that mind that structures human relationships, and so reproduces the dominant culture. The production and reproduction of the dominant culture require the production and reproduction of the dominant ideology as a necessary prerequisite, and this occurs in the relationship between the adult and the child, as the child learns to forget the felt experiences of the real conditions of her existence and then substitute for them an imaginary idea of her existence. "Unfortunately," Althusser writes, "this interpretation leaves one small problem unsettled: why do individuals 'need' this imaginary transposition of their real conditions of existence in order to 'represent to themselves' their conditions of existence in imaginary, that is, in ideological forms?"[3]

THE DETACHMENT CHILD

From the infant's first days, ideology interrupts his ability to meet basic biological needs: namely, in the first months of life, attachment to the mother remains a biological necessity, until the infant signals a readiness to separate from the mother. Ideology interrupts and structures the relationship of the adult and the child in the form of technology, medical science, and the belief in the salvific force that technology and science supposedly embody. Yet for the infant, technology augers something other than salvation. Technology in the form of baby formula, rubber nipples, cribs, intercoms, and even strollers goes hand in hand with premature detachment from the mother and the resultant emotional and physical deprivation. Ideology goes hand in hand with detachment and abandonment. Baby formula, nurseries, cribs, intercoms, and other tools that facilitate physical and emotional detachment from the infant influences the child's development in profound ways and makes difficult, if not impossible, the child's attempt to navigate a separation from the mother when an earlier state of oneness outside the womb never fully prevailed. There can be no separation without the child's first having experienced attachment.[4]

Children have been prematurely detached from their mothers and fathers for millennia, but not everywhere. Jean Liedloff, in *The Continuum Concept*, makes the point quite clearly that other cultures, cultures described by Daniel Quinn as "Leaver" cultures, have a completely different way of understanding what they mean when they say "us." For the "Leaver" culture, "us" includes the subject and the object, the adult *and* the child, the self *and* the other. Western dualism and its cultural manifestations maintain a gap between subject and object, knower and known, and in this gap posits a "unique" and "individual" personality often at war with everything else around it, including itself.

Detachment parenting is a distinctly cultural phenomenon practiced and perfected in particular by Western child-rearing ideologies for so long that it has become an ambient reality, an ideological obviousness. Blaming the child for adult detachment is a central element of this tradition. Western history might be read—and will be read in this book—as one long, intensifying series of responses to the suffering of emotional deprivation that the adult inflicts upon the child, and the child then inflicts upon the world.

LOOKING BACKWARD

Consider the book of Genesis. As text, it contains stories that define the Western mind. After creating Adam, God sets him in the Garden and gives him some rules to live by:

> Then the Lord God took the man and put him in the garden of Eden to till it and care for it. He told the man, "You may eat from every tree in the garden,

but not from the tree of the knowledge of good and evil; for on the day that
you eat from it, you will certainly die." (Gen. 2:15–17)

Soon after, the Lord God gives Adam a helper, Eve, "and both were naked
and were not ashamed."

In spite of their ostensible happiness in the Garden of Eden, Eve chooses
to disobey God, having first been led astray by the Devil dressed up as a
snake, and so indulges her appetite and invites Adam to do the same. When
God discovered their disobedience,

> He said, "the man has become like one of us, knowing good and evil; what if
> he now reaches out his hand and takes fruit from the tree of life also, eats it
> and lives forever?" So the Lord God drove him out of the Garden of Eden . . .
> He cast him out. (Gen. 3:22–24)

According to the Judeo-Christian tradition, Adam's sin defined the
human race as a *fallen* race. Among the lessons we learn from the Book of
Genesis one of the most ambient and so invisible has to do with the child:
there is nothing worse in the history of the universe than the child's disobedience of the father. The child's disobedience is the seed and source for all
human misery, and even the source for death itself. Finally, the child's misery
is, according to biblical myth, the child's own fault. The child is wayward and
destructive. Hence Solomon reminds his adult audience that to "spare the rod
is to spoil the child."

That the story of Adam and Eve may have been ideological propaganda
for a dominant culture that produced it should not be ignored. For, as the agri-
culturists began to dominate Mesopotamia long before the books of the Old
Testament were written, they required a source of labor to till their fields and
bring into submission other uncultivated lands. The child undoubtedly
offered one of the quickest, cheapest sources for a farmer in need of inexpensive labor, hence the biblical injunction: "Happy is the man whose quiver is
full of them."

In one sense, then, God sets His children up to fail and thus justifies His
treatment of them as a result not of *His* child-rearing ideology, but of the
child's nature, which, by the way, is prone towards disobedience, destruction,
and damnation through no fault of the Creator. As a result, God the father sets
His children to work in the fields after casting them out of the Garden.
Detachment from the father, hard labor, and suffering are their punishment
simply for being born. Detachment-style parenting and ideologically justified
suffering are also self-serving propaganda for the master who requires obedient labor.

In *Thou Shalt Not Be Aware,* Alice Miller outlines the way in which adult
pedagogues maintain power over their child-charges. One manner is to pre-

sent the child with an "impossible pedagogical situation" so that, once the child has failed, the pedagogue can demonstrate to the child her utter reliance, subjugation even, to the adult pedagogue. The "impossible pedagogical situation" sets up the child to fail, and the pedagogue has proclaimed it as his duty to show the child just how she has failed. When love becomes a currency, and when it is given only conditionally by the parent upon successful completion of a task assigned to the child, the child is introduced to a parenting pedagogy that, according to Miller, represents an original scene of anxiety-producing narcissism. This pedagogical parenting practice teaches the child to constantly look "outside" his own body to the parent-pedagogue with these questions in mind: Am I okay? Do you love me? When shame, punishment, and humiliation are the response, the child learns not the intellectual lesson the pedagogue has set before him, but rather another, more important lesson about hierarchy, power, subjugation, fear, and obedience.

Detachment parenting serves to sever the child's cognitive mind from her experience of herself as a mind-body. As a result, the child's cognitive mind becomes identified with her status as a "social subject." The child's ego-mind becomes the site of overt ideological indoctrination while the body is merely the vehicle, a container. The child's body is rarely neutral, for according to the adult, it is the site of wicked or sinful or oedipal desires, and so must be itself dominated by the ego-mind's idea of itself. An affective theory of ideology identifies the ego-mind's idea of itself as a cultural construct, no more and no less real than any cultural construct, which is to say, the ego-mind's idea of itself is a relative no-thing, historically determined and without any absolute or essential content.

The culturally enforced split between the head and the body has disastrous consequences for the child, and these primarily relational consequences become the material of the larger culture. When the child is split from his body, he is split from his heart, the seat of his emotional response to the world, the place from which compassion for the other is experienced, and from which intuition whispers. When severed from his body, then, the child has already become a victim of the dominant ideology, and so, a victimizer as well. The process by which the child learns simultaneously the role of victim and victimizer—and later reenacts this emotional experience—becomes the driving force in the production and reproduction of the ideologies that inform the lived relationships on the personal as well as the cultural level.

In detachment-style parenting the infant learns early and often that the adult—a force outside the infant's body—determines the rightness or wrongness of the child's physical or emotional condition. When the child's needs or feelings are deemed inappropriate by the adult, the process of repression and cultural reproduction has begun. The child's mind internalizes adult ideologies that determine whether the child's needs—and the expression of those needs—result in further detachment, emotional trauma, and chronic longing.

As a result, certain needs and feelings are bound up with the felt experience of detachment: longing, hunger, shame, and anger. Rather than reading a child's behavior as a way of reading and supporting her emotional needs, the adult instead reads the child's behavior as "misbehavior," as a sign of the child's willfulness or inappropriateness. The child learns early and often from the lived relation with the adult that the rules and regulations of adult culture will not tolerate this or that in the child, though the rules are inconsistently applied, and so always in the child's unconscious mind to varying degrees is *confusion.*

Along with the adult's domination of the child's experience of herself, the child is frequently required to repress her emotional energy, certain emotional expressions are inherently against the rules imposed on by the adult. The child's expression of anger, for example, is often disallowed, though for no conscious reason other than that the child's anger seems to represent a serious threat to adult authority and control and, ultimately, to the adult's idea of himself as a parent who is in control. Anger, then, must be disallowed, by either forbidding it or meeting it with a greater force. For the child to survive and be deemed acceptable and appropriate by the adult world, she learns to hold in or hold off certain feelings that threaten the adult. The more that is held in, the deeper the need for release later. If this emotional release is prohibited by the adult, and if this prohibition against an abreaction is internalized by the child and practiced against herself as a way of conspiring with the adult against the wicked child within, neurosis develops. As a result, coping behaviors take the place of spontaneous experience. Addictive behavior develops. Most importantly, human relationships develop out of the need to control or to be controlled by another, all of which represents the unconscious reenactment of the child's relational experiences with the mother and the father. The repressed emotional energy that resulted from the child's relational experiences with the mother and the father becomes fused with the contents of the ego-mind as well as the larger unconscious mind.[5] The conscious and unconscious mind, driven by repressed affect, gives rise to what will become the adult's "character structure" or, as Althusser would say, the individual's status as a "social subject."

The consequences of detachment-style parenting not only impact and structure the individual's reality, but the culture's reality as well. Those cultures that have practiced a particularly intense version of detachment-style parenting—as did the seventeenth-century Puritans in America and the nineteenth-century Germans in Europe (all of which will be discussed in some detail later)—soon after enacted or allowed to be enacted genocidal practices that, to have occurred on as massive a scale as African slavery, colonialism, and the Jewish Holocaust required an adult "social subject" well acquainted with, and in fact informed by, an ideology of domination and subjugation that did not appear to be anything other than normal and obvious.

This is not to say that there were not individuals who protested and worked against these atrocities. Rather, this is to say that the culture from which genocidal practices spring must first be practicing the rudimentary ideologies required on a wide scale in its human relationships—in its child-rearing practices primarily—in order to bring to fruition such massive horrors.

To teach the child to deny the body is, ultimately, to teach the child to deny the center of human experience and the source for all creative, spiritual, and emotional connection, first to oneself and then to everything and everyone else. The birth of the atomic age and the proliferation of weapons of mass destruction remain a case in point in spite of the ending of the Cold War. Because of weapons of mass destruction, genocide is always already only moments away, or the time it takes a nuclear missile to find its target. Like our predecessors, however, we tolerate this chronic threat of violence as an inevitable condition, and justify the constant threat of annihilation as the surest way of ensuring "peace." Only the beguiled, abused child believes that violence is love, war is peace, or that work will make us free. Yet, the child invented by detachment parenting is quite frequently, for a time, a malleable child, an obedient child, and so for the adult bent on exercising control and demonstrating his or her power, the detached child can, for a time, appear to be the "ideal" child.

As the detached child grows older, he is offered ever more complex approaches to the cognitive description of life even as the physical experience of being alive becomes, quite often, intolerable. The coping mechanisms learned in childhood intensify in adulthood and become neuroses, and addictive behaviors, including eating disorders and compulsive spending. Even so, the adult world continues to teach the child to embrace a cognitive life which denies the body, encourages emotional repression, and celebrates obedience as an absolute good. As a result, the child falls victim to the only game in town and becomes a part of the making and remaking of the dominant ideology. Cut off from his feeling, intuitive center, the child is left to navigate the world according to the dictates and commands of the hegemonic order of the adult world, even though it more often than not produces in the child half-felt feelings of anger and deep sadness that, when the child becomes an adult, turn to feelings of bitterness, unpredictable explosions of rage, chronic violence, chronic anxiety, and chronic suffering. This is precisely what Henry David Thoreau meant when he wrote in Walden that "most men lead lives of quiet desperation." Depression, in other words, is—and has been—the dominant culture's emotional legacy.

Unconscious ideology reassures us that the adult has always invented the child. Ideology reassures us that there can be no other way for a society to perpetuate itself: the child must be made to conform. Yet other cultures—driven to the margins of awareness by Western culture's ongoing colonial and economic conquests—prove otherwise.[6] The invention of the child and the production and reproduction of the dominant culture go hand in hand, and this process is a distinctly *cultural* phenomenon. More plainly, it becomes clear that in order to reproduce a culture devoted to unconscious ideologies of superiority and domination—and the attendant genocidal violence that has gone with these ideologies in an ever-intensifying way over the past four hundred years—the child must be made to believe that domination, superiority, violence—even genocidal violence—are inevitable sacrifices made necessary by the need for civilization to "progress."

Progress is an illusion, yet in its name innumerable atrocities are justified, for progress is linked to the idea of tomorrow, and tomorrow will be better, and so the suffering of today is, ostensibly, ameliorated. The idealized and transformed tomorrow never comes for the child, however, in spite of the promises of the dominant adult culture. The popularity of the musical *Annie* exemplifies the way in which adult ideology is placed in the mouths of babes as a sign of their need to acquiesce to the dominant ideology. In spite of her abandonment, her abuse, and her longing, or because of it, Annie sings, and she sings not about her sadness, anger, or confusion, but rather, about the promise of tomorrow: "Tomorrow, tomorrow, I love you, tomorrow, you're always a day away." These are not the child's words, but the adult's words put in the child's mouth. Annie's gleeful belief in tomorrow is the adult's nostalgia, the adult's longing for a Daddy Warbucks to save the day. Annie's story is a particularly pronounced version of how contemporary culture tells itself a story about the child in order to defend its treatment *of* the child. Annie's emotional state—her unflagging high spirits, angelic voice, and distinctly American optimism—grows out of the adult-inspired ideology of the child's "resiliency." This is self-serving, to say the least. After all, Daddy Warbucks, the rich industrialist with ties to the dominant political culture—a hard-nosed raconteur—is also, when the chips are down, a "lover" of the child. Ultimately, Annie's story is a paean to the child's experience of adult hegemony.

Unfortunately, the adult tends to confuse cultural idealizations of the child with his or her own emotional experiences as a child. For the adult, childhood nostalgia and stories that idealize the child and create delusional descriptions of childhood take the place of the adult's ability to feel and remember his or her physical, emotional life from its earliest moments. Children who have been abandoned either physically or emotionally by the adult do not sing about it, at least not in the way Annie sings. Children who have been abandoned and abused tell their story though their behavior, especially in the ways in which they connect, and ultimately fail to connect, with other human beings in a satisfying way. Detached relationships breed detached relationships.

Unfortunately, Western child-rearing practices have been detachment practices in one form or another for thousands of years, though not exclusively. There have been—and continue to be—other ways of parenting along other cultural lines forgotten by Western culture.[7] As Louise Kaplan writes in *Oneness and Separateness,*

> It is ironic that the vital importance of a human infant's attachment to his mother should be subverted by shame and impatience at the very moment in history when the complaints of human detachment are loudest. Modern social forces conspire to interrupt the elemental dialogue between mother and infant—the dialogue that insures our humanity.[8]

CHARACTER

What we experience as children structures our reality and determines in large part the nature and the quality of the dialogue we have with ourselves and with others we are in relationships with. Character structure represents the ideology of child-rearing pedagogy turned into a physical and emotional "reality" for the individual.[9] Character structure corresponds to what Freud called the unconscious. Our character structures, "real" as they are to us, leave us vulnerable to beguiling ideologies, manipulative people, and dangerous politics. Character structures take on a life of their own in that they structure the body and the ego-mind. Because at the most basic level our child-rearing pedagogies split the child off from the energetic body, the feeling heart, and the body's intuition, we take the ideas we learn about ourselves as realities. Still, these realities are nothing more than delusions or ideologies. Character structure is another way of describing how the epistemological form of ideology represents "false consciousness."[10]

Character structure retains its viability as a result of repressed affect from childhood. In other words, rigid, masochistic tendencies feel real to the masochist because they structure the world and how the masochist interacts and makes contact with it. The masochist, for instance, looks out and sees a world trying to rob him of his independence, but within he feels that he must comply and please the world in order to "get on," even if it means denying himself to the breaking point. The masochist is often angry, and resentful and hates "playing the game," but it is a game and the rules have been clear since childhood: submit. All of this delusional thinking is fueled by repressed rage just beneath the surface. Yet the masochist must hold in his rage or risk offending the powers-that-be. Holding it in proves the masochist's strength to himself. And this is key: denying one's feelings is central in the process by which one denies one's true material history and lives, instead, what Althusser calls an "imaginary relationship" to the conditions of one's existence. To deny feelings, then, is to deny felt experiences as a child, and so as an adult the individual lives a life determined by the dominant culture's dominant ideology. A real relationship to the conditions of my existence is impossible unless the individual lets out the rage that is within him. This is prohibited by the dominant ideology that says his angry feelings are "bad," and to feel them is an explicit and implicit rejection of the mother. He does not want to feel his rage and so reject the mother for fear of losing her. That he has already lost her decades before as a child has little impact on his holding onto the hope that perhaps someday she will see him and provide him with what the infant needs: oneness, attachment, well-being, contentment.

No matter which character structure dominates the personality, each individual has relational styles that correspond, though one or two character structures do tend to dominate. Nevertheless, they all begin developing for the same reasons: each character structure develops as a compensatory behavior as a result of the original split inflicted on the child's mind/body system in childhood. That is, character structure relies on the ideological notion inflicted on the child through years of pedagogical training, which teaches, in short, that we are not our body, our feelings, and our intellects working in a system. Rather, ideology teaches that we are our *ideas* of ourselves, and our bodies and feelings must be tamed, for they get in the way of our living out our own ideas of ourselves. The end result is that when the mind and body are split, the individual sees everything in the world from a dualistic perspective. For instance, if the child learns that there is "good" behavior and "bad" behavior, then this must mean to the child that there is a "good" child and a "bad" child within, and so the child splits off from this "bad" child or conversely, splits off from the "good" child out of anger and resentment. In any event, the split mind sees the split within its own consciousness and, as a result, the world becomes split into manifest pairings of oppositions, including "self" and "other." Along with this split comes an interjected voice of shame from the adult world, what Freud called the superego, to judge and condemn, measure and compare, and always keep the "self" on guard against the "other." The other is first and foremost an aspect of the individual—frequently it is the body itself; also, the other represents the one side of the split ego-mind. Or, the split might run between the intellect and the affect, with the affect being the other.

The split mind, then, is not the mind split into two, but rather the mind that sees the world in pairs, in oppositions, as a fundamental dualism. In this way, a dualistic mind is not a stable pairing, but rather a multiplicitous collection of splits that leads to a sense of disconnection and fragmentation within oneself and in the world. The split mind constructed out of anger, resentment, and deprivation later in life begins to project this anger and rage and deprivation into all relationships that the individual adult engages in. So, at any given time, the adult's ego-mind is the self, while the poor, or the ethnic minority, or the homosexual, may be the other and therefore deserving of the exact same treatment he received as a child while in the hierarchical position of other in the relationship with the adult.[11] When, however, we "can thoroughly realize that crying, sulking, self-doubt, apathy or rebellion were correct human responses to . . . incorrect treatment, [one's] whole feeling about [oneself]— as the wrong one—changes appropriately."[12]

THE MYTH OF PROGRESS

Western culture and its child-rearing practices have, according to conventional wisdom, improved since the fifteenth century.[13] In the fifteenth and sixteenth centuries, wet nursing, swaddling, and exposing infants as a way of "rearing" them meant that in some cases, institutions that wet-nursed children often had infant mortality rates as high as 90 percent, while a 50 to 60 percent mortality rate was common. Parents often had ten children simply as a matter of course because so many children died. In sixteenth-century France, a mother who gave birth to ten children in her child-bearing years might see two reach adulthood. Five, six, even seven of her children would die in their first year. Historians of childhood such as Lloyd DeMause, Philippe Aries, Alice Miller, and others observe that infant mortality was high not because children were vulnerable creatures ill-suited to life in a harsh world, but because they were mistreated due to parental ignorance perpetuated by the dominant culture, which was largely blind to the consequences of its child-rearing practices.

Infant mortality rates dropped in the nineteenth century as European mothers began to breast-feed their infants rather than ship them out to wet nurses, who, in the past, could offer only "pap" to the many children they had contracted to "nurse." Infant mortality rates dropped, the Industrial Revolution dominated Western economic fortune, and the family became a "safe haven" against the outer world.

Falling infant mortality rates in nineteenth-century Europe in no way suggest that the child's position in the family had greatly improved. In fact, the position of the child vis-à-vis the hierarchical culture he found himself in remained largely the same. The culture was a patriarchy; the male/husband/father-as-paterfamilias ruled the hierarchical roost. By the end of the nineteenth century in Europe, the family costumes had changed, but the child nevertheless occupied the same hierarchical position in the community and in the family that he had occupied since the Agricultural Revolution: he remained at the bottom of the hierarchical totem pole as the adult's God-given property. Freud would come into his own as a scientist and thinker of the first order in an attempt to puzzle out the Victorian adult by working backwards to the Victorian child. For the first time childhood had become a site of disinterested inquiry. As a scientist, Freud was interested in, at first, a general way of approaching the etiology of his patient's neurosis. What he assumed about the nature of the child and the nature of the adult in his hunt for the causes of his patient's illnesses is taken up in some detail in the next chapter.

THE PURITANS, THE CHILD, THE PSYCHOPATH, AND THE MASOCHIST

As English colonization of the New World gained momentum, John Winthrop wrote in 1630 one of many Puritan tracts that spelled out individuals' responsibilities to their brother and to God. At the beginning of *A Model of Christian Charity,* Winthrop describes a cultural phenomenon so ubiquitous as to make it seem an inevitable reality of the human experience:

> God Almighty in His most holy and wise providence, hath so disposed of the condition of mankind, as in all times some must be rich, some poor, some high and eminent in power and dignity; others mean and in subjection.[14]

Winthrop offered nothing new to this congregation; rather, he reminded the Puritans of what they already knew: the world of human relations was a hierarchical patriarchy created and ordained by God. At the bottom of this hierarchy were the apostate, the native, and the child. At the top, of course, were God and His earthly agents: kings, ministers, and adult males. Finer distinctions could be made here, but suffice to say that the baptized male resided near the top of the ideological hierarchy of the Puritan world, and the child somewhere near the bottom.

The three most popular texts for the Puritan reminded every individual of this ideological state of affairs, but because the Bible—especially the Old Testament— was the word of God, any community that patterned itself after such a text was patterning itself according to God's Word. After the Bible, the *New England Primer* was the most well-known New World text, and the colonial child was exposed to it and its ideological hierarchy constantly. Third in familiarity, preached from the pulpit as if it, too, were Holy Scripture, was Michael Wigglesworth's epic poem of God's judgment, *The Day of Doom.* How the Puritans used these texts to indoctrinate their children and reproduce their culture is of particular interest to us.

The nature of the human relationship reproduced by Calvinistic ideology is not always obvious or apparent, and yet it remains a pronounced and significant part of Puritan theology. In part because of Calvin's loyalty to the doctrine of original sin, Calvinism's reproduction of caste was, at the same time, an intensification of caste and of the human relations that consequently developed. This was nowhere more pronounced than in the adult's rearing of the child. For the Protestant, each congregation became its own petty principality responsible for deciphering God's Word and enacting it as the head of that principality—along with the guidance from his spiritual community—saw fit. After the Reformation, then, the family became all the more important for the production and reproduction of the dominant culture, especially in the New World, where the old institutions and the civilization that sprang from them were thousands of miles away. Even so, the hierarchical ideology of the institution lived in each individual, having been exposed to it since birth. It was inevitable that the shape and content of the institutions of Europe should reproduce themselves first in personal relationships and later in political ones.

In one sense, then, when the Reformation decentered papal authority it did nothing to dilute its ideological grip on the conscious and unconscious minds of the masses; rather, the ideological and cultural power of the Catholic church, when traumatized by the firestorm of Reformation, reseeded itself in much the same way an ancient pine tree requires fire to release the seeds in its cones. Hundreds of tiny versions of the parent tree soon spring up around the burnt-out carcass.

So, too, when Copernicus, Newton, Luther, and Calvin stoked the fires that would scorch the Roman Catholic Church of sixteenth-century Europe, smaller "Protestant" versions found soil and grew from the same ideological gene pool. Theologically, Protestantism—especially Calvinism—distanced itself from Catholicism. Though the ideological apparatus had changed, the ideology from which the institution—now institutions—sprang remained largely intact, especially when it came to the child's place in the hierarchy of human relations.

For the child, then, New World Protestantism delivered an even more concentrated dose of ideological oppression: the family, the congregation, and the school. These smaller institutions were vastly more effective—and still are—in reproducing the status quo due to the personal and often violent nature of ideological indoctrination, all the more effective for the fact that adults, having been indoctrinated themselves, believed that the violence done to children was, in fact, "for their own good."

Consider one of the most popular colonial texts of the seventeenth and eighteenth centuries in America: The *New England Primer,* which dates back to the 1680s. The *Primer* flourished as a school text for close to two centuries and remains representative of the way in which the dominant culture reproduced itself through a process that fused cognitive development and emotional trauma through institutionalized repression. As such, language exists primarily to remind the child that he is a sinner, for as the letter *A* teaches in the *New England Primer's* alphabet, "In Adam's Fall we sinned all." The letter *F* reminds the child of the ambient nature of violence, punishment, and judgment, for "The Idle Fool is whipped at School." The letter *H* speaks unconsciously to the process taking place as the child experiences the fusion of pedagogy and ideology: "My Book and Heart Shall never part." The letter *J* reminds the child to accept his place no matter how unjust it might feel, and to thank the one who whips him, for "Job feels the Rod, Yet blesses God." Primers usually contained alphabets, prayers, and promises to be memorized "by all dutiful children." Along with the alphabet, the *New England Primer* included "The Dutiful Child's Promises":

I will fear God and honour the King.
I will honour my father and mother.
I will obey my Superiours.
I will submit to my Elders.
I will love my Friends.
I will hate no man.
I will forgive my Enemies, and pray to God for them.[15]

This interesting list of promises makes the ideological hierarchy clear to the child. Above all, the *New England Primer* teaches the child his place and how to remain there. It is important to note that it makes little difference to the production and reproduction of the dominant culture whether the child resists the content of the *New England Primer* or fully embraces it. A child's rejection of the *Primer* represented an exception that proved the rule. The *Primer* represents the coming together of ideology, pedagogy, and text in a powerful and influential way. In the *Primer* the child learns a hierarchy in which God and king stand first and foremost, and in their place the child must honor father and mother as superiors and as elders. In fact, the child must obey and submit to superiors, named here as "elders." In short, the child must submit to and obey all who demand that she submit, based on their claim to superiority or the fact that they are an elder. This works out clearly in relationships between the child and the adult, but it works out less clearly between two adolescents or two children. Rivalries of dominance and submission often manifest themselves in some children in the form of school yard violence. When the repressed rage demanded by the institution's pedagogy is combined with the child's emotional isolation from a supportive witness, and if the child has been trained at home to deny the body and the release of stored affect, violence will be the result. School yard violence becomes school yard massacre when, along with the process of abuse, repression, and isolation, the child is also interpolated by violence as a result of the lived relationship between the adult and the child, founded as it is on an ideology of subjugation made real by the child's lived and repressed experience of violence at the hands of adults.[16]

When teaching the letter *K*, the *Primer* invites the schoolmaster to teach the child about the appropriateness of a hierarchical society in which the rich and powerful rule not because they are rich and powerful, but rather, because they are closer to God, who is the source of their many blessings. The king, after all, was something other than human, at least according to the *Primer*, in instruction on the letter *K* the *Primer* reminds children where their fears and loyalties should lie: "Our KING the good/No man of blood."

This is not to say that the schoolmaster did not have his own political ideas and may very well have taught the children under his care his own particular brand of royalist or dissenter politics. In spite of this, or perhaps because of it, the ideological content of the *New England Primer*, combined with the pedagogical methods of instruction, represents a seventeenth-century example of the psychodynamic process of cultural production and reproduction. Language acquisition, then, is never an ideologically neutral process. Rather, it is synonymous with ideological acquisition.

From the point of view of the adult schoolmaster, the *New England Primer* represents the opportunity to enact the ideas essential to the preservation of the status quo. In other words, the letter *J* teaches about the human relationship between God and man, kind and subject, and, most important, adult and child. As children learn to decode the letter *J* in their primer, they are reminded of what they have already learned at home and at church. The dutiful child submits to authority, even when that authority uses brutal and violent methods to demonstrate love. To inculcate this most difficult yet necessary lesson of submission, the schoolmaster implicitly and explicitly teaches the child to submit, for in submitting to the schoolmaster's violence, the child—like Job—learns to submit and to bless God. The colonial schoolmaster teaches the ideological structure of human relations while at the same time enacting them, which is essential for the psychodynamic process of ideological acquisition. Ideological acquisition occurs as a psychodynamic process by which adult culture is produced and reproduced by way of adult attack on the child's biological system. The adult attack on the child is always ideologically driven, violent, and emotionally traumatic. The degree to which the adult requires the child to repress the emotional experience—to bless God for His rod—is the degree to which the child's repressed affect—usually rage and deep sadness—becomes fused with the ideology of the dominant culture and the hierarchical structure of its human relationships.

To the Puritan adult's way of thinking, the child came into the world as a wayward sinner in need of stern measures so that she might be made docile and obedient and pleasing to God. As an upstanding Puritan, the father *must* control his children or risk admonition or other forms of ostracism from the community. This is, in part, why Puritan parents tolerated the unmitigated assault on their children by the schoolmaster. The child was, like Frederick Douglass, sent to a "slave-breaker." The slave-breaker worked the slave hard, broke his will, and sent him home to his master to surrender his life. The school house of Puritan New England was a place in which the child's will was broken with abandon. Is it any wonder the Puritans could not achieve a New Jerusalem? The peace and abundance of Christ did *not* extend to children, for who knew if the child was elect or not? Only God knew. Michael Wigglesworth makes this plain in his epic poem, *Day of Doom*. As group after group approaches God's bar of judgment on the last day, each is informed of its failure to have lived up to God's standard. Generally speaking, there need be no judgment in Calvinistic Puritanism, for, according to Calvinism, the saved are predestined by God in an irresistible fashion to be His elect. The rest, well, the rest go to Hell, but they should take pleasure in living a life for the elect and for Christ, in spite of their eternal fate. Who was elect, and who was not was a difficult question however. Wigglesworth produces the anxiety of the Puritan's insecurity in much the same way an adult confounds and confuses a child, all toward manipulating the child's behavior. That the *Day of Doom* played fast and loose with Calvinism made no difference in the poem's popularity, for it confirmed what the Puritans already knew about "the Master." He was violent, inscrutable, loved whom He loved, and hated whom He hated. One's behavior had little to do with influencing God's love, but with little else left to the Puritan, the morality of behavior became of primary concern to the community elders and adults in relation to the children.

The plight of the child according to Puritan doctrine is made clear in *Day of Doom* in stanzas 166–68, for the child who died in infancy is doomed to Hell not for any wrongdoing or sinful thought, but simply for being born into the world. The child, in other words, is blamed and condemned for her existence. God does the same with the adult in earlier stanzas, but the ruthlessness and the self-loathing are pungently clear when applied to the infant:

> *Then to the bar, all they drew near / Who died in Infancy,*
> *And never had or good or bad / Effected pers'nally,*
> *But from the womb unto the tomb / Were straightway carried,*
> *(Or at the last ere they transgressed) / who thus began to plead:*
> *"If for our own transgression, / or disobedience,*
> *We here did stand at Thy left hand / Just were the recompence:*
> *But Adam's guilt our souls hath spilt, / His fault is charged on us;*
> *And that alone hath overthrown, / And utterly undone us. . . .*
> *How could we sin that had not been, / Or how is his sin our,*
> *Without consent, which to prevent, / We never had a power?*
> *O great Creator, why was our nature / depraved and forlorn?*
> *Why so defiled, and made so vile / whilst we were yet unborn?*

Rather than wait for God to explain Himself, the infants simply accept their vile state and ask God for mercy. Although God attempts to explain Himself in stanza 171, it is not Calvin's God who answers these infants, for God responds to the infants' situation with what appears to be a fair and understanding mind, for He acknowledges, at least at first, that the infant's condition is, in fact, different from the average adult sinner's condition. With this in mind, God explains Himself:

> *God doth such doom forbid / That men should die eternally*
> *For what they never did. / But what you call old Adam's fall,*
> *And only his trespass, / You call amiss to call it his*
> *Both his and yours it was.*

Because the infants are born from the same source that gave life to Adam, his sin stains them all. This concept was familiar to the point of redundancy to the Puritan congregation primarily because it confirmed what they had already learned at home and later, what they would learn at school each time children learned their letters in the *New England Primer:* Children come into the world broken, incomplete, and in need of adult reform.

But, God contradicts Himself by indirectly implying that this whole ideological scheme is unjust when in stanzas 180–81, he says to the infants,

> *You sinners are, and such a share | as sinners may expect,*
> *Such you shall have; for I do save | none but Mine own elect.*
> *Yet to compare your sin with their, | who lived a longer time,*
> *I do confess yours is much less, | though every sin's a crime.*
> *A crime it is, therefore in bliss | you may not hope to dwell;*
> *But unto you I shall allow | the easiest room in hell.*

The point in the infants' argument is that *they did not sin,* yet, according to Wigglesworth's God, "every sin's a crime." So, though their sin is small, they must burn in hell. Oddly, none of the infants is chosen or elect. As infants who died at birth, they are doomed as unregenerate and must, according to God's law, be detached from Him eternally. Yet the doctrine of predestination and irresistible grace suggests that at least some of the infants must have been chosen *before* birth to enter Heaven. But the notion of the child's inherent wickedness had been so impressed on the community, and on the Puritan child, that this unconscious traumatic experience found its way into Wigglesworth's poem. Though the poem takes liberties with Calvinistic doctrine, it seems to speak a deeper truth to Puritans, a truth of their own unconscious mind, which was structured through childhood trauma and which they confused with the mind of a transcendent deity.

The popularity of *The Day of Doom* suggests that Wigglesworth's mind was, in many ways, a tolerable representation of the Puritan mind. As such, the *infant* must go to Hell. Why is not clear, even though God explains it: on the one hand, the infant is stained by Adam's guilt, and this in itself is, somehow, a sin, and "every sin's a crime." Yet, the infants' sin is less, and so they go to the "easiest room in hell." In Wigglesworth's mind, God was a grand scorekeeper, measuring, weighing, and comparing sin to sin. Oddly, this is not Calvin's God; rather, it smacks more of the pre-Reformation Catholic God who gladly exchanged indulgences for sins and let repentant sinners, "buy" their way into heaven. Wigglesworth combined the harshest qualities of both the Catholic and Puritan Gods and came up with a master who could calmly and coolly send infants to Hell simply for being born. God always obeyed His own rules, whatever they were at any given moment.

It should be noted again that the popularity and longevity of Wigglesworth's poem suggest that his view of the Puritan condition made sense to his audience and to the Puritan ministers who led the community. *The Day of Doom* was, according to Sacvan Bercovitch and others, quoted by ministers as frequently as—or more frequently than—biblical Scripture, so powerful and moving was the story Wigglesworth had wrought. The idea of a loving God, who reserved the right to judge, condemn, and reject the infant, simply confirmed what, in childhood, the Puritans had internalized about the Master at the hands of *their* adult masters.

John Robinson, a Pilgrim preacher, wrote in *Children and Their Education* that children must be "broken and beaten down so that the foundation of their education being layd in humilitie and tractablenes other virtues may in their time be built thereon." From the workhouse to the schoolhouse, the child's body frequently became the site of ideological contestation, for in it, the adult believed, lay something that resisted the dominant culture, and this resistance was sure proof that the child, not the adult, must be broken and reformed. If the farm and workhouse often numbed the child's mind and body, the schoolhouse and its rigorous pedagogies of obedience, violence, and repetition aimed at achieving a similar result. The justification for relationship of master and pupil came from economic as well as religious premises: the child must learn or he will fail in life, or, similarly, the child must learn or else she will go to Hell. The adult, however, has no more idea of the child's fate than does the child, and so all religious and secular education frequently amounts to nothing more than the process by which the adult codifies his anxiety into beguiling ideologies and then projects them onto and into the child, thereby reproducing the dominant ideology that condones violence, terror, and domination as something "for the child's own good." In fact, the adult is merely acting out the powerlessness and terror he experienced at the hands of his schoolmaster, and is now passing them on in exactly the same way they were passed on to him. This cycle of "poisonous pedagogy" implicitly and explicitly teaches the child that violence, terror, and subjugation—and the attendant suffering that results—are normal and to be expected and ultimately, to be passed on.[17]

The disciplinary rod of the seventeenth-century schoolmaster took on many shapes, including the ferule, a ladle-shaped piece of wood used for striking the child's hand, and a bunch of birch twigs used for whipping boys who "either lye or will not learn." The "flapper" came from Boston: "It was a heavy piece of leather six inches in diameter, with a hole in the middle. This was fastened to a pliable handle. Every stroke on the bare flesh raised a blister the size of the hole in the leather."[18] No less effective in punishing the child was the "tattling stick, a cat-o-nine tails with heavy leather straps." Some children were whipped on the back, on the bare ass, on the head, on the hands, on the soles of the feet, and anywhere else the adult felt was necessary in order to break the child's will and inculcate automatic and unhesitating obedience.

The degree to which the schoolhouse's twin towers of pedagogical violence and ideological hierarchy interpolated the child with the dominant ideology was the degree to which the child experienced the schoolhouse ideology as something more than mere ideology, and instead, as an all-encompassing reality that went beyond the schoolhouse doors and justified violence and subjugation as a way of life. When schoolmasters whipped the child and that child reported the experience, at home, the child might be whipped again for having caused the whipping at school. This is not uncommon, and it is not only a seventeenth-century phenomenon. Adults often espouse and enact relationships of violence as a form of loving the child because it happened to them when they were a child. As a result the beaten child carries the belief into adulthood that as a child he deserved the violence, shame and terror, and is "better off" for it. The repressed terror and rage at having been beaten without the ability to defend himself leave a lasting impression on the child, namely, a character structure that determines his perception of reality in adulthood. This victim compensates for his pain, terror, and humiliation by detaching from the site of his experience, namely, the physical body, and retreating into the world of ideas. The unconscious emotional need that is left over from this retreat—the need for love, compassion, understanding, and support for the child's subjective reality—along with the repressed affect —rage, terror, and shame left over from the child's child-rearing experiences at the hands of the adult order—lead to later behavior that the adult world defines as the child's "misbehavior" and therefore confirms the original premise that the child has a "foolish," "sinful," "willful," or "animal" nature. According to this self-fulfilling prophecy, corrective training measures must therefore be continued, all the while producing and reproducing the dominant culture even as it creates a relationship between the adult and the child based solely on the adult's violent subjugation of the child, though the violence is often masked behind a façade justified by appealing to "adult" authority.

In 1692 the new charter of the Massachusetts Bay Colony revised entirely the covenant by which the community had originally defined itself. Before 1692 an individual claimed his right to vote based on his membership in the local congregational church, which in turn was granted as a result of his conversion experience either in England or subsequently in America. After 1692, because church membership remained flat while the population grew, the new charter decreed that suffrage would be based not on one's religious experience but on one's economic power. Property ownership became the requirement for an individual to claim his voting right. The dream of a New Jerusalem in which the lion and the lamb would lie down together was lost to the Puritans, for the European predator could not change his predatory practices, especially when it came to the predatory relationship between the adult and the child.

Those at the bottom of the human hierarchy, in other words, could and should be preyed upon and treated harshly, even violently. The sublimated feelings of terror, horror, rage, and deep-seated insecurity were, as a result of child-rearing experiences, fused with the ideologically driven assumptions about race and worth and "progress." Puritan Calvinism was, in effect, a confirmation of the world the Puritan had already internalized while a child.

The Puritan's evangelistic pedagogies were at the most fervent when dealing with their children. The harsh and punitive measures the adult used in his or her dealing with the child—especially the schoolmaster to his student—are absolutely accounted for in Calvinistic dogma, for if beating the child could not regenerate her soul, then at least battle against Satan was being waged, for in beating a child, the adult beat one of the "limbs of Satan" into submission. It was a win-win proposition for the Calvinistic adult, and a lose-lose proposition for the innocent child, for in either case, the child was beaten, and the world was born.

The production and reproduction of the Puritan's dominant ideology at first took a decidedly new course at the close of the seventeenth century. Economics rather than religion occupied the children of the Puritans. The children of the abusers rejected the conscious ideology of their masters, and the theocratic state of the Puritans ended, and instead, the children sought to become masters themselves. As the colonial errand into the New World shifted from a religious experiment into an experiment in economic opportunity, the hierarchical structure of human relationships that defined the adult's relationship to the child remained largely unchanged. In fact, it became an ideological justification for the enslavement of the "child-like" Africans, who required the master to save them from barbarism, indolence, and waywardness.

Cultural intensification is one particularly distressing aspect of ideological acquisition, as the practice of African slavery in the New World suggests. Intensification occurs in part because ideological acquisition is an unconscious phenomenon that requires the child to remain ignorant of what is in fact happening to her, and at the same time, requires the child to thank, obey, and even worship adult abusers and the power they represent. Intensification of ideological reproduction, then, is a transgenerational phenomenon. The repression of trauma is in no way a form of healing, however. Rather, it guarantees the reproduction of the ideology through the reenactment of the ideology that gave rise to the trauma in the first place. From adults children learn what it means to be victimized and at the same time are equipped with the ideological justification, pedagogical method, and unconscious drive in the form of repressed affect to become victimizers in their own right.

In other terms, the process by which the adult reared the child in seventeenth- and eighteenth-century America led to a preponderance of psychopathic and masochistic character structures at work in human relationships. The point to remember here is that character structure develops in the child as a result of "normal" child-rearing pedagogy. As character structure develops, ideological acquisition takes place simultaneously, for the dominant child-rearing ideology determines the nature of the relationship between the adult and the child; as the adult invents the child's character, the dominant culture reproduces itself via the child's ideologically determined character structure. The implications of this formula are far-reaching, for the nature of the relationship between the adult and the child is unconsciously taken by the child—when an adult—as the natural and obvious order of things. In other words, as a result of the child's domination, the adult believes in the subjugation of the other as a necessary and obvious given and so practices—sometimes with vehemence—the unconscious and conscious ideology of domination and subjugation. In this way, the dominant culture's institutions represent an exponential enlargement of the original relationship between the adult and the child.

It bears noting at this point that none of the child-rearing pedagogies of the Puritans and early colonists were considered cruel or unusual at the time. Rather, the unending physical and emotional violence that so many children experienced at home and at school did not appear to the adults at the time as violence, but rather as a necessary and effective measure of the adult's love of the child. This is not to say that the ambient violence between the adult and the child went entirely unnoticed. John Locke, Jean-Jacques Rousseau, William Wordsworth, Ralph Waldo Emerson, and other figures of the seventeenth through nineteenth centuries considered the dominant child-rearing pedagogies to be deleterious to the child's well-being and so to the culture's well-being. In spite of these occasional voices of resistance, the dominant culture remained inexorably and unconsciously committed to its course, a point I take up in more detail in Chapters 2, 4, and 5 as I consider the dominant ideology of Victorian child-rearing.

SLAVERY AS HUMAN RELATIONSHIP

In *The Peculiar Institution*, Kenneth Stamp details how important it was for the Southern slaveholders to learn how to handle their slaves, for the slave did not willingly submit, but always had an eye to resistance, even in the face of the harshest of punishments. Slaves who obeyed were prized. Slaves who chronically disobeyed were whipped, sold, or killed. How might the ideal relationship between slaveholder and slave be cultivated? By the 1830s in the South, slave owning had become an essential part of the regional economy and, in particular, to the Southern way of life. Slave owning, according to one South Carolina pamphleteer, was a science that, when learned, might be profitable for all, even the slave. Accordingly, the ideal relationship between master and slave required the master to be a student of "human nature," reading his slaves and their behavior and knowing when to step in *before* the disobedience or insurrection occurred. Overt physical violence was always an option, but the ideal master dominated his slave emotionally, psychologically, intellectually, and physically. If done well and in proportion, overt acts of violence would be less necessary and so, when performed, more effective in terrorizing others who might otherwise be considering an act of disobedience. Stamp writes,

> a wise master did not take seriously the belief that Negroes were natural-born slaves. He knew better. He knew that Negroes freshly imported from Africa had to be broken in to bondage; that each succeeding generation had to be carefully trained. This was no easy task, for the bondman rarely submitted willingly. Moreover, he rarely submitted completely. In most cases there was no end to the need for control . . . How might this ideal be approached?
>
> The first step of slave management was to establish strict discipline. "They must obey at all times, and under all circumstances, cheerfully and with alacrity," wrote one Virginia slaveholder. Unconditional submission is the only footing upon which slavery should be placed. *It is precisely similar to the attitude of a minor to his parent or a soldier to his general.*
>
> The second step was to implant in the slave a consciousness of personal inferiority. They had to know and keep their place, to feel the difference between master and slave, to understand that bondage was their natural status.
>
> The third step in the training of slaves was to awe them with a sense of their master's enormous power. The only principle upon which slavery could be maintained was the principle of fear not only of the master's power to do violence, but of the master's sacred position *as master*. Few slaves could free themselves altogether from the notion that their masters were invested with a sort of sacredness.
>
> The fourth step was to persuade the slave to take a personal interest in the master's business and to accept his standards of good conduct. The master should make it his business to show his slaves that the advancement of his individual interest is at the same time an advancement of theirs. Once they feel this, it will require but little compulsion to make them act as the master desires.
>
> The final step was to impress the slave with a sense of helplessness, to create in the Negroes a habit of perfect dependence upon their masters. Slaves were taught that they were unfit to look out for themselves, and so then directed their energies to the attainment of mere temporary ease and enjoyment. The masters calculated on this—and did not wish to cure it—and *by constant practice encouraged it.* (emphasis added) [19]

I cite the proceeding material at length because it so aptly reproduces not only the ideology that informs the relationship between master and slave, but also the relationship between adult and child, especially between teacher and student. Those in power, the slave owner understood, had a God-given right and responsibility to dominate those who were "beneath" him. The slave, like the child, must be actively constructed by the adult-master in a continuous process of emotional and physical indoctrination framed by violence—and the ongoing threat of violence—which represented self-evident justification for the master's domination. In other words, violence justifies itself by violence. Both the child and the slave understood this keenly in the antebellum South, in New England, and elsewhere.

The Southerner's pedagogical method of gaining and maintaining mastery of his slaves was drawn quite consciously from other extant institutions that practiced a similar kind of domination and subjugation. The school, the military, and the family were three such common models from which the slave owner learned lessons in slave management.

What I mean is this: the slave owner himself had been treated as a slave when a child. Thus slavery—here understood as the domination and subjugation of another for the master's narcissistic use—was familiar and obvious to anyone who grew up in a world marked by the kind of violence known to the child in the colonial schoolhouse. Slavery confirmed what the adult always already knew about the world, having learned firsthand as a child that violence, domination, and subjugation were a part of "human nature."

The violence inherent in the slave model of human relationships has transgenerational antecedents and consequences. On the one hand, the ideology of slavery as an obvious, necessary given for the plantation owner was constantly affirmed, though indirectly, by the father's detachment-style domination of his children. The rage and longing left behind in the child at the hands of the adult expressed themselves in a willingness to dominate and subjugate the other, in this case, the African.

The slaveholder understood that the only way to maintain power over another human being was to demand strict obedience, and the only way to guarantee strict obedience, was to inculcate an ideology of personal weakness and inferiority. Weak, submissive, terrified people submit. The significant point here is that the slaveholders did not invent a new way to dominate and humiliate others, but rather enacted an already existing pedagogical practice that almost everyone in the dominant culture had experienced firsthand. The slave owner adapted and enacted the contents of his unconscious mind—both ideological and affective—to pedagogy of human relationships that practiced power and violence as a way of life.

That the slave was a "grown-up child" and should be treated as such was a common euphemism of the age. George Fitzhugh, an outspoken defender of slavery and of the "universal law" of racial inequality, wrote in 1857 that "the Negro is but a grown up child, and must be governed as a child, not as a lunatic or criminal. The master occupies toward him the place of parent or guardian." But what did it mean to be a "grown-up child"? According to the slave owner, Africans—like children—could not possibly fend for themselves and therefore required the master's guidance. Slavery, then, "relieves the slave from a far more cruel slavery in Africa, or from idolatry and cannibalism, and every brutal vice and crime that can disgrace humanity; and that it christianizes, protects, supports and civilizes him."[20] In other words, Fitzhugh reproduces an argument that was undoubtedly used *against him* as a child: violence and the threat of it are "for the child's own good."

When an entire class of people—children—is routinely dominated by ambient methods of violent coercion and exploitation, more often than not the people grow up and reenact the ideology and pedagogy they internalized in childhood. Simply put, the child-as-slave becomes the adult slave owner. However, the slave owner remains himself a slave and a victim in spite of his need to enact the victimization of the slave, who, he understands, should be treated just like a child or, in other words, *just like the master was treated when he was a (slave) child.*[21]

Before we begin to bask in the idea that slavery was abolished almost a hundred and fifty years ago, it bears repeating that the inherent violence of the relational structure between the adult and the child continues to be written across Western culture as an ever-intensifying need to dominate and subjugate the other through ever-intensifying means of cultural violence. Often this violence takes the form of economic subjugation justified by "first" and "third" world hierarchies, which differ little from John Winthrop's 1630 proposition that "some are born rich, some mean and in subjection." In short, we live in a world today in which cultural hegemony is made real by the threat of genocidal destruction. This is, in one sense, the master's relationship to the slave writ large across the globe, for the way to maintain hegemony over the other is to constantly remind them that the master has the power to utterly destroy *when the need arises.* Yet, economic, militaristic, or technological domination is the only way to assure Western security, or so the dominant ideology incessantly reminds us. We listen to the ambient story of cultural hegemony that goes on all around us and do not know that we are listening and quite frequently do not even realize that we are obeying because, as children, we were taught with rewards and threats, stories of success and failure, and countless other invisible acts, all of which amounted to one and only one lesson: the child must obey the adult.

Ongoing habitat destruction, the continued stockpiling of weapons of mass destruction. and the potential for global population to double yet again sometime in the next century—to name only a few of the serious threats to the global habitat—all come as a result of *cultural* practices or, in other words, as material expressions of *ideology.* The ambient nature of the intensifying cycle of human violence and habitat destruction—along with a dominant ideology that demands the idealization of childhood—makes only the most grotesque forms of violence perceivable, and soon even these scenes will seem trivial and inevitable. Even so, the survival of the human species is not, in any way, inevitable. Oddly, though, the road to self-destruction that Western culture currently finds itself racing down is too rarely linked with how ideology invents the child, the adult, and the hierarchical nature of the relationship. Understanding the ways in which the dominant culture is produced and reproduced in the simplest, most mundane relational acts between the adult and the child reveals that whatever happens between warring nation-states, between the dominant and the subjugated, between the rich and the poor, happens first between the adult and the child, no more and no less than it ever has, even as the twentieth century, labeled by the child rights activists "the century of the child," has closed.

LOOKING FORWARD

The Puritan story of the child is our story of the child, punctuated as it is by violence, domination, humiliation, and subjugation of the child as a God-given necessity, made necessary as a result of the child's nature. As a result of the lived enactment of these beliefs, the child learned his or her place in the world, and it was a lowly place, a place for the most abject and despised members of the community. Even the schoolmaster, not a favorite citizen of the community, retained absolute power over the child. Violence, domination, humiliation, and subjugation represented the ideological status quo of the Puritans.

The Puritans read each of their favorite texts—the Old Testament, the *New England Primer,* and *The Day of Doom*—in a similar fashion, and one of the ideas they came up with—justified by all three texts—is that the child is a "limb of Satan." The child is unregenerate and bound for Hell simply for being born. Children need the "adult" to save them from their wicked nature. God has created this situation, and this is a fact proved by the Bible. The child-rearing pedagogy of Puritan adults was in many ways familiar to them, for it was detachment parenting made necessary by the demands of the cultural moment. The Puritans swaddled and detached from their children just like their English cousins did. They had every reason to, for they lived, especially in the very early days of the Colonies, at the edge of life and death. They trusted God, and God's Word encouraged—even required—them to dominate their children or risk spoiling their community.

The New World experience did quickly put an end to three generations of overt Puritan ideological domination, or so it seemed. In fact, the Puritan ideology went through a kind of a dispersal in 1692. This dispersal was not a disappearance, but rather more of a reseeding. In many ways Puritan ideology has never entirely released its grip on the dominant ideology. In fact, though the vocabulary had changed by the end of the nineteenth century, the ideological position of the child vis-à-vis the adult culture had not changed at all, and in fact, children experienced what might be seen as an intensification of their experience as subordinates at the hands of the adult world.

Sigmund Freud's work makes this abundantly clear. The psychoanalytic child, for all of his biological psychologies was, like the Puritan child, "flawed" from birth. The child's flawed nature, however described, continued to represent a destablizing threat to the adult status quo. Whether Puritan or Victorian, the response to the child was strikingly similar: adult *ideology* was required to assess and address the biological nature of the child in the name of the adult's conscious and often unconscious acceptance of the cultural status quo as *obvious*. Freud's Oedipus complex implicitly relies on a sensibility about the child's nature that was left over, or transposed, from the seventeenth century in spite of the work of Locke and Rousseau. In the next chapter, I explore this issue in more detail, while at the same time reading history as a human relationship in which the ideological status quo is produced and reproduced in the child via the adult's unconscious child-rearing pedagogies. The individual's mind is also the communal mind, or the collective unconscious. The structure and the emotional content of the individual mind represent a fractal-like microcosm of the macromind. The community reproduces its macromind in its cultural institutions, which are nothing more than material expressions of the mind. After many generations, the material reproduction of mind appears to be "obvious" and "natural" when in fact it is a relative, subjective, highly modifiable cultural phenomenon resulting not from God's plan, or from biological necessity, but rather, from the nature of the human relationships experienced and internalized by the child at the hands of the adult.

Freud suspected the unconscious mind and childhood experiences were intimately connected. The child, Freud discovered, exhibited something he called "the drives"—those deep-seated impulses that motivated human behavior. For Freud, the child's impulses—or drives—came with the child from birth. The adult must help the child to contain these deep biological drives—often taking the form of murderous rage and sexual appetite in the small child, all of which, not unlike the Puritan's child, came into the world from beyond. As brilliant as many of Freud's observations were, his Oedipal theory inadvertently reproduced the dominant ideology regarding the nature of the child, and with the child's nature firmly established, the hierarchical relational structure of the adult to the child remained intact. The adult had to help the child redirect her energies, which meant to properly repress them if the child was to join the adult world as a functional member of the dominant cultural order of the Victorian era.

It is worth noting that Freud became skeptical about the fate of the human race—especially as he watched two world wars and the rise of the nuclear weapon. When asked by Albert Einstein to sign a letter that demanded the outlawing of the development of nuclear weapons, Freud, in his old age, balked and believed the effort to be in vain; attempting to outlaw new weapons was, for Freud, the same as outlawing human aggression and hostility. The predilection for destruction, he had come to believe, was in our nature and not in our nurture.

Detachment-inspired pedagogy is still widely practiced today. In the classroom, in the home, and in the stories we tell about ourselves to our children—on television, in film, in books—the nature of the child and the child's place in the adult world continue to remain "obvious," at least to the adult. Violence has evolved into a subtle, chronic hum that can be almost completely ignored. The child lives and breathes and, ultimately, *becomes* an expression of a dominant culture that practices violence and domination even in seemingly mundane relational moments.

NOTES

[1]For a discussion of twenty-first century population projections, see Nichola Eberstadt, *The Tyranny of Numbers: Mismeasurement and Misrule* (Washington, D.C.: American Enterprise Institute Press, 1995).

[2]I am indebted here to Daniel Quinn's work, including *Ishmael* and *The Story of B,* and the work in critical theory that Theodor Adorno and Max Horkheimer's did as members of the Frankfurt School of Critical Theory.

[3]Louis Althusser, *Lenin and Philosphy and Other Essays,* trans. Ben Brewster (New York: Monthly Review Press, 1971), p. 237.

[4]See Louis Kaplan, *Oneness and Separateness: From Infant to Individual* (New York: Simon & Schuster, 1978) for a discussion of the stages of oneness and separateness the infant moves through on his way, ideally, to "constancy."

[5]This is indebted to the Gestalt approach to human awareness.

[6]For an in-depth exploration of the child's place in a culture other than our own, see Jean Liedloff, *The Continuum Concept: In Search of Happiness Lost* (Reading, Mass.: Perseus Books, 1977).

[7]In *Ishmael: An Adventure of Mind and Spirit* (New York: Bantam, 1992), Daniel Quinn argues persuasively that "western" culture is too narrow a term for what is really a world wide phenomenon, accept for a few indigenous, aboriginal cultures that still exist. One culture, albeit with subcultures within the dominant culture, has spread and dominated human existence, and it has become so prevalent that we mistake this one dominant culture, which Quinn calls "Taker" culture, with life itself. To be in Taker culture, the dominant ideology whispers, is to be more fully human.

[8]Kaplan, *Oneness,* p. 27.

[9]See Frederick Perls, Ralph Hefferline, and Paul Goodman, *Gestalt Therapy Verbatim* (New York: Dell, 1951). The basic principle underlying these disturbances is the environmental demand to be what he is not "the demand to actualize an ideal rather than to actualize himself. He becomes lopsided. Some of his potential is then alienated, repressed, projected. . . . Finally, this deep split between our biological and our social existence leads to more and more conflicts and [personality] "holes." Some of us have no heart or no intuition, some have no legs to stand on, no genitals, no confidence, no eyes or ears" (p. x).

[10]Alexander Lowen, M.D., researcher and therapist, writes,

> the different character structures are classified into five basic types. Each type has a special pattern of defense on both the psychological and the

muscular levels that distinguishes it from the other types. It is important to note that this is a classification not of people but of defensive positions. It is recognized that no individual is a pure type and that every person in our culture combines in different degrees with his personality some or all of these defensive patterns. The personality of an individual as distinct from his character structure is determined by his vitality—that is, by the strength of his impulses. (*The Language of the Body* [New York: Collier, 1958])

To summarize Lowen, in terms of the energetic processes of the body, there are five basic character structures that child-rearing pedagogy inflicts on the child: "schizoid," "oral," "psychopathic," "masochistic," and "rigid." The schizoid character structure describes someone with a diminished sense of self whose ability to connect with the physical reality of the body and its feelings is equally diminished. Most "modern" adults experience the world through a schizoid character structure even though their childhood experiences may not have been traumatizing. This is so because of the basic assumptions Western culture makes about the child and that nearly every adult assumes to be true. The child is other and needs to be trained, taught, and molded into a good citizen. These beliefs lead to a split in the child between the head and the feelings, thereby cutting the child off from feelings of power, aggression, sadness, and joy. This makes an obedient child, but a depressed and confused adult. The end result is a person who is all head and no heart and is often unaware of the murderous rage within. The rage is unconscious in nature and will never be taken seriously until adults take seriously their own emotional needs and, by extension, the real emotional needs of infants and children. Our culture has been reaping the consequences of the schizoid split more frequently as the ideology of the dominant culture offers the schizoid character inappropriate, fantasy release of murderous rage. Those killed by the release of murderous rage, however, do not experience it as a fantasy.

[11]In *The Drama of the Gifted Child: The Search for the True Self,* trans. Ruth Ward (New York: HarperCollins, 1997), and *For Your Own Good: Hidden Cruelty in Child-rearing and the Root of Violence,* trans. Hildegarde, and Hunter Hannum (New York: Farrar, Straus & Giroux, 1984), Alice Miller details the process by which the repression of childhood affect turns into adult neurosis.

[12]Liedloff, *Continuum Concept,* xix.

[13]The relationship of the adult to the child in Western culture appears to be so obvious that it frequently goes unquestioned, even in times of inexplicable acts of violence done by children to other children. Ideology absorbs this feedback not as information by which we might reconsider our most basic assumptions about the human community, but rather as proof that the child, indeed, requires even *more* taming than we at first thought. Nevertheless, histories of childhood do exist that take up the child's experience as much as this is possible, as in Philip Aries's ground-breaking study of childhood as a history of abuse in *Centuries of Childhood: A Social History of Family Life* (New York: Random House, 1962) and Lloyd DeMause's "psychogenic" view of history in *The History of Childhood* (Northvale, N.J.: Jason Aronson, 1995), which develops his own thesis, though indebted to Aries' original project nonetheless. Still, these histories of childhood have been found wanting by some theorists and historians, and sometimes for good reason. In fact, other histories of childhood take on

this thesis and have argued that, in fact, childhood was not so bad. Those who believe in childhood abuse as a history of Western culture are simply not looking at all of the evidence. In *Forgotten Children: Parent-Child Relations from 1500–1900* (Cambridge: Cambridge University Press, 1983), Linda Pollock argues that DeMause and Aries were simply too extreme and that the relationship between the adult and the child is one of continuity these past four hundred years. Violence, for Pollock, was the exception rather than the rule.

Pollock's view that the history of the relationship between the adult and the child is one of continuity in which love and care have been largely constant has merit, but so, too, does DeMause's psychogenic view of history. DeMause's psychogenic theory of history argues that the relationship between the adult and the child represents a primary drive of historical process. Both the DeMause thesis and the Pollock thesis suffer from their own unconscious blind spots. DeMause and Aries have been taken to task for looking at only a "minority" of children and then generalizing about the condition of children as nearly universally exploited and abused up until the nineteenth century. Pollock, on the other hand, argues that the majority of children "were wanted," and that this has been so even as cultural ideas about what constitutes a childhood have changed over the centuries. Some children are abused, Pollock admits, but only a small minority.

Other ways of understanding the history of the relationship between the adult and the child exist, outside or perhaps between the DeMause and Pollock lines of inquiry. This work, as Hugh Cunningham describes it, is reminiscent of Pollock's position, and it "undermined the old sociological assumption that there had been a transition, generally associated with industrialization, from extended families to nuclear families; the nuclear family now became the norm. It thus became possible to argue that loving relationships within nuclear families had a perdurance in history and a power to withstand the onslaughts and intrusions of church, of state, and of economic change" (*Children and Childhood in Western Society Since 1500* [New York: Longman, 1995], p. 15).

There are significant problems with what appear to be contradictory views of the history of childhood. On the one hand, DeMause chooses to see history as a process of evolution and improvement, for children especially. DeMause maps out the history of childhood as evolving through different "child-rearing" modes. He begins with the most violent child-rearing mode, "infanticidal," and links it to the earliest date in his historical analysis, "antiquity to the fourth century, A.D." The modes continue, moving steadily towards the present. The closer we come to the present in DeMause's history, the more civilized our practices are, he observes. After infanticidal mode comes the "abandonment mode," the "ambivalent mode," the "intrusive mode," the "socialization mode" and, finally, the "helping mode."

Though DeMause acknowledges that these modes tend to overlap in any one particular historical moment, he relies heavily on the specious notion that we were savages to our children "way back when," and we have tamed ourselves, and so have found a more humane way to tame our children. A psychogenic view of history must accept the possibility that human civilization has not evolved towards a helping mode. Parents always helped their children, as Pollock and others have argued. Nor did infanticide end in the fourth century A.D. Adults have always felt ambivalence for their children from time to time. The question of whether this erupted into violent and deadly forms of child-rearing depends on the cultural and historical context. In other words, what did the dominant culture say about adult ambivalence towards children? If exposure or abandonment were the norm, then an adult may act out his or her feelings of deep ambivalence in this way. Or perhaps the dominant culture condoned infanticide, the drowning of second daughters. Perhaps the economic strain might appear so great to a family that a second daughter, defined by the dominant culture as weak and as a drain on the family's economic viability, might be drowned outright, or perhaps exposed at the local garbage heap either to die or to be picked up by some other adult more inclined to raise a daughter.

[14]John Winthrop, *A Model of Christian Charity*. The text is from Samual Eliot Morison, ed., *Old South Leaflets* (Boston: Old South Association, 1837).

[15]From Patricia Demers and Gordon Moyles, eds., *From Instruction to Delight: An Anthology of Children's Literature to 1850* (Toronto: Oxford University Press, 1982), pp. 29–33.

[16]See Paulo Freire, *The Pedagogy of the Oppressed* (New York: Continuum, 1995).

[17]See Miller, *For Your Own Good*. In it, she cites numerous pedagogues who discuss the countless ways violence and the fear of violence are used to manipulate the child into obedience that serves adult ends.

[18]Alice Morse Earle, *Child Life in Colonial Days* (Stockbridge, Mass.: Berkshire House, 1993), p. 197.

[19]Kenneth Stamp, *The Peculiar Institution: Slavery in the Ante-Bellum South* (New York: Random House, 1956), p. 144–48.

[20]George Fitzhugh, *Cannibals All or, Slaves without Masters* (n.p., 1857).

[21]The ideology of submission, domination, superiority, and inferiority runs like a sedimentary deposit across the geology of the ideological landscape. John Locke makes a similar argument at the end of the seventeenth century not about slaves, but about the king to his subjects in *The True End of Civil Government*. When Locke discusses the power the father has over the child he likens it to that of the monarch over his subjects. It is absolute and necessary, for the children like slaves, "are not born in this full state of equality." Though Locke argues that the two powers, "political and paternal," are distinct and separate, he cannot resist detailing how, in fact, similar they are. The father is a king of his house. The father demands perfect obedience and submission. The father is a priest over his family. All of these qualities the monarch should assume as well over his subjects. Locke, *The True End of Civil Government* (London: Oxford University Press, 1960).

CHAPTER 2

Freud, Shakespeare, and *Hamlet* as Children's Literature

> *The tendency for adults to use their children as best they can to meet [adult] needs is so widespread and so taken for granted in world history that most people do not refer to this form of sexual abuse as a perversion; it is simply one of the many ways adults exercise power over their children.*

—ALICE MILLER, *For Your Own Good*

THE SEDUCTION THEORY

In 1896 Sigmund Freud published "On the Aetiology of Hysteria," a controversial paper advancing a theory that explained adult psychological disorders as latter-day expressions of childhood sexual trauma, otherwise known as the "seduction theory." Freud would later call this his "first great error." For a short time, however, Freud believed that he had found the root of adult hysteria: the use and abuse of the child as a sexualized object by the adult. According to the seduction theory, early sexual experiences up to the age of four were necessarily traumatic and so necessitated the ego-defense Freud called "repression." Freud began to suspect that adult hysteria—what we call neurosis today—was repressed affect from childhood emerging in disguised form.

Throughout 1896 Freud was beginning to suspect that his entire culture abused their children routinely, and that it all too frequently took the form of sexual abuse, or what he called "premature sexual shock." Adults seduced children for adult pleasure. This made sense to an adult raised in an ideology that implicitly accepted that the "other," the child-object, was there for the dominant adult-subject. As Freud and others were exploring the new world of the unconscious and attempting to map it out and discover its connection to our waking life, most adults routinely believed that what happened to a two- or three-year-old would not be remembered later by the child any more than a potted plant would remember. So, it followed that the adults might exercise their power over the child in any manner they felt necessary.[1]

The degree to which the adult suffers from hysterical symptoms corresponds to the amount of repressed affect, which in turn corresponds to the degree to which the child experienced abuse and was then implicitly required to deny the event and the attendant emotional response, which included terror, horror, confusion, rage, powerlessness, and deep sadness. According to the seduction theory, the child's repression reappeared in the adult as hysterical symptoms including varied physical illnesses, identity disorders, and long-standing emotional depression. In "On the Aetiology of Hysteria," Freud documents his seduction theory with eighteen patients—six men and twelve women—all of which in the course of treatment discovered memories of sexual abuse.

Freud understood the controversial nature of the seduction theory. It indicted adult Victorian culture even as it sought to explain it to itself and it left Freud open to popular attack and professional disgrace, for if he was right, most adults in Victorian England probably experienced abuse of one form or another as children. This was too much for his contemporaries to accept, for as adults they were well-educated members of the scientific aristocracy, and as such represented the leading edge of the most "civilized" culture in the Victorian world. How could a Victorian culture that considered itself to be the most civilized, most evolved, and most technologically advanced of all the world's cultures hide such a bizarre and unsettling nightmare in its closet?

Not unmindful of the professional risk he was taking in advancing the seduction theory, Freud wrote to Fliess, his confessor and closest confidant, defending his conclusions and his theory. His patients' memories were real, Freud concluded, because when his patients recalled "these infantile experiences to consciousness, they suffered under the most violent sensations of which they are shamed and which they try to conceal."[2] "I therefore put forward the thesis," Freud wrote before the Oedipal theory, "that at the bottom of every case of hysteria there are one or more occurrences of premature sexual experience, occurrences which belong to the earliest years of childhood but which can be reproduced through the work of psycho-analysis in spite of the intervening decades."[3]

Freud was in no way pleased with his seduction theory in that it shed such a harsh light on Victorian culture, *his* culture, his father's culture, and one from which he sought approval and success. Nevertheless, for a time he pushed the theory forward and named names. Adults who had ready access to children were responsible. "Foremost among those guilty of abuses like these, with their momentous consequences," he wrote, "are nursemaids, governesses and domestic servants." Perhaps the most unsettling implication of the seduction theory is in the indictment of the parent, for hysteria was not transmitted genetically from father to child, but rather as a result of child-rearing practices.

It is no wonder then that the seduction theory was given, according to Freud, an "icy reception from the masses. . . . And this after one has demonstrated to them the solution to a more than thousand-year-old problem—a 'source of the Nile!' " For Freud, in 1896, the seduction theory was *the* breakthrough theory that explained the neurotic behavior of individuals as well as entire cultures. Yet in finding the psychodynamic "source of the Nile," Freud had unknowingly discovered his own family, for in early 1897 Freud began noting in his own sister signs of "psychoneurosis," a psychological disturbance brought on by—according to the seduction theory—the sexual abuse of the child by the adult. This was a crucial moment for the seduction theory, for the death of Freud's father in the autumn of 1896 left Freud emotionally reeling, doubting himself and the aggressive, condemnatory nature of the seduction theory. And by the fall of 1897 Freud had officially abandoned the seduction theory, for to go on believing in it meant that he had to accept its dire logic. Almost a year after his father's death, Freud wrote to Fliess that "in every case the father, not excluding my own, had to be blamed as a pervert" if the seduction theory as it then stood were to remain intact and consistent with itself.[4] This meant that Freud's sister's psychoneurosis had its root and source in the child-rearing practices of Jacob Freud, Sigmund's father. This conclusion the son could not finally accept.

Nevertheless, "Freud might have continued to believe in the seduction theory had it not been for the death of his father in the autumn of 1896 and his own self-analysis to which he turned so much energy after that death."[5] After his father's death Freud felt "torn up by the roots," and became convinced that the death of the father was the most significant event in a man's life. Though this may be true for some, it is not true for all. The birth of one's child, or the death of one's mother or spouse, may supersede the death of one's father as the most significant event in one's life. Still, for Freud, the death of his father *was* deeply unsettling, dredging up as it did feelings about his father that had been buried within him for years. By the end of Freud's self-analysis he had come to believe that the seduction theory was a "great error" and a near disaster for his career.

By October 1897, Freud had pursued his self-analysis to the point where he recognized his own "love of the mother and jealousy of the father" as the root and source of his own neurotic tendencies. It should be noted that only after the death of his father did "jealousy" become a congenital feature of the child's character. From the point of view of the seduction theory, the child's jealousy of the father may be understood not as a congenital condition, but as the result of the child's emotional needs going unmet by the adult world, including but not limited to the father and the mother. In Freud's case, however, like so many other Victorian children, the child was separated from the father by cultural requirements of filial loyalty, obedience, an oppressive work ethic, and a family life that gave little credence to the child's emotional life. Specifically, Freud as a child, learned early that his family required filial loyalty, even if it meant that the child must pretend not to see what he has in fact seen. Freud's observation about his relationship to his father in *The Interpretation of Dreams* "raises . . . the possibility that even the most sacred of Freud's beliefs owed more to personal experience than is usually admitted."[6]

Freud was more than a Victorian child—he was a Jewish child as well, and this, along with the prevailing child-rearing pedagogies of the time, informed his relationship with his father. Freud's own memories of his father as a gruff, distant, and occasionally violent adult offer some insight into the child's growing character: sure of his Jewishness, even though his father at times questioned it, and sure of his difference, even though his father did not recognize it. Freud would spend much of his life—especially his professional life before 1896—finding surrogate fathers to fill his emotional need for support, approval, and guidance. From Jean-Martin Charcot at the Salpêtrière asylum in Paris in the mid-1880s, Freud began to suspect that it was perhaps nurture rather than nature behind a patient's neurosis. Equally important, perhaps, is Freud's idealization of Charcot. He writes to his new wife, Martha Bernays, about his work at the asylum with Charcot and what a revolutionizing experience it was: "what I do know is that no other human being has ever affected me in the same way." Charcot, a genius in Freud's eyes, had taken notice of Freud, and this—not unlike the death of Freud's father ten years later—"revolutionized" Freud's soul. Josef Breuer later took the place of Charcot as Freud's mentor and surrogate father. By 1887 Freud would be in practice for himself in Vienna and his famous correspondence with Wilhelm Fliess would begin and continue for seventeen years.

Professional relationships and personal friendships are unremarkable in and of themselves. The nature of Freud's relationships with Charcot, Bruer, and, finally, Fliess, should be noted, for the intensity with which Freud threw himself into these relationships—so unlike his relationships with women, for instance, and so frequently one-sided as Jeffrey Masson documents—speaks to Freud's emotional need for a connection with a figure that, like a father, might help to stabilize and approve of his brilliant and careening mind.

Soon after the death of Freud's father, the seduction theory was abandoned and the Oedipal theory was born, and so, too, the father, for the Oedipal theory recasts the father not as a perpetrator of sexual abuse, but as the victim of the child's compulsive sexuality and inborn need to destroy the father and possess the mother. In 1900 Freud outlined his Oedipus theory in

The Interpretation of Dreams. The destiny of King Oedipus, he wrote, "moves us only because it might have been ours—because the oracle laid the same curse upon us before our birth as upon him. It is the fate of all of us, perhaps, to direct our first sexual impulse towards our mother and our first hatred and or first murderous wish against our father."[7]

Even as Freud propounded the Oedipal theory, he was loath to abandon his previous work altogether, and he continued to collect evidence in support of the seduction theory from his patients. Yet the theory was doomed for one reason: Freud was a driven, ambitious, public man, driven to achieve professional fame with the same intensity with which he attached himself to Fliess. He desired fame and notoriety, and his publications and lectures on the seduction theory had won him little of either by 1896. Freud realized that pursuing the theory would all but guarantee professional isolation, which for him was synonymous with the emotional abandonment, betrayal, and rejection he had experienced as a boy with his father.

The death of Jacob Freud in 1896 led to the son's lengthy period of self-analysis. Eighteen months later Freud had abandoned the seduction theory, concluding that "it was hardly credible that perverted acts against children were so general. Perversion would have to be immeasurably more frequent than hysteria, as the illness can only arise where the events have accumulated and one of the factors which weaken defense is present."[8] If the seduction theory were correct, and hysteria was as common as it seemed to be to Freud in 1896, then it followed that sexual and other forms of abuse adults inflicted on children were far more common—in fact almost universal—than he could at the time come to accept. In short, Freud could not continue to develop a theory that indicted an entire culture and moreover cast his own father as the victimizer. Instead, Freud drew upon the dominant ideology of the Victorian era—an ideology of the child that stretched back to the Old Testament—and constructed the Oedipal theory, a description of human relationship's that inadvertently cast the *child as the seducer*. From this point of view, memories of sexual abuse were the fantasy of the child, an expression of the child's inborn nature.

The Oedipal theory had a number of consequences for the development of psychoanalysis, for it meant that Freud stopped short his inquiry into the cultural and ideological antecedents that informed the nature of the relationship between the adult and the child. Had he pursued the seduction theory, Freud might have expanded his definition of seduction beyond the narrow confines of "sexual" events and so come to understand the ways in which the child's seduction might be understood in terms of ordinary Victorian child-rearing practices. Instead, he clung to the ideological status quo of Victorian adult culture and abandoned the seduction theory altogether. What Freud could not understand at the time was that neurosis might develop from abusive and traumatizing events experienced as a child as a result of the adult's domination over the child, even though that domination may not have become sexualized, and even though it was sanctioned and even required by the dominant culture. Read in this way, the seduction theory offers a way of seeing Victorian child-rearing pedagogies that celebrated adult power and the child's obedience—and the emotional repression that resulted—as part and parcel of a broader understanding of Freud's aetiology of adult hysteria. Sexual seduction, in other words, is one of the most intense forms of the adult's seduction and betrayal of the child, but by no means is it the only form.

Even so, by the autumn of 1897—a year after his father's death—Freud had recanted and exonerated his father concluding his suspicions about him were groundless, all as a result of what he described in his letters to Fliess as the beginning of his "self-analysis." Freud's self-analysis—a practice he would continue for the rest of his life—ultimately begs the question: can one analyze oneself and find accurate information? Freud's self-analysis confirmed not so much the truth or falsity of his patients' claims about their past—or about his own past—as Freud's own subjective, heartfelt need for a father and a connection to a meaningful if idealized past that the father represents to the son, especially when that father has been emotionally gruff, and aloof in life. At death, suddenly, the father becomes all, a demigod full of "wisdom and imaginative light-heartedness" and this is nowhere more true than in Freud's recollections of his father after his death. In short, the seduction theory dethroned Jacob Freud, traduced him even, and left Sigmund alone, and cut off from his culture, his family, his own past, and perhaps, his professional future. After 1897 and his self-analysis, Freud "discovered" the error of his ways. Freud now believed that the suspicions about his father's guilt were false and instead pointed to the son's inborn desire to destroy the father and therefore to the child's guilt. Jacob Freud's assumed molestation or seduction [of his sister] was "no more than the figment of Freud's own imagination."[9] His sister's psychoneurosis, then, had to come from some source, other than her childhood experiences at the hands of her father. So, too, that of all of Freud's other patients. And so as Freud exonerated his father—and castigated himself for his disrespectful suspicions of him—he exonerated every adult everywhere and is forced to work not with the memories and suffering of his patients, but against them. The all-knowing authority of the father had been reestablished.

THE OEDIPAL THEORY

After 1897 the seduction stories of Freud's most troubled patients came to be recognized not as *memories*, but as *fantasies*. According to the Oedipal Theory, "parents do not actually abuse their children in order to fulfill their own needs but children supposedly fantasize this abuse, repressing their own aggressive and sexual desires (instinctual drives) and experiencing these desires—through the mechanism of projection—as being directed against them from the outside."[10] Whereas the seduction theory believed in the toxicity of repressed memories, the Oedipal theory believed in the necessity of repressing the "Oedipal phase" in an appropriate way. The seduction theory believed that children should be spared from premature sexual shock; the oedipal theory argued that children necessarily bring it on themselves. The seduction theory argued that adults seduce children for their pleasure; the Oedipal theory argued that children seduce adults because it is in the child's nature to be "sexual." The seduction theory believed in the child's nurturing environment as the determining factor of his or her psychological health as an adult, the Oedipal theory focused squarely on the child's nature as the significant determining factor for psychological health as an adult. According to Freud's daughter, Anna, a fervent believer in her father's psychoanalysis, nothing in the child's relationship with adults "is pathogenic, even if it is significant for the formation of the ego and personality."[11]

What this means is that the child's nature, or what we today call the child's genetic makeup, determines the child's later psychological life. Nothing is pathogenic; that is, nothing can cause illness from the outside. Freud's world is a determined world from "outside." It all comes from within, and apparently, the child brings this along from birth. This is an extreme view, yet it is necessary if one is to take seriously the Oedipal theory and the theory of infantile sexuality. We have to be born conflicted, in order for Freudian psychoanalysis to make sense. From this perspective Freud comes close to recapitulating his Jewish roots and the Judeo-Christian ideological belief in "original" sin, which states that man is a fallen creature as a result of Adam's "first" sin, a sin of disobedience against God, "the Father." Obedience has *always* been a highly valued element in child-rearing pedagogies indigenous to Western culture.

For Freud, then, the child comes into the world poised to project onto the parents murderous rage and sexual desire, and when this tumultuous stage is not properly repressed, neurotic psychological illness—and the conflict-ridden history of Western civilization—are the result. This is "original sin" recast, and it remains a heavy load for the child—and the culture—to bear.[12]

CULTURE, IDEOLOGY, AND THE SEDUCTION THEORY REVISITED

The adult draws the ideological line that separates "acceptable" childhood trauma—which from this point of view is not really *trauma* after all—from unacceptable sexual trauma of the kind inflicted on the child by pedophiles and sociopaths. Questioning how and where this line is drawn, however, can be a tricky business, as Freud himself discovered. On the one side are the acceptable child-rearing techniques that the dominant culture sanctions and often requires the adult to practice in order to enjoy community membership. Any trauma to the child that results from these culturally sanctioned practices is always already necessary and "for the child's own good." The majority then define the minority in terms that offset the violence inherent in the child-rearing practices of the majority. As a result, according to the dominant culture, a tiny minority of freaks do exist. They are monsters who attack and use the child for their own perverted pleasure. The dominant culture has nothing to do with the other, even though the other throws in sharp relief by their monstrous acts the ostensible normalcy of the majority. The pedophile, as James Kincaid argues in *Child-Loving: The Erotic Child and Victorian Culture,* is always something "other," and never *us.* In this way the dominant culture needs the pedophile—even revels in his existence—in order to justify the dominant culture's own sense of obvious rightness. That the pedophile *defines* adult culture, however, is difficult to discuss or approach directly, as Kincaid's elliptical study of the Victorian child and Victorian culture implicitly communicates.[13]

Nevertheless, Kincaid reminds us that we should make no mistake when considering the Victorian culture and its predilection for pedophilia: Victorian culture is the dominant culture, and any line contemporary culture draws between itself and the oppressive world of Victorian sexuality merely reinscribes the line yet again; on the one side the prudish, pedophilic Victorians, and on the other, the so-called enlightened majority of contemporaneity. The dominant adult culture has always reared the child through what should be understood as a chronic, ambient process of seduction, and what makes it difficult to discern this process is its ambient, ideological, unconscious nature. The seduction and its negative consequences for the child and the culture can be seen only in their most extreme and grotesque manifestations: pedophilia, for instance, or children shooting children. Freud used just this type of argument to finally justify his abandonment of the seduction theory: it could not be true, he convinced himself, because if it was, then *everyone* was implicated. That everyone might be implicated and not realize it, however, is precisely what those who study ideology and the unconscious find so fascinating.

If we understand Victorian child-rearing pedagogues as a culturally enshrined rape of the child's original mind—so commonly enacted that it was, and remains, invisible—then the chronic and ambient nature of neurosis that Freud discovered before 1896 makes more sense. From this point of view it can be safely claimed that all children suffer from a broad definition of sexual abuse even when the abuse has not been overtly "sexualized" by the abuser. Rather, emotional trauma as an energetic, physical experience impacts the child's sexuality to the degree to which certain ideas about the body become fused with the child's repressed affect, all of which results from the relationship between the adult and the child in the most mundane, ordinary moments. This is so because all abuse is based on an imbalance of power in a relationship in which the one believes one has an absolute cultural, spiritual, or biological right to dominate and subjugate the other.[14] At its most basic, the relationship between the adult and the child in almost any era of Western culture conforms to this hierarchy. When the adult demands obedience from the child while prohibiting the child an emotional discharge, the repressed emotional energy is stored in the body in the form of cellular information, just as Freud suspected before 1896. Moreover, stored emotional energy might lead to diseases of all sorts, including anxiety disorders, chronic fatigue disorders, depressions, and even cancers, all of which Freud suspected before to 1896—and others have explored more recently.[15] Child-rearing experiences, Freud believed before 1896, might indeed be what he called at first the "source of the Nile" for not only the adult's psychic and physical existence, but the culture's as well.

THE OEDIPUS COMPLEX AND FREUD'S *HAMLET*

Freud turned to literature and discovered stories that exemplified his newly constructed Oedipal theory. In 1897 Freud writes yet another letter to Fliess in which he sees in *Hamlet* Shakespeare's unconscious portrayal of every man's Oedipal dilemma. In the Oedipal dilemma, according to Freud, the inborn desire to sexually possess the mother's body has not been successfully repressed in Hamlet, and it is these desires that drive him to distraction—he lives in and through them unconsciously his entire life. The sexual desire for the mother—along with the attendant rage at the father, who stands between the son and the mother—surfaces in a tangled and confused way in the form of what Freud calls Hamlet's "melancholia," his hysterical depression. When, at the beginning of the play, Hamlet learns of his father's death, he is confused, hurt, angry, despondent, and hopeless, and lacks motivation to do anything except contemplate suicide. Hamlet, according to Freud, has such a difficult time in avenging his father's death—once he learns of it through the ghost of his father—because Young Hamlet unconsciously recognized his own desire in Claudius's murderous, jealous deed. This unresolved desire resurfaces in the form of Hamlet—now an adult—unconsciously pursuing his mother in a confused and desperate attempt to possess and dispossess himself of his desire for the sexualized, idealized love object the mother represents.[16] Freud finds a similar conflict in Sophocles' *Oedipus the King,* a story that takes place two thousand years prior to Hamlet.[17]

Freudian psychoanalysis has given way to theories of ego development that directly challenge Freud's deterministic claims. Barbara Schapiro writes, for instance, that the post-Freudian relational model of the developing self might be better understood as a tapestry in which the whole cannot be so easily separated from the part. Schapiro writes that contemporary psychoanalysis believes that "the model of the universe is no longer one of separate working parts; the lens of the new sciences delineates a view of the universe as a dynamic patterning of interactions, connections, and interrelationships."[18] Relational models of the developing self observe that character structure—or self—develops all within a context, and that, unlike Freudian claims, everything is pathogenic in the child's development. This means that one's character is determined as much by one's genetic makeup—one's nature—as one's nurture. In other words, human relationships determine the nature of the child's self.[19]

According to the relational model of the developing self the child brings the potential for strong affect with him, but there is no preordained biological requirement for the son to develop murderous rage towards the father. Rage is not a fact of nature; rather, it is a fact of nurture. From the relational model, strong affect and strong desire—once thought to be primordial realities by Freud—are in fact consequences of the relational matrix the child is born into. From this perspective, then, to understand how the relational matrix in which the adult and the child interact and have their being—and so produced and reproduce the dominant culture of which they are a part—we must consider the basic ideological assumptions that govern the pedagogical practices of the relationship between the adult and the child. As Freud suspected, the stories a culture tells itself about itself—a culture's literary production—speak sometimes brazenly, sometimes subtly, and almost always often unconsciously—to the basic ideological assumptions that govern the relationship between the adult and the child.

THE RELATIONAL MODEL AND *HAMLET* AS CHILDREN'S LITERATURE

The relational model of the developing self underscores the dynamic, dialectical, pathogenic nature of how adult culture produces and reproduces itself through the child. This is nowhere more apparent than in texts produced by adults for children. Though often dismissed as inconsequential, children's literature nevertheless represents a unique field of literary study in the larger arena of literary studies in that none of the literature consumed by the audience is produced by the audience. This alone raises serious ideological questions. Whose interests are served when one group determines what another group will read? When reading children's literature in any of its manifold forms—from the fairy tale, to the picture book, to the cartoon, to the novel, to the animated film—the child is always already consuming a version of him or herself through the ideological apparatus of the dominant adult culture.

Historians of childhood note that the adult production of "children's literature" began in earnest in the seventeenth and eighteenth centuries in Europe and America. Though texts for children—usually didactic in nature—

have existed in one form or another for millennia, the rapid rise in children's literature coincided with the rise of the middle class, public schooling, and the colonization of the New World. The intensification of the production of children's literature has been hailed as a change for the better, linked as it is to Western culture's ideological understanding of children and the rise of what we call "childhood." The rise of a literature targeted specifically at children signifies, according to nearly all concerned, a broadening, more sympathetic view of the nature of childhood and the needs of the child. This claim will be discussed and questioned in subsequent chapters. For now it is sufficient to note that children's literature did not exist in Europe and America as a cultural *commodity* or as a part of school curriculums prior to and through seventeenth and early eighteenth centuries.[20]

Nevertheless, a kind of children's literature did exist in, say, Shakespeare's England, for in one way or another all literary production is a record of, among other things, human relationships, human conflict, and the ideologies that give rise to the cultural field in which human relationships take place. In this way *all* literary production is a reproduction of the author's experiences as a child at the hands of the adult world, for in those generative experiences as a child the adult's character is invented, and as an adult author, he reinvents himself and the relational world that invented him in his literary work. This is almost always an unconscious process, with some exceptions.

In this way, then, an "adult" literary work speaks directly to the nature of the relationship between the adult and the child as it exists in the unconscious mind of the author. The author's literary text can then be read as a site of unconscious projection—or ideological representation—of his unconscious experiences as a child. From this perspective *Hamlet* can be understood as children's literature in that it dramatizes the story of how a culture built on the quest for power, violence, domination, and subjugation produces and reproduces itself first and foremost in the relationship between the parent and the child.

Hamlet remains a remarkable and contemporary story precisely because, as Freud suspected, it sheds light on the process by which a human being is made into a cultural being and the trauma, conflict and suffering that result. In *Hamlet* Shakespeare gives us, a story of family, monarchy, and the sovereign nation-state, showing that when the workings of one are considered, the others are automatically invoked. At the heart of this story is the relationship of the parent and the child—and it is not, as Freud consciously suspected, an Oedipal story, but rather, is what he *unconsciously* suspected though could not allow himself to see for fear of betraying the father: *Hamlet* is the story of the adult's seduction of the child.

All of the children in *Hamlet*—Hamlet, Laertes, Ophelia, and Fortinbras—are fused to the dominant adult culture and can imagine no other reality, even if their beliefs about themselves result in suffering, self-betrayal, and self-destruction. The dominant ideology of the adult culture governs the child's relationship to "reality" in *Hamlet,* and that "reality" is always one and the same with adult culture. "His will is not his own," Laertes says to Ophelia about Hamlet. Laertes believes that Hamlet's will belongs to the people of Denmark, who must choose his fate, for in Hamlet's fate is the fate of the nation. Though this may be true according to the dominant story of monarchy and election, it is equally true that Hamlet's will is not his own because it belongs not to himself, but to a myriad of others, all of which Shakespeare brings to life in Hamlet's story. In other words, Hamlet's mind is not his own because it is cathected to a myriad of idealized abstractions that then unconsciously structure the nature of his "lived" relationships with himself, Claudius, Gertrude, Ophelia, and others.

To understand the nature of the relationships between the adult and the child in *Hamlet,* we need to view the text as a crossroads of culture, ideology, and metaphor. Stephen Greenblatt describes such a text as

> a focal point for converging lines of force in the sixteenth-century culture;
> their significance for us is not that we may see through them to underlying
> and prior historical principles but rather that we may interpret the interplay
> of their symbolic structures with those perceivable in the careers of their
> authors and in the larger social world as constituting a single, complex
> process of self-fashioning, and through this interpretation, come closer to
> understanding how literary and social identities were formed in this
> culture.[21]

The quest here, then, is to provide a way of accessing the *Hamlet* text—and the larger social world that gave rise to it—in such a way that the root and source of Hamlet's idealized abstractions—and the repressed affect that drives them and his conflict with himself—might be understood to be the symbolic projections of Shakespeare's mind, invented as his mind was in his time as a child in sixteenth-century England. In this way Shakespeare's *Hamlet* gives us access to characters who have been, by and large, seduced and betrayed by adult culture while children and, by the time of the drama, continue to live out this oppressive relational hierarchy forced on them as a child by the parent, which is the source of their undoing.

SHAKESPEARE-AS-CHILD

Queen Elizabeth began her reign in 1558. Shakespeare was born six years later in 1564. This section does not present an argument about Shakespeare's genius. Rather, I propose that understanding Shakespeare's childhood is understanding his ordinariness. There is every reason to believe that his experiences as a child growing up in Straford-upon-Avon in the latter half of the 1560's were wholly ordinary.[22]

Even before the great educational reforms of the seventeenth century, the education of the child was alive and well. The child was taught continuously by adults of every sort, but especially those adults who held political or ideological power: the parish priest, the schoolteacher, the political official, and the parent. All must be obeyed, respected, feared. The child was taught curricular content only in as much as it produced and reproduced ideological realities: the child must know his or her lowly place in the hierarchical scheme of things.

In 1564, England was in the middle of a cultural crisis—tensions were high. The rising market economy was creating unemployment as it had never been known in England. Furthermore, the political and religious unease unsettled the ideological foundations of English society even as the economic foundations crumbled for the ordinary English yeoman. At the end of the sixteenth century, Queen Elizabeth toured her kingdom and, upon returning to London, exclaimed "Paupers are everywhere!" Only a hundred years before Elizabeth's tour, one historian writes, "the English countryside consisted in large part of peasant proprietors tilling their own lands, the yeoman, the pride of England, the largest body of independent, free, and prosperous citizens in the world."[23] By the end of the sixteenth century, enclosure laws and the rising market economy had displaced many thousands, who became unemployed and without access to their previous manner of subsistence. They and their children would become the inexpensive labor force behind the ever-rising market economy, the middle-class, and later, the Industrial Revolution. As Robert Heilbroner notes, "The problem of survival was henceforth to be solved neither by custom nor by common, but by the free action of profit-seeking men bound together only by the market itself. The system was to be called capitalism. And the idea of gain which underlay it was to become so firmly rooted that men would soon vigorously affirm that it was an eternal and omnipresent part of human nature."[24] The rise of capitalism and the market economy merely shifted the terms of the ongoing process of cultural domination of the many by the few, while concentrating the power to direct the cultural domination into fewer and fewer hands. Capitalism was an intensification of the already extant ideology of hierarchy, superiority, and domination, and so the economic process by which class and caste became a lived political and cultural reality made unconscious sense to the many, since it tallied with their experience.

Along with the economic upheavals of the sixteenth century came political and religious turmoil. By the time of his birth Shakespeare's parents, John and Mary, had witnessed the transformation of England from a Catholic to an Anglican nation when, in 1534, Henry VIII decreed the Act of Supremacy and declared himself the supreme head of the Church of England. Men and women lost their lives as a result of their refusal to swear allegiance to Henry as the supreme head of state *and* church, including Sir Thomas More, whom

Henry ordered beheaded in 1535 in the Tower of London for failing to take the Oath of Supremacy. Edward VI, Henry's only son, assumed the throne at the death of his father in 1547. In 1549, fifteen years after the beginning of reformation in England, Edward introduced uniform Protestant services in England based on Edward VI's *Book of Common Prayer.*

In 1553, on the death of Edward VI, Lady Jane Grey was proclaimed Queen of England by the Duke of Northumberland; her reign lasted nine days. Mary I, daughter of Henry VIII and Catherine of Aragon was crowned Queen of England. Mary immediately began the Restoration of Roman Catholicism in England by restoring to power the Roman Catholic bishops deported by her father. By 1555 England officially returned to Roman Catholicism. Mary ordered Protestants persecuted, and about three hundred were burned at the stake. In 1558 Mary died and her half-sister Elizabeth became Queen. Elizabeth repealed Mary's Catholic legislation and reestablished a nominal protestant Anglicanism in England.

Pope Clement VII's Catholicism, Henry VIII's Anglicanism, Mary I's Catholicism, and Elizabeth I's Protestantism are more alike than they are different when considered as cultural ideology. The Catholic Church before the Reformation taught that good citizenship was obedience to God, and because God was not always on hand, the good citizen, the good Christian, obeyed God's representatives, represented by a top-heavy hierarchical bureaucracy known as the Catholic Church. That the monarchical state has a bureaucratic structure very like that of the Church offered a seamless ideological reality to the masses. That popes crowned kings helped to maintain this ideological illusion as a necessary and inevitable reality. In other words, according to the dominant ideology, the masses—rhetorically referred to as "the children"— need the great father, the king, the pope, for these men are somehow more than men, for they are closer to God, closer to what it means to be human, and so "the children" tolerate their masters as a result of having been taught to need them, even to worship them.

The dominant culture reproduces itself in the production of the child-as-cultural being, and William Shakespeare is no exception. The reproduction of the dominant culture through the child may be done in the form of apprenticeship for the middle-class child, agricultural labor for the peasant child, and prolonged schooling for the upper-class child. Regardless of the class and the manner in which the child is trained, *the child is trained* according to the precepts of the dominant culture. Schoenbaum notes that when William Shakespeare was two years old, his brother Gilbert was born "into impeccably bourgeois circumstances, and his life would follow a middle-class pattern," at least until the father's debts began to catch up with the family. There were eight children born to John and Mary Shakespeare; the first daughter, Joan, did not survive childhood, a not-uncommon fate for children in the sixteenth century. Common causes of death among children in Renaissance England usually involved poor nutrition. Either the mother had not the nutrition to maintain her own health and thus sustain a nursing relationship with her child, or she put the child out to a wet nurse, a surrogate mother, who, while nursing her own children nursed others as well. According to some histories of the family, wet-nursing is said to have been the cause of an extraordinarily high death rate among infants, especially in France during the Renaissance. In *The Making of the Modern Family,* Edward Shorter maintains that upper- and middle-class families who could afford to send the child to a wet nurse suffered infant mortality rates often as high as 90 percent. The high mortality rate of the child, according to Shorter and DeMause, confirmed the adult's belief that the world was no place for a child. As a result, the adult's belief in the child's weak constitution—rather than the wet nurse's economic situation in which she found it necessary to take in as many infants as were offered to her—was to blame for the high rates of infant mortality. The wet nurse played an active part in maintaining this ideology, for otherwise she might lose what income she could generate during her years as a nursing mother.[25]

The causes for Joan Shakespeare's death are undocumented, but there is a record of plague in Stratford-upon-Avon in 1564, which perhaps took the eldest Shakespeare daughter. Quite possibly Joan was sent to wet-nurse and this made her even more susceptible to viral and infectious diseases. In 1562, according to some histories of childhood, it was not uncommon for the father to determine whether the child should be sent to a wet nurse, and to which one. John Shakespeare's desire of upward mobility and middle-class standing suggests that, perhaps, like other townspeople, he sent his first daughter out of town and into the countryside to wet-nurse. Then, as now, the middle class could demonstrate their rising wealth, their social power, and their overall community status—and their desire for more status—by adopting such practices.

How did Mary Shakespeare mother William? In all probability, Mary swaddled her son. If she nursed him, she nursed him for only a short time for in 1566 a second son, Gilbert, was born and in 1569 another daughter, the second Joan, was born. If Mary swaddled her son—and there is no reason to believe that she did not—she did so because it was believed to be the right way to love your infant child. Swaddling offered a way to immediately begin molding the child, quite literally. Swaddled babies are passive, quiet babies and sleep most of the time. The heart rate drops and with it the usual squawking and noisome behavior disappears. Swaddling, William Dewees explains, "consists in entirely depriving the child of the use of its limbs, by enveloping it in an endless length bandage, so as to not ineptly resemble billets of wood . . . the circulation nearly arrested; and the child without the slightest power of motion. . . Its head is compressed into the form the fancy of the midwife might suggest; and its shape maintained by properly adjusted pressure" (p. 4).

Sixteenth-century swaddling practices perpetuated the myth that a quiet baby is a good baby. Swaddled babies were rarely beaten. Swaddling served to slow down the infant's respiration so that swaddled babies cried less, seemed to require less, and could be left immobile for hours while the adult tended to other tasks, other children, or, in some cases, activities outside the home.[26]

Swaddling physically restrained the infant, and along with this restraint went the commensurate adult desire to morally and emotionally shape the child. In short, then, swaddling represents an early introduction to child-rearing pedagogies of the adult world. That swaddling served the adult cannot be denied. That swaddling served the infant by molding her body, making her "straight," protecting her from scratching her eyes out or tearing at her hair, or preventing her from touching her genitals and thus morally protecting the child from her animal instincts, is the stuff of adult projection.

Aside from the manner of birth and the manner of nursing, swaddling represents one of the earliest and most profound experiences of child-rearing pedagogy for the infant. No other animal has ever swaddled its newborn. That humans swaddled their newborn children represents one of the purest expressions of culture and ideology interrupting the energetic relationship between the mother and the child. Contrary to the assertions of some historians of childhood, this interruption has never ceased, but rather, has only taken on variant forms since the sixteenth century. The way in which we swaddle our children in the twentieth century will be considered later. For now, it is enough to know that the infant does not require swaddling; rather, the adult requires the infant to be swaddled. The infant neither requires nor asks for "molding"; rather, the adult requires the infant to be molded according to the dictates of the dominant ideologies of the particular historical moment. The process by which the adult invents the child begins at birth, and there is every reason to believe that William Shakespeare experienced the dominant, ordinary child-rearing pedagogies dominant in England in 1564.

What this means is this: when in need of a mother, the ordinary sixteenth-century child was either swaddled, placed with a wet nurse, or both. If with a wet nurse, the child competed for the adult's attention with as many as a dozen or more infants. It was difficult for the child to receive the emotional and nutritional energy needed to thrive. This accounts for the high infant mortality rate among wet-nursed infants. On the other hand, if the infant remained in the home, the swaddled child appeared quiet and calm; "a good baby" for whom the mother, left alone while the father worked his way up the social ladder, labored twenty-four hours a day in an attempt to love and nourish her growing family. The swaddled child lives according to the dominant culture's timetable. The child's biological need for contact and for energetic exchange with the mother—even when not nursing—cannot happen if the infant remains tied to a board and hung on a peg on the wall or placed near a stove to keep warm.

It would be a mistake to name poor nutrition as the sole cause of high infant mortality rates during the sixteenth century, unless we broaden our understanding of what it means for the infant to be nourished by the adult. Nourishment includes skin-to-skin contact between infant and adult, of which the swaddled infant receives only the bare minimum while nursing. Nourishment includes holding, carrying, and attachment to the mother's body so complete that it provides an experience of oneness reminiscent of the infant's time in the womb. The swaddled infant is the detached infant. Nourishment includes sleeping with the adult so that nursing on demand might be possible through the night. The swaddled infant, like the twentieth-century crib baby, sleeps alone, detached from his or her main source of energy. Swaddling-board death was, undoubtedly, not unlike today's crib death, in which the baby passes so deeply into sleep that respiration stops and the baby wilts and dies like a plant left in the dark.

The swaddled child of the sixteenth century, having survived infancy and early childhood, begins his ideological training through church and, perhaps, school. By the time the child reaches the age of six his earliest experiences with his culture's child-rearing experiences have been "forgotten," though remembered in the child's body unconsciously. At the center of the child's body remains a host of stored affect that has accumulated as a result of the first six years, and depending on the adult ideology about the expression of that affect, may or may not be accessible to the child as he grows and becomes an adolescent. By the time the child reaches the age of overt indoctrination, approximately the age of six for school children, the dominant ideology of the institution often serves as an apologist for what has happened to the child in his first six years. The child learned overtly in Renaissance England that he is wicked at heart, that his desires are the desires of the devil, and that to be a proper gentleman, and a proper servant to the queen, he must confess his sins, deny himself, and remake himself in the image of the master.

For the alert and sensitive individual, the inconsistencies between the lessons at church, at school, and at home offered cracks in the dominant ideology that the child might exploit, or hide in. Still, avoiding the dominant ideology is, ultimately, impossible, especially when a dominant culture feels itself imperiled from without or within, as did sixteenth-century England. In 1569 the plague that ravaged London, Stratford-upon-Avon, and elsewhere had abated. The northern rebellion against Elizabeth's rule had been suppressed, but safety and security seemed uncertain in a time of ongoing political and economic unrest. In 1570 Shakespeare heard in church "An Exhortation to Obedience" in three parts, and later, "An Homily against Disobedience and Wilfull Rebellion" in six parts. "Each installment of the latter appropriately ended with a prayer for the Queen and the security of the realm. These Homilies on obedience and rebellion, delivered over nine Sundays and Holy Days, instilled political submissiveness in the simple people." On

Sundays and on Holy Days the vicar "instructed the children of both sexes in their catechism. . . . At school the boys learned *Nowell's Catechism* in Latin."[27]

As a boy, then, Shakespeare learned the dominant political ideology right along with his Old and New Testaments. School curriculum complemented and supported what children learned in church, and children experienced these ideological exercises with a uniform pedagogical hierarchy of master and pupil, of priest and parishioner, adult and child. Obedience to the teacher, the priest, and the adult became synonymous with obedience to the Queen and to God.

Yet the particular form of this hierarchical relationship between adult and child—whether Protestant or Catholic—could never be completely controlled. Records indicate that one of Shakespeare's schoolmasters was brother to a Catholic priest, "tortured on the rack and in 1582 put to death, a Catholic martyr. His school master brother resigned in the previous year. . . . Thus it was possible, in Elizabethan grammar schools, to receive tuition from papists or popish sympathizers, despite the severe penalties to which recusant schoolmasters were subject."[28]

This all makes some sense when considering that people, great and small, refused to abandon their Catholic faith, a faith that may well have been a thousand-year-old family legacy, simply because the King decreed it. Shakespeare's own faith has remained a puzzle for scholars for three hundred years. His plays reveal a man well-versed in the Bible, and one who dips freely and perhaps unconsciously from both Protestant and Catholic theologies. *Hamlet* is no exception.

For so many children their adult character structures grow out of unconscious rage at the adult world left over from childhood, long forgotten as a result of chronic intellectualizing, repression, and the indoctrination of a nationalistic spirit—the spirit of obedience—that does not allow the child to question the dominant order; to do so is evidence of the child's worthlessness. Indoctrination often terrifies the child, for it is a time of extreme aloneness in which the child fears that he may be going crazy, yet has no advocates or "helping witnesses." The result is the suppression, the repression, or the holding in of the child's intense feelings. This process can be disastrous for the community, for the suppression of justified rage in childhood makes a person violent and blind, according to Alice Miller.[29] Furthermore, a personality prone to depressive episodes along with bouts of rage characterizes the adult who was reared in an environment prohibiting release of strong affect. During the Renaissance, depression—or melancholy—had been identified as a mental disorder associated with agitation, sleep disorders, hallucinations, and suicidal ideations.

In *A Treatise of Melancholy* (1586), Timothy Bright, a Renaissance clergyman and physician, analyzed melancholy and other emotional disturbances. Bright's was only one of many books on melancholy during the sixteenth century in England. Apparently the subject fascinated Elizabethans so that, whether Bright's text had any influence on *Hamlet* or not, the fact remains that Hamlet was, in some ways, a familiar character. If the repression of emotional trauma experienced as a child is "the root cause of psychic disorders," it follows then that Elizabethans shared relational experiences due to traditional child-rearing practices shared by the dominant culture. It also follows that in *Hamlet,* we see not so much a representation of Danish family life, but rather, Elizabethan family life.[30]

Of John and Mary Shakespeare's eight children, the first was baptized Catholic, for Mary I still reigned. The other seven children were given Anglican baptisms. William Shakespeare's father recognized the shifting winds of economic and social forces and sought to work with them rather than against them. He left husbandry and agriculture for glove-making when the future of the English Yeoman appeared bleak. He then moved from the production of commodities to the production and reproduction of the political life of Stratford-upon-Avon when he secured public office. Up until 1578 records speak specifically of his loyalty and his high standing as a public official, until his own personal and public collapse, due to bad debts incurred on his climb up the social ladder.

John Shakespeare was an ordinary Englishman in his response to the social instability of his time. The first known record about John Shakespeare indicates that he was a farmer, perhaps in cattle, perhaps in sheep, but soon after he is documented by town registers as "a glover." Having undoubtedly witnessed or experienced first-hand the effects of the enclosure laws, John Shakespeare decided that he should join the rising middle class if possible, and so he entered into glove-making, a trade he maintained from 1568 until he was elected Stratford-upon-Avon's bailiff, for which he then acted as the town's "almoner, coroner, escheator, and clerk of the market." He also served as the justice of the peace for which "he issued warrants, dealt with cases of debt and violations of the by-laws, and carried on negotiations with the lord of the manor. . . Appropriate ceremony accompanied his exalted station."[31] Up until 1578 John Shakespeare was a busy, driven man, with his political ambitions seemly nearly realized. The economic tenor of the times, however, brought him down.

As quickly as he climbed the social ladder, John Shakespeare fell off. By 1576, he had fallen into considerable debt, having made his way up the social ladder through bad loans and improvident spending, and so he assiduously avoided church and town council meetings—having attended for years with consistency—as a way of avoiding debt collectors. In his desperation he "mortgaged part of his wife's inheritance" and sold his land for ready money, but was nevertheless plagued by debt until he died in 1601, the year in which *Hamlet* was first performed. John Shakespeare was not alone in his economic ill fortune. One of Shakespeare's biographers writes that "other townsmen experienced similar problems. Travelers in the west Midlands, and government officials also, noted what today we would describe as an economic recession."[32]

Like so many men, John Shakespeare mortgaged the emotional life of his children, hoping to be able to repay them later with an inheritance, a public reputation, a coat of arms, and an "exalted station." He had none of this to give his children by the time they were grown. Following this historical reconstruction of Shakespeare's probable emotional experience as a child, a speculative psychodynamic profile reads something like this:

- As an infant, William needed his mother's breast but instead was sent out to wet-nurse, as decent "middle-class" families did if they could afford it. He suffered childhood illnesses, mild malnutrition, and was exceptional for surviving. Though he had some physical contact with a mother figure, his need for the mother's breast would dominate his character structure. He would always seek to find an adequate substitute for it. Swaddling exacerbated the experience of emotional deprivation and disconnection from the mother's body.
- William needed a father, having been abandoned emotionally by John Shakespeare for career, reputation, and wealth. William's character structure would be dominated by, on the one hand, longing and need and a sense of melancholy, inclining him to existential hopelessness, while on the other hand, internalization of a sense of rage at having been unrecognized, ignored, abandoned, all within the confines of culturally sanctioned relationships.
- The child—especially the male child—learns early and often that the anger, longing, and sadness he feels is a sign of his sinful nature, and not to be encouraged or acknowledged. The father projects his own emptiness onto the son as a story of hardness with the attendant contradictory message: obedience is freedom.
- The institutions of church and school represent sites of ideological confirmation of what the child has already experienced and internalized in relationships with adults. The child will learn ancient and unquestioned stories of his lowly state, his need for reform, and that violence, domination, and subjugation are the adult's—and God's—preferred methods to accomplish the child's reform.

Obviously, other mitigating factors also influenced William Shakespeare's character. The point here is not to oversimplify Shakespeare, but rather to explore the *basic* ideological context that gave rise to culturally determined child-rearing practices, and so shaped his first years of life. In this way we might come to understand how and why he speaks to the human condition in such a way that not only do his contemporaries understand the basic conflicts of his stories, but four hundred years later, so do we. The fact that contemporary minds still recognize their own emotional experience in Shakespeare's dramas indicates that we share something with Shakespeare and his characters: Freud's Oedipal theory argued, for instance, that it was a basic trait of human nature that connects the audience to *Hamlet*. When we see *Hamlet* through Freud's seduction theory, however, what we witness in *Hamlet* is not so much a character's human nature in conflict, but rather the conflicted symptoms of the child's human nurture.

(NO) ORDINARY SEDUCTION

Just as *Hamlet* came to the stage in 1601, Louis XIII, the heir to the Bourbon throne, was born in France. Louis represents a kind of hyperreal version of the projective nature of the nurturing that always already goes on between the adult and the child, and he seems a striking example of the extent to which the grandiose narcissist can justify any kind of child-rearing behavior when it confirms him in his idea of himself. Louis XIII's experiences as a child also provide a fascinating perspective from which we might speculate about *why* Hamlet is so conflicted, despondent, and vulnerable to the Ghost of his father as the play opens.

First, consider Louis XIII briefly as a kind of historical doppelganger to Hamlet's fictional character: during the first three years of his life, according to Jean Herorard's diary, court nobles, nannies, and even his mother and father sexualized the young prince's relationships with all those around him and encouraged Louis to do the same, at least until he was seven years of age, at which time he was taught that he was now "a little man . . . and at that time . . . had to be taught decency in language and behavior."[33] The point Herorard implicitly and unintentionally makes over and over again is that the adults involved with Louis as a child are not conscious of seducing the child any more than sixteenth-century English parents who swaddled their children realized that they were seducing the child as a result of their own confused narcissistic projections, among them: the seduction of the child is always for the child's own good. The child desires to be seduced. The child will not remember the seduction. The child will learn important lessons from the seduction, especially regarding power, domination, and human relationships.

Herorard records that members of the Bourbon court "amused themselves by training the one-year-old to offer his penis instead of his hand to be kissed."[34] Louis's erections as a three-year-old occupy a special place in Herorard's journal, for in the young prince's erect penis the adults saw the phallic potency of the Bourbon dynasty, the future, the past, and the power to produce and reproduce themselves. The adults in Louis's life did not see a three-year-old boy in need of what all ordinary three-year-old boys need.

Rather, the child Louis is, according to the adults in his life, something more than human. He invites their sexualized treatment of him because he is precocious; precocity is proof of Louis's superior, royal blood and therefore of his God-given right to rule, all of which flatters the mother and the father, the king and the queen.

When Louis XIII came of age and assumed power in France, he banished his mother. The son's rage—Louis's or, for that matter, Hamlet's—comes as a result of his deeply felt sense that she—and by extension all women—has betrayed him in a fundamental way. For the ordinary child, however, there is no escape from this ideological confinement, for betrayal and seduction are so ordinary, so matter-of-fact, and such an ambient part of the dominant culture that these acts have become almost invisible. Any complaints of the child are understood as the result of the child's wickedness, and the child is encouraged to believe in this, or his own genetic weakness, or his own debilitated attention span. Louis's mother (or Shakespeare's mother, or Hamlet's mother; it makes little difference) tells the same story of the mother's unconscious projection onto the child of adult powerlessness, fear, and insecurity. As a result of adult projection—justified by the dominant culture and unconscious ideology—the child becomes an object from which the mother gratifies her emotional needs, all in the guise of "loving" the child. The mother possesses the child and sees in him an object of use-value: the child represents a site of psychogenic projection and retroflection as well as cultural reproduction, for as the mother works out the unconscious anger and powerlessness she experienced when a victim of the same kind of narcissistic seduction, she recreates the ideological and emotional environment for her child, and so her character structure is passed on to her child via emotional trauma. In this way the child's body becomes the site of cultural and ideological production and reproduction. The defense mechanism of repression—which saves the child at the time of the trauma—guarantees that the child will forget and so repeat what he has learned at the hands of the adult. Remembering, according to the dominant ideology, is not allowed.

And yet we try. Literature is often a covert, subversive expression of the human mind's need to remember, even in a coded form. Consider again Hamlet's character as an expression of Shakespeare's experiences as a child as well as a refraction of the dominant culture's treatment of the child. Hamlet has a deep sense of having been betrayed by his mother when she remarries Claudius, and he is convinced that this is the betrayal that offends him. He cannot remember having been betrayed by her at any other time. Yet Hamlet's obsession with Gertrude has been characterized as evidence for the Oedipal theory, of the son's innate desire to sexually possess the mother. The seduction theory, on the other hand, suggests that Gertrude's marriage to Claudius reminds Hamlet of an earlier, forgotten betrayal—the abandonment of the child by the mother. Hamlet's need for Gertrude is the child's need for emotionally engaged mothering. His great, towering offense at her remarriage then speaks not so much to her morality as it does to his repressed rage at her for having abandoned him, betrayed him, and quite probably used him as the mother's narcissistic site of projection.

Hamlet was an only child, for when he was not in the hands of a wet nurse, a nanny, a governess, a schoolmaster, or Yorick the court jester, the prince-child may have suffered a fate similar to Louis XIII. The seduction and betrayal of Louis's childhood by well-meaning adults speaks directly to the blindness and amnesia adult culture fosters in itself regarding the basic emotional needs of the child. As a product of this cultural moment, Hamlet might be understood as a kind of ideological cousin to Louis XIII, especially in regard to dominant child-rearing practices of sixteenth-century France and England. As cultural inventions, then, Louis XIII and Hamlet share a family resemblance and, when juxtaposed, offer a striking moment of hyperreality in which Shakespeare's fancy and historical reality merge and begin speaking one to the other.

HAMLET AS HUMAN RELATIONSHIP

The point here is simply this: the mind—both its conscious and unconscious parts—is invented by the dominant culture in *childhood* as a result of lived human relationships. With this in mind, then, *Hamlet* represents the unconscious mind of Elizabethan England as it is refracted and represented through the character structure of Shakespeare's unconscious mind. Its contents are ideologically motivated; its meaning is relative, temporal, and historically contextual. One's mind appears "real" and substantial to the individual due to repressed affect buried since childhood, thus giving force and substance to the mind's structure, its patterns of thought, and its apparently fixed nature. Shakespeare's vision is the vision of the third eye, or what Keats described as his "negative capability." Like Hamlet's epiphanic surrender to the larger mind that "shapes our ends," Shakespeare's wisdom comes from his ability to detach himself from his individual, dualistic ego-mind and so experience and persuasively portray a myriad of different personalities in his dramas, though none of them his own. He remains in between, fixed nowhere.

Shakespeare's subversive, antiauthoritarian stance in Hamlet contains the recognition that subversion is a difficult thing to pull off, and that the ideological status quo manifests a gravitational force akin to the magnitude of a black hole. It pulls all things into it, even light. Yet, in a culture that must have felt as claustrophobic to Shakespeare as contemporary culture does to the twenty-first-century Englishman, Shakespeare finds a position from which to write that can only be described as "elsewhere."

This is what makes *Hamlet* so contemporary and still accessible to audiences after four hundred years. Hamlet feels one thing, but he thinks about another, and another, and another. He has the split mind that each of us has been raised with in Western culture, and as a result, Hamlet is overburdened with self-consciousness. He lacks spontaneity—and for good reason. Spontaneity in the child threatens the dominant ideological order of the dinner table, the classroom, the church; self-consciousness, on the other hand, perpetuates the status quo by inculcating the constant awareness of judgment, leading to anxiety and, ultimately, inaction. The split mind is the fractured mind, the mind of "shreds and patches"; it is the modern mind, it is Hamlet's mind, and it is Shakespeare's mind; the split mind is the suffering mind.

The effects of the split mind are nowhere more apparent than in the structure and nature of the human relationships that *are* the play *Hamlet*. To understand a character's behavior, however, one must have access to a character's child-rearing experiences that do not appear directly in *Hamlet*. And yet every text has its own unconscious mind, the heteroglossia of the cultural moment that speaks in a myriad of voices, some of which represent the author's many voices, and some of which the author remains unaware.

Consider the nature of Ophelia's primary relationships in the play as an example of how the adult relationship depicted by Shakespeare speaks to the relationship between the adult and the child that lies latent in the drama. When overhearing a conversation between his son and daughter, Polonius demands—as a slave owner might demand the business between two slaves—what the matter is. She obeys as, undoubtedly, she always has. She is female. She is daughter. She is child. Therefore, she obeys.

Ophelia explains that Hamlet "hath, my lord, of late made many tenders of his affections to me" (I.3. 99–100). Polonius's response is reactionary, and ultimately, inaccurate. He assumes that Hamlet, like himself, cannot really mean what he says, and does not love Ophelia, and that he only wants sex, and that Ophelia, at least in Polonius's eyes, could never be a queen, for a queen is strong, brave, and his daughter is, well, just a "green girl." Polonius tells her to think herself "a baby" and states plainly that she "does not understand herself," and that he knows her better than she does. In the relationship between the father and the child, Ophelia accepts the position of incompetent object forced on her by her father, and as a result she agrees to deny her love for Hamlet and his for her, and instead, accepts Polonius's domination of her as the determining factor in all of her relationships. Domination and subjugation then become the substitute for the father's love, and for Hamlet's love as well. The child accepts the domination of the parent because domination has always been offered as love since childhood.

Polonius, like Claudius and Old Hamlet, acts out disturbing and destructive narcissism when interpreting Young Hamlet's madness and Ophelia's role in it. Polonius tells Claudius that he believes young Hamlet's madness is the result of lovesickness for his daughter, and he reads Young Hamlet's behavior through this assumption until his death. In act 2, scene 2, Polonius provides his interpretation of Young Hamlet's madness to the King and Queen, and his tale hinges on the part Polonius played as a faithful servant to the king when he forbid his daughter to spend any time with the prince. "Lord Hamlet is a prince out of thy star," Polonius tells Ophelia. "This must not be." The irony here is of course that Gerturde had hoped Ophelia would be Young Hamlet's wife. Polonius's assumptions, his actions, and his need to see Young Hamlet's madness as a result of Ophelia's withdrawal from him—which is Polonius's doing, he reminds the King and Queen—mark him as a consummate narcissist, the meddling fool, the betrayer who betrays because he was betrayed.

When Polonius demands that Ophelia reject Hamlet, he thereby repeats an injunction familiar to Ophelia since childhood: deny your own needs and obey the father, for this is the path to peace and security. Shakespeare demonstrates, however, that Polonius's fathering of his daughter is nothing more than an expression of ideological hegemony over the child; unreal though it may be, it *feels* real to Ophelia, made real by her ongoing, chronic, unconscious need for *fathering,* understood here as emotional support for the child's autonomous nature, the child's autonomous needs, and emotional support for the child's developing humanity. When Ophelia's father dies at the hand of Hamlet, Ophelia spirals into a psychopathic break not from "reality" but from her father's ideologically scripted delusion of "reality." In short, at her father's death, Ophelia meets "the real" for the first time, and it terrifies her. She is without structure, having been structured by the father. She personifies emptiness and experiences for the first time the intensity of her emotional need that will now never be filled by the father, a need that has always informed her, but that has remained in the background of her mind her entire life. Polonius's death manifests negatively the psychodynamic nature of the ideological hegemony that governs the relationship between the adult and the child. When Ophelia loses her father, she does not lose her emotional support, for she never had it from him. Rather, when she loses her mind, it is not her mind that she loses, but the mind of the father, the ideological signifier who has scripted her since birth according to his own understanding of the dominant culture. At his death Ophelia comes face-to-face with what is left of her own self and finds, apparently, only emptiness and desperate need; she sinks into hopelessness and death. "Her death was doubtful," the priest says at her funeral in act 5 scene 1, and as such he cannot offer her the sanctification of Christian burial, for she did not die in the arms of Mother Church, but rather, she died in the arms of no mother at all.

Ophelia and Gertrude share a great deal in common. They lack autonomy, and have lacked autonomy since birth. Gertrude's hasty remarriage to Claudius represents, in part, her unconscious need to submit to a master, for without a dominant father figure in her life, she too might go mad. Yet Gertrude's distracted passivity suggests that she is in a kind of delusional world of her own making, so much so that she is, somehow, innocent of Old Hamlet's death *by reason of insanity.*

In *Hamlet* it seems the whole world is on the verge of wholesale violence. This might be understood as the symptom of a culture of seduction and power in which the seduced child as an adult desires independence from the adult world but is trained from birth to ignore these desires. The act of denying one's needs builds into a tension that often explodes into an outburst of violence and negativity at oneself and often others. The explosion, however, is not recognized as negativity by the individual exploding; rather, the explosion represents a move towards "independence." Gertrude's marriage to Claudius is an example of this self-justifying madness. Of course she must have recognized the questionable and controversial nature of her marriage to her husband's brother. Nevertheless, she marries, and it represents a strong, independent, bold move for Gertrude, in her own mind. Even so, her son cannot understand it, for he interprets it as an insult against him, against his father, and against custom. Gertrude remains blind to these interpretations until Hamlet brings them to her attention in act 3, scene 4. Before this moment, Gertrude's anger is unconscious and passive. From Gertrude's perspective, her remarriage may seem to be a move towards autonomy as she acts on her own desire, dances on the edge of taboo, and flouts custom by marrying her brother-in-law. Her unconscious and therefore unrecognized emotional need will be her downfall.[35]

In act 1 Claudius attempts to talk Hamlet out of himself—as all the fathers do with their children in the play—and into the "right" frame of mind, which in this case is Claudius's mind. The loss of fathers, according to Claudius, is common and ordinary, for the son must lose his father. To feel "obsequious sorrow" to the degree Hamlet feels it is, according to Claudius, a "fault to nature, to reason most absurd, whose common theme is the death of fathers." Hamlet's need to mourn and to puzzle over his feelings is, according to the new father, Claudius, a sign of weakness, of unmanliness, and Claudius subtly reminds Hamlet that the weak will not inherit the throne. Claudius's command is clear: choke it up and get over it. Claudius's threat is subtle, but also clear: if you do not get over it, you may not be next in line to the throne for long.

This makes Hamlet angrier than ever, for it touches his vulnerability in a way that Old Hamlet undoubtedly touched him as a child, since the crown prince cannot be "weak" or "unmanly," and it is the father's job—whether it be Old Hamlet or Claudius—to harden the son. This is done in part by threats of punishment and fatherly—or Royal—abandonment.

Yet Claudius would have Hamlet think of him as a father, and for good reason. Even so, Hamlet will have nothing to do with Claudius as a father even before the Ghost appears and stirs up Hamlet's rage. In act 1, scene 2,

Hamlet's response to Claudius is already angry and disdainful, describing himself and his relationship to Claudius as "a little more than kin and less than kind." The irony is, of course, that Hamlet is Claudius' child, for the culture of Claudius and Old Hamlet are one and the same. The genetic blood line is one and the same. The two brothers that Young Hamlet believes to be so different, so alien to one another, are, in fact, doppelgangers. The difference in character between Claudius and Old Hamlet—and between Young Hamlet and Claudius—lies only in the idealized projections of Young Hamlet's mind.

In act 1, scene 2, Hamlet compares his idealized notion of his father to Claudius and finds Claudius sadly wanting. Hamlet believes that his father was an "excellent" king, and compared to Claudius, Old Hamlet was a "hyperion to a satyr," a god compared to a beast. Young Hamlet needs to believe in these differences. They are automatic and unconscious yet bear little resemblance to the truth. Nevertheless, Young Hamlet's idealized projections of his father justify his idealized grip on the past and so reject the reality of the present, which is simply this: the father is dead—there is no father, and there never was. Only in the idealized past does Old Hamlet live and walk; and it is the idealized past made "real" by Young Hamlet's unmet emotional needs for fathering that the Ghost exploits in order to seduce his child.

Both Old Hamlet and Claudius are grandiose narcissists and so interact in their relationships in a similar fashion; seduction defines them. With this in mind, then, it seems likely that Old Hamlet ignored the feelings of his son to the same degree and probably with the same unctuous tone that Claudius used when dismissing Hamlet's feelings in act 1, scene 2. Indeed, it seems clear that young Hamlet's emotional needs had been neglected all along by his father, and instead, an idealized notion of duty and filial obligation was instilled in him in the same way school boys learn to idolize the king. Would Old Hamlet have been sensible to Young Hamlet's emotional needs aside from his role as "crown prince"? This is doubtful, for Old Hamlet was insensible to a great many things, chief among them the traitorous brother planning a royal coup in his midst.

Claudius and Old Hamlet rule Denmark in much the same way. Both enjoy a provocative, warlike stance; both enjoy the idea of themselves as having dominated "Old Norway"; and it seems that both drink and revel in the same way—for this is where the tradition that Hamlet reports in act 1 becomes known to him. Finally, and when the time calls for it, Old Hamlet and Claudius undoubtedly kill, use, and abuse others in the same way.

Yet Hamlet's emotional need for a father represents not two brothers acting out the dominant political culture—and perhaps ongoing sibling rivalry. Rather, Young Hamlet sees in the death of his father a world of idealized absolutes gone bad. King Claudius reigns the "unweeded garden," which, Young Hamlet implies, was once beautiful and well cared for. Young Hamlet holds himself and Claudius to a standard of judgment that neither can achieve, and yet, one that he implicitly assumes Old Hamlet exemplified.

Claudius's murder and theft of the crown mark him as a narcissist, a craven and "adulterate beast" according to Young Hamlet. Yet, when the Ghost appears to Young Hamlet he recounts the story of his murder and this alone marks Old Hamlet as a towering narcissist, for the narcissist needs control and can only operate in a relationship when he is in control. As an expression of Old Hamlet's character, the Ghost refuses to surrender his control over those relationships he controlled—or failed to control—in life. Moreover, the Ghost's presence makes patently clear that the father sees his son only as a vital object to manipulate for his own purpose. Even after death, the child exists only to be used by the father as an instrument of his wrath and vengeance.

This is clear in what the Ghost *does not say* in act 1, scene 5: "Thus was I, sleeping, [deprived] by a brother's hand of life, of crown, of queen." Nowhere does the Ghost refer to the relationship he had with Young Hamlet, for it seems implicitly clear that they had no relationship outside of the ideological obligation the prince has to the king. Old Hamlet's Ghost does not count the loss of his son as one of the crucial relationships he was deprived of when murdered. Rather, Old Hamlet remains focused on exactly the same things Claudius finds so desirable: his life, his crown, his queen.

On the other hand, the Ghost also represents a projection of Young Hamlet's mind, and as such, marks both Young and Old Hamlet as grandiose narcissists. From this point of view, Young Hamlet might be understood to be at war with himself, the one side of his mind in conflict with the other, the narcissist trying to control and dominate the masochist, the masochist trying to appease and serve the terrifying narcissist. Nevertheless, whether the Ghost is "real" or merely a projection of Young Hamlet's mind, the Ghost is a manifestation of the Father, and how the relationship between the Ghost and Young Hamlet speaks to the origins of Young Hamlet's relationship to himself, which is always already about the child's relationship to the father.

The relationship between Polonius and Laertes represents another example of the narcissistic seduction of the son by the father in *Hamlet*. In this case the son is bound to the father as the slave to his master. Laertes must "wring" from Polonius his "slow leave" when desiring to return to his life in France. Moreover, when he does return, Polonius hires Reynaldo to spy on his son, ostensibly to keep an eye on his son's moral growth. To do so Polonius encourages Reynaldo to tempt his son into the very activities he would wish his son to avoid. Polonius's actions are the actions of the narcissist, bent on proving to himself that, in fact, he has control over those things he thinks he should control. His narcissism is a defense against his unconscious sense that he has no control and is powerless. Though Polonius does not outwardly suspect that his powerlessness and his fear of powerlessness drives him, Shakespeare invites the audience to suspect it when he implicitly reminds us that Polonius failed to warn his king, Old Hamlet, about a threat to his crown.

Hamlet dramatizes Shakespeare's understanding that the child raised by wolves becomes a wolf. In other words, the child seduced by the adult develops a character structure—a way of being—that feels real as a result of repressed affect stored as energetic information in the cellular structure of the body. This state of being, as Freud argued in his Oedipus theory, appears to be so real to the individual that it can easily be confused with human nature. Nevertheless, the child reared by seduction develops human relationships characterized by an unconscious need to repeat the past in an attempt to remember it, and so find release from it. The production and reproduction of the dominant ideology requires the adult to remain unaware of what happened to him as a child, and so remain unaware—and thus a perpetual victim—of internalized feelings:

- Rage at having been seduced and betrayed by adults as a child,
- Terror at having been physically violated and powerless to stop it,
- Horror at having been abandoned in his most desperate need,
- Shame at having been taught explicitly and implicitly that whatever he received or did not receive from the adult was deserved,
- Profound sadness.

TO BE OR NOT TO BE

By act 3, scene 1, Hamlet asks, "to be, or not to be, that is the question." The question is important, but so too the a priori assumptions Hamlet makes about being. For the child raised to deny his feelings believes that his cognitive intellect is the seat of his ego-identity. He identifies himself with his thinking mind rather than, say, his beating heart. As an example of a Renaissance humanist Hamlet enacted the belief that his intellectual mind was the seat of his being, and it is in his mind that he thinks that he lives, and this is nowhere more clearly stated than in his "to be or not to be" soliloquy. Shakespeare seems to be as skeptical of humanism as he is of supernaturalism, since by the end of the play he leaves both philosophical positions behind for what John Keats called Shakespeare's position of "negative capability." Yet in act 3, Hamlet is caught up squarely in the workings of his own conscious mind. "To be," for Hamlet, is to think, and to think is to be conflicted, constrained, and confused. As a result, Hamlet considers what appears to be the only other option, "not to be," which in this context suggests "not thinking about one's being," which for Hamlet can only mean death, for letting go of the thinking mind—the mind of "deep plots," the mind that seeks evidence "more relative," the mind that "by indirection finds direction out," the mind that makes him man and not animal—is tantamount to letting go of life itself. Yet all of Hamlet's fears of being and not being are merely the dominant ideology that resides in Hamlet's conscious mind and is given reality by the stored terror and rage left over from his childhood experiences. It is a state of being he appears to transcend by act 5 as an individual, though in his newly won freedom from fear, he inadvertently, perhaps inevitably, reproduces the dominant culture.

In act 5 Hamlet finds release from his ideologically determined ego-mind, which is a release from the schizoid, narcissistic character structure that separates him from the world. In other words, he has released his rage and is free from his terror, for there is no such thing as "Young Hamlet" to protect anymore. Death will come. He has had a kind of mystical experience grounded solely in his intuition, his feeling, and his body. In act 5, scene 2 Hamlet shares his conversion story with Horatio.

> Sir, in my heart there was a kind of fighting that would not let me sleep. Methought I lay worse than the mutines in the bilboes. Rashly and prais'd be rashness for it: let us know our indiscretion sometime serves us well when our deep plots do pall; and that should learn us there's a divinity that shapes our ends, rough-hew them how we will.

Hamlet has suspected the truth of what he says from the beginning of the play; however, it is only after his sea voyage and the extremity of need brought on by the sea voyage that he had the undistracted leisure to listen to his own heart, the "fighting" that went on inside him, and the mortal danger he intuitively knew his trip to England represented. Hamlet explains that, for reasons he did not understand, he "grop'd" in the dark and found in Rosencrantz and Guildenstern's belongings his death warrant signed by the King.

Hamlet acts, and he acts without restraint or moral consideration, but rather, he uses his "father's signet ring" and seals Rosencrantz and Guildenstern's fate. He feels no pangs of conscience for their deaths, though Horatio seems awed, perhaps frightened, for when he hears how Hamlet dispatched his one-time friends, he says, "what a king is this!" For Hamlet has become like a king in his new-found ability to spontaneously act. Judge and jury for Rosencrantz and Guildenstern, Hamlet has done a kingly deed, and the nature of the deed is not lost on Horatio, for Young Hamlet has thrown off his character and become his father, he has become Claudius; in short, young Hamlet comes into his own as a political animal during the sea voyage. Young Hamlet commands with the authority of the royal seal and his royal lineage, and his command is a familiar one: death to traitors.

By the time Hamlet reaches Denmark act 5, scene 1, he is prepared to fully appreciate the lessons of the graveyard, for he suspected as much on his sea voyage: death can come at any time and is not to be avoided, so act while ye may. Hamlet's sea voyage, then, represents a symbolic passage from the earlier world of the play in Denmark to a world of liberated action in which his "deep plots" of control and of god-like knowing—his character—are transcended, and he accepts his mortality along with the consequences of his prior actions. "The readiness is all," he says, for that is all one can be when death arrives: ready.

The ghost no longer appears in the play in act 5. In fact, it is as if the ghost never existed by the time Hamlet returns from the sea voyage. He has come to terms with the distant, idealized authoritarian father as well as the betraying, angry mother. Shakespeare can only provide the barest of outlines for how this liberation from character structure takes place, but it has everything to do with Hamlet's acceptance of how little he knows and how little he can control, and that even one who ostensibly conquers the world—like an Alexander or a Caesar—still dies, returns to the earth, and becomes nothing more than a "stop for a beer barrel."

Having accepted the insecurity of his mortal condition, Hamlet appears to have settled into a deeper understanding of himself, one that goes beyond his rage at Gertrude and Claudius and beyond his role as revenger. Yet in the final act of the play, the subversive quality of Shakespeare's political inquiry is turned on its head. Hamlet becomes the avenger and kills Claudius even as Claudius kills Gertrude with his poisoned drink. Laertes falls as Hamlet immediately and without question avenges the treachery Laertes employed in their fencing match. And in his final kingly act, Hamlet gives his "dying voice" to Fortinbras in an attempt to sway the fortunes of Danish politics once he is dead. Fortinbras represents the Old Order of King Hamlet, in that the frame of *Hamlet* goes beyond Castle Elsinor and into Poland, for in Poland we learn that the father and the child are having their dispute, and to prove himself correct in his need to undo what he considers his father's failure to be, he marches into Denmark and fills the political vacuum. In giving his dying voice to Young Fortinbras, Hamlet gives his voice to Old Fortinbras. And in giving his dying voice to Old Fortinbras, he gives it in proxy and in principle to Old Hamlet as well, for Old Fortinbras and Old Hamlet are twin kings, perpetually fighting each other for frozen patches of worthless ground, using their loyal subjects as they use their children: as so much royal firewood. After all is said and done and the carnage of the Old Order lays strewn about the stage, Hamlet inexplicably says yes to this political history and gives his dying voice to its reproduction, to Young Fortinbras. What else can he do? Shakespeare the playwright provokes a catharsis in his audience, drawing forth a kind of abreaction of their longing, their need, and their sadness by the end of the tragedy. This alone is a subversive political act, for it makes the masses less vulnerable to ideological manipulation; that is, except for the ideological designs that the play itself has for the audience, for it teaches as well as delights. It should be noted, then, that Hamlet's dying voice is as

conservative as it is politically motivated, and it must have pleased Shakespeare's royal audiences *very much.*

A GRIM TRADITION

Classical psychoanalysis as it developed from Freud's Oedipal theory leads
to a relationship between analyst and patient in which the dominant adult ideology manifests itself as the analyst's narcissistic countertransference of
unconscious need onto the patient. What this means is this: the analysis
enlists the patient into an adult conspiracy to deny the plight of the child, a
plight both analyst and patient experienced, yet the trauma remains so
painful—even as it lies buried in the unconscious minds of both analyst and
patient—that the analyst encourages the patient to continue practicing the
defensive mechanism of repression in order to spare the analyst. The patient
often does this willingly, for this is the exact same relational requirement
demanded of them as a child by the adult. The adult-centered analytical pedagogy serves to deny the patient access to his past, his intuition, his body, and
his emotional life—thereby reenacting and so reproducing the original ideology and pedagogy that led to the original seduction trauma. Rather than real
identification with one's physical and emotional reality, the Oedipal pedagogy requires the patient to identify with the analyst's intellectual interpretations of the patient's seduction traumas—all of which, according to the
Oedipal theory, did not really happen, but rather, were simply the projected
fantasies of the child. From the Oedipal perspective, the patient can recover
only by further repressing his Oedipal desires—for though they are "natural,"
they are at the same time "sick." The successful patient represses and then
transfers his Oedipal desires onto a suitable substitute.[36]

Oedipal pedagogy leaves untouched the individual's unconscious emotional life, buried since childhood, which will continue to give rise to neurotic
character disorders, including conflicted and unsatisfying relationships,
chronic anxiety, depression, and addictive behaviors. Freud's genius, however, lies in how close he came to exposing the age-old tradition that denied
the child his subjective, emotional reality, for by extension the seduction theory implies that the emotional reality of the child is no more and no less real
for the child than it is for the adult—and so when a child is seduced, violated,
manipulated, coerced, overpowered, abused, beaten, sexually molested, or
ignored, the emotional responses to these events are predictable and, in fact,
appropriate *and need to be acknowledged and supported by the adult.* For this
to happen, however, the adults must acknowledge and support their own emotional reality, not only as adults, but as children. Understanding this, then,
allows the adult to treat the child's emotional life not as something to be conquered, fixed, or disregarded, but as substantial and necessary for the individ-

ual's well-being, for the individual's human growth and development, and by extension, for the human community's growth and development as well.

Freud's seduction theory was a direct challenge to the age-old tradition of adult exploitation and manipulation of the child for adult purposes, adult power, or adult pleasure, a challenge that Freud ultimately could not make, for it meant exposing, as he wrote, "even my own father." Instead, like so many Western intellectuals before and since, Freud retreated into intellectual theory and denied his—and his sister's—emotional experience as children, and so even as he attempted to diagnose the dominant culture, he inadvertently helped to reproduce it.

Freud was not alone in this process. His own European tradition conspired against him, however, for in the eighteenth and nineteenth centuries in Germany countless books on child-rearing were published, chief among them Dr. Schreber's series on child-rearing. Dr. Schreber's child-rearing pedagogy—along with many other texts of the same period—would later come to be known as the *black pedagogy,* a hierarchical structure of physical and emotional domination and subjugation practiced by the adult on the child, all "for the child's own good." The ideology of the child as willful and wicked would later reappear in classic Freudian psychoanalysis.[37]

In an historical irony, Freud would later treat Dr. Schreber's paranoid son, a young man suffering from symptoms of the same nature as Young Hamlet. The reasons for Freud's inability to help Young Schreber are complicated, but Freud's failure can be attributed in part to the ideology of the child that lay at the foundation of Freud's theory of the unconscious mind, for the Oedipal child's governing nature was one and the same with the nature of child as invented by Dr. Schreber's *black pedagogy.* The upshot here is that as children, Freud and Young Schreber and Young Hamlet all suffered a similar kind of emotional seduction—in their cases in the form of domination and subjugation—by fathers who were themselves grandiose narcissists. With Oedipal theory in hand, however, Freud inadvertently reenacted the role of authoritarian father as he encouraged Schreber's son to repress his rage at the father and so deny his emotional suffering as the consequence not of the child's lived experiences with a tyrannical narcissist, but rather, as a result of the child's Oedipal fantasies.

Before Dr. Shreber's child-rearing manuals codified the *black pedagogy* of German child-rearing tradition in 1858, the Brothers Grimm attempted a codification of their own, and invented one of the most popular books for adults and children of the nineteenth century, *Kinder-und Hausmårchen* (Children's and Household Tales), first published in 1812. The Brothers Grimm figure largely in the German and the European tradition, for the rise of folklore as a serious scholarly concern is also the story of the rise of the German-nation state, and with this story is another one of central importance:

the rise of children's literature proper, and like *Hamlet*, Freud, the Brothers Grimm and their fairy tales represent a telling moment of cultural reproduction and ideological intensification.

NOTES

[1]See James R. Kincaid. *Child-Loving: The Erotic Child and Victorian Culture* (New York: Routledge, 1992). The sexualized child of the Victorians was also the "asexualized" saintly child, for, as Kincaid argues, making the child pure and saintly in Victorian culture was an act of sexualization of the child, in that the "pure" and "innocent" child represented a sublimation of adult desire. Yet Victorian culture, according to Lytton Strachey, James Kincaid, Richard Wallace, and others, had developed a cult of the child that fetishized the child and her innocence as eminently desirable. Kincaid writes,

> by attributing to the child the central features of desirability in our culture—purity, innocence, emptiness, Otherness—we have made absolutely essential figures who would enact this desire. Such figures are certainly not us, we insist, insist so violently because we must, so violently that we come to think that what we are is what these figures are not. They come to define us: they are the substance we feed on. The pedophile is thus our most important citizen, so long as he stays behind the tree or over in the next yard. . . . the pedophile acts out the range of attitudes and behaviors made compulsory by the role we have given the child.

Also, see Michel Foucault's *The History of Sexuality,* vol. 1, *An Introduction,* trans. Robert Hurley (New York: Pantheon, 1978).

[2]Quoted in Alice Miller, *Thou Shalt Not Be Aware: Society's Betrayal of the Child,* trans. Hildegarde and Hunter Hannnum (New York: Meridian, 1984) p. 194. One important thing to keep in mind about recovered memories: it may not matter if they are true or not. If the memories are accurate descriptions of earlier events—and there is no reason to believe otherwise—then this is as significant for the suffering patient. If the memories are not accurate, then this is as significant for the patient—and the analyst—for why would an adult desire to despoil their filial relationship and lie to an authority figure of Freud's type? A "fictional" account of sexual abuse, in other words, is as important and significant for the patient and for the analyst as a "real" account, for it suggests that the adult felt a sense of betrayal at the hands of the adult world the depth of which could only be understood in the form of sexual abuse Stories of abuse, whether true or false, are always stories of the relationship between the adult and the child. Keeping all of this in mind it is important to remember that Freud felt convinced of his clients' truth-telling, as it was always accompanied by strong emotions, a desire to keep the past hidden, and a sense of guilt and shame of having been a part of the sexual experience.

For more on the story of the rise and fall of the "seduction theory" through 1896 and 1897, see *The Complete Letters of Sigmund Freud to Wilhelm Fliess, 1887–1904,* trans. and ed. by Jeffrey Moussaieff Masson (Cambridge, Mass. Harvard University Press, 1985). Also, see Masson, *Assault on the Truth: Freud's Suppression of the Seduction Theory.* (New York: Farrar, Straus, & Giroux, 1984).

[3]Sigmund Freud, *The Standard Edition of the Complete Psychological Works,* trans. James Strachey, Anna Freud, Alix Strachey, and Alan Tyson. Vol. 3 (1893–99) (London: Hogarth Press and the Institute of Pychoanalysis, 1961); pp. 202–3.

[4]Quoted in Ronald W. Clark,*Freud: The Man and the Cause* (London: Jonathan Cape/Weidenfeld & Nicolson, 1980), p.159.

[5]Ibid. p.160.

[6]Ibid. p. 13.

[7]Freud, *The Interpretation of Dreams.* trans. James Strachey (New York: Avon, 1965), p. 262.

[8] Sigmund Freud, *The Origins of Psychoanalysis: Letters, Drafts, and Notes to Wilhelm Fliess,* 1887–1902, ed. Marie Bonaparte, Anna Freud, and Ernst Kris and trans. Eric Mosbacher and James Strachey (Garden City, N.Y.: Doubleday, 1957), pp. 215–16.

[9]Clark, *Freud,* p.161.

[10]Miller, *Thou Shalt Not Be Aware,* 110-11.

[11]Anna Freud, *The Ego and the Mechanisms of Defense* (New York: International University Press, 1966), p.17.

[12]Freud's theories produce and reproduce the dominant ideology of his era, which are premised "on a Cartesian duality," that the world is made up of self and other, subject and object, inner and outer. This worldview grows out of Newtonian and Cartesian scientific paradigms still dominant at the time. See Barbara Shapiro, *Literature and the Relational Self* (New York: New York University Press, 1994).

[13]In Chapter 4, I explore in detail Victorian child-rearing ideology and its relationship to the dominant culture.

[14]Again, a topic that will be taken up in more detail in Chapter 4.

[15]Countless authors, scientists, therapists, medical doctors, and others have been exploring the relationship between the mind and the body and between Eastern and Western approaches to medicine and healing. An exhaustive list is impossible. For a primer, see Depak Chopra's *Quantum Healing: Exploring the Frontiers of Mind/Body Medicine* (New York: Bantam Books, 1988). Also, see the work of Dr. Andrew Weil, Carolyn Myss, Alexander Lowen, Joan Borysenko, and Norman Cousins, to name a few.

[16]In 1900 Freud published *The Interpretation of Dreams,* his first full account of the Oedipal theory and its relationship to the unconscious and to the notion of infantile sexuality. In it Freud writes, "in the [story of] *Oedipus* the child's wishful fantasy that underlies it is brought out into the open and realized as it would be in a dream. In *Hamlet* it remains repressed; and—just as in the case of a neurosis—we only learn of its existence from its inhibiting consequences." All Hamlet can do, according to Freud, is to take vengeance on the man who murdered his father and married his mother, "the man who shows [Hamlet] the repressed wishes of his childhood realized" (298–99).

[17]Consider what Miller observes about Sophocles' *Oedipus, the King.*

> Oedipus punishes himself by putting out his eyes. Even though he had no way of recognizing Laius as his father; even though Laius had tried to kill his infant son and was responsible for this lack of recognition; even though Laius was the one who provoked Oedipus's anger when their paths crossed;

even though Oedipus did not desire Jocasta but became her husband thanks
to his cleverness in solving the sphinx's riddle, thus rescuing Thebes; and
even though Jocasta, his mother, could have recognized her son by his
swollen feet—to this very day no one seems to have objected to the fact that
Oedipus was assigned all the blame. It has always been taken for granted
that children are responsible for what was done to them, and it has been
essential that when children grow up, they not be aware of the true nature of
their past. In return, they are given the right to treat their own children in the
same fashion. . . . His blindness saves his life, because it serves to pacify
and reconcile the gods. (*Thou Shalt Not Be Aware,* pp.143–44)

[18]Shapiro, *Literature and the Relational Self,* p. 3. Also, see Stephen Mitchell's
Relational Concepts in Psychoanalysis: An Integration (Cambridge, Mass.: Harvard
University Press, 1988).

[19]Ibid.

[20]The rise of the public school and the rise of children's literature run a parallel
course. The necessity for the one is always found in the other. Whether both are, in
fact, necessary, is another matter—capitalism, the needs of the labor market, and the
potential for school and text to effectively indoctrinate the child play a central role.
See Hugh Cunningham, *Children and Childhood in Western Society Since 1500* (New
York: Longman, 1995).

[21]See Stephen Greenblatt, *Renaissance Self-Fashioning* (Chicago: University of
Chicago Press, 1980), p. 6.

[22]Shakespeare's literary sources for *Hamlet* include François Belleforêt's collection, *Histories Traqiques,* published in 1580; also, a twelfth-century Latin work, the
Historiae Danicae by Saxo Grammaticus, first published in 1512, which harkens back
even further to an Icelandic saga from the ninth century. Perhaps Shakespeare read
Timothy Bright's *Treatise on Melancholy,* published in 1586, and Montaigne's essays
published in 1595, along with numerous other authors whose ideas circulate in
Hamlet.

[23]Robert Heilbroner, *The Worldly Philosophers: The Lives and Times and Ideas
of the Great Economic Thinkers* (New York: Simon & Schuster, 1980), p. 29.

[24]Ibid. p. 36.

[25]Abandonment, conscious and unconscious neglect, and outright murder
account for infant mortality, along with disease—often the result of adult ignorance as
well Edward Shorter, *The Making of the Modern Family* (New York: Basic Books,
1975).

[26]See Lloyd DeMause, ed., *The History of Childhood* (Northvale, N.J.: Jason
Aronson, 1995).

[27]See S. Schoenbaum, *William Shakespeare: A Compact Documentary Life* (New
York: Oxford University Press, 1977), pp. 50–60.

[28]Ibid. p. 66.

[29]Alice Miller, *The Drama of the Gifted Child,* trans. Ruth Ward (New York:
HarperCollins), p. 4.

[30]According to Timothy Bright, the melancholy individual is "given to fearful
and terrible dreams. . . " and his house "seemeth unto the melancholic a prison or dun-
geon, rather than a place of assured repose and rest" (*A Treaty of Melancholoy,* 1586,

quoted in *Shakespeare: The Essential Reference to His Plays, His Poems, His Life and Times and More* [New York: Dell, 1990, p.75]). Still, others suggest it is not necessary for Shakespeare to have read a treatise on melancholy to understand it. Of course, both can easily be true, for though some of the language Hamlet uses echoes Bright's language when describing his shifting moods, it is arguable whether the character of Hamlet could have grown in the hands of any author without the author having first-hand experience of melancholia.

[31]Schoenbaum, *William Shakespeare,* p. 36.

[32]Ibid. p. 42.

[33]Quoted by Philippe Aries, *Centuries of Childhood: A Social History of Family Life* (New York: Random House, 1962), p. 162.

[34]Jean Herorard, *Journal sur l'enfance et la jeunesse de Louis XIII,* ed. Eud. Soulié and E. de Barthélemy (Paris: 1868) quoted in Aries *Centuries,* pp.51–60.

[35]Emotional need is another way of understanding what Aristotle meant by *hamartia,* or "overweening pride." Overweening pride in this case is really overweening insecurity compensated by unconscious ego-projections of grandiosity. These projections are ideological in nature and driven by an overwhelming emotional need left catastrophically unmet since childhood.

[36]Miller, *Thou Shalt Not Be Aware,* p. 24.

[37]Katharina Rutschky, *Schwarze Pädagogik* (Berlin, 1977).

CHAPTER 3

The Brothers Grimm, the Black Pedagogy, and the Roots of Fascist Culture

*Of all our institutions public education is the most impor-
tant. Everything depends on it, the present and the future.
It is essential that the morals and the political ideas of the
generation which is now growing up should no longer be
dependent upon the news of the day or the circumstances
of the moment. Above all we must secure unity: we must be
able to cast a whole generation in the same mould.*

—NAPOLÉON, *Letters*

THE EMPEROR'S NEW CLOTHES

Napoléon's "La Grande Armée" defeated Alexander I's Russian army in the
Battle of Friedland on June 14, 1807.[1] The result was the Treaty of Tilsit (July
1807), which was simply one in a long series of treaties that resulted from
French conquests in Europe during the first decade of the nineteenth century.
The Treaty of Tilsit forced Frederick III, King of Prussia, to cede large por-
tions of German territory to France. This was not a complete disaster for the
Germans, however, for Germany was at the time a fragmented territory of
petty principalities, none of which could unite Germany into one nation-state.
Cultural and geographical unification, however, was on the minds of many
Germans. The Treaty of Tilsit represented at least in part a step towards a
united Germany, albeit a Germany under French rule.

As Napoléon's military conquests continued successfully through the
first decade of the nineteenth century, he used his success as a way to legitimate and justify the founding of a Bonaparte family dynasty throughout
Europe. Napoléon's military prowess might be understood not so much as an

example of the divine right of dynasty in action as the use of military power to define the meaning of "divine right" and thus legitimate itself. In this way Napoléon might be understood as a truly modern tyrant. In the process of legitimating his own power, then, Napoléon institutionalized Napoleonic rule and named his brothers ruling monarchs of conquered European nations, including Joseph, "King of Naples," and Louis, "King of Holland." When Napoléon's only son, Francis Charles Joseph, was born in 1811, he immediately proclaimed him "King of Rome," the crown prince of Napoléon's empire.

When Napoléon consolidated his military victory in the Treaty of Tilsit he proclaimed a large region of Germany the "Kingdom of Westphalia" and placed Jérôme Bonaparte, his youngest brother, on the throne. Jérôme's monarchy demonstrated Napoléon's occasionally disastrous judgment. Nevertheless, Napoléon's overarching plan for the domination of Europe made ideological sense from the point of view of the colonizer: he understood that to maintain political power gained as a result of military conquest he must institutionalize the means of control so that the majority would, by and large, tyrannize themselves without the enormous costs incurred by maintaining a large occupying army. In short, military domination must be completed by ideological subjugation, or all was lost. This meant that the conqueror must appropriate existing cultural and political institutions that would then be handed back to the conquered peoples Frenchified, which meant, to Napoléon, civilized. In this transposition of his ideological beliefs Napoléon was no different than any other military colonizer before or since. Napoléon—like Hitler after him—understood that the colonizer must dominate the colonized early and often, so much so that the colonizer's culture— even if it is a culture of violence and subjugation—appears to be inevitable and as such, necessary if the colonized are to become *civilized*.[2]

Before Napoléon's conquest, the Germany of the Brothers Grimm was a collection of over three hundred petty principalities, duchies, and kingdoms; and "each petty prince considered himself an absolute ruler and reigned with unquestioned authority within the boundaries of his territory, however small it might be."[3] Before the French occupation, Wilhelm IX ruled Kassel—one of the principal residences of the Grimm family—and as one of the petty princes of over three hundred German principalities, he "represented a dull mixture of stupidity, greed, and unenlightened notions of absolutistic grandeur and his hand often lay heavily on his subjects. . . . But he nevertheless commanded the loyalty of most of his subjects, who *instinctively respected and obeyed him in spite of all the abuses of his regime. Patriotism seems to have been a matter of habit and ingrained loyalty to the region without regard for the person of the ruler*" (italics added).[4] It seems unlikely that the subjects of Wilhelm IX, "instinctively" respected him, as the above passage claims. Rather, Wilhelm IX's subjects, like all subjects in all sovereign nations, are taught as children to respect and obey the authority figure so that respect and obedience might come from the subject *as if* it were an instinctual response, *as if* patriotism, nationalism, and unconscious obedience to the dominant ideology were in the child's nature. In fact, emotional and physical needs are part of the child's nature; yet these needs can be used against the child and can become a political resource in reproducing the dominant culture, as Napoléon, Hitler, and other political leaders well understood. As a result, incompetent leaders like Wilhelm IX and Jérôme Bonaparte relied on the "instinctual" obedience of the majority of their subjects, for their subjects had been trained since childhood to obey and to regard their obedience as a service to God, king, and father.

By the time of Jérôme's coronation in 1807, many of the residents of the newly constituted Kingdom of Westphalia—especially those who lived in the capital, Kassel, greeted their new king not so much as a colonizing aggressor, but rather, as a curiosity—and no more and no less legitimate a state power than Wilhelm IX. Perhaps the Bonaparte family could establish order, peace, and prosperity to Europe after all.[5]

THE BROTHERS GRIMM

As aspiring members of the rising bourgeoisie, the Brothers Grimm sought nothing less than German unification; that they would exercise their national-istic desires as folklorists—rather than as politicians or military leaders—only at first appears unusual, for they understood what Napoléon understood: political unification among the disparate and diverse German people could be realized any number of ways, not least of which included the production of a "unified" culture through the propagation of the story of *das Volk* collected from an oral tradition that provided access to an ancient German past—an idealized German past—in which the German lived a life of language and story that transcended temporal political boundaries. By evoking this period in their folklore, fairy tales, and philology, the Brothers Grimm hoped, in part, to lead the reader to an ideological and emotional identification with an idea of a past Germany that might then serve to provoke a felt need for the creation of a newly organized political German state, discovered and realized through the production—and reproduction—of the ancient German *folklore*. The Brothers Grimm operated from the assumption that the stories of *das Volk* provided access to the real, the pure, and the truly German. The question of what "real" and "pure" meant to the Brothers Grimm, however, has been hotly disputed by recent critics. Nevertheless, most agree that the Brothers Grimm were keenly aware of their political and ideological situation as they proceeded to collect, edit, and publish *Kinder-und Hausmärchen* (Children's and Household Tales) in 1812.

Jack Zipes describes the Grimm's agenda as a kind of war, waged not on the battlefield as Napoléon waged it, but rather as an ideological battle for which the combatants fought for access to the dominant culture through its ideological apparatus. In *The Brothers Grimm*, Zipes suggests that Jacob and Wilhelm Grimm were both keenly aware of the ideological state of affairs in early-nineteenth-century Germany, for the brothers desired their own personal and political access to the dominant culture and were routinely denied it due to their Hessian ethnicity, which identified them with the illiterate and benighted *Volk*. The brothers, however, considered themselves enlightened intellectuals with decidedly bourgeois aspirations who made it a priority to identify the *Volk* and their own Hessian background not with illiteracy or backwardness, but rather, with a tradition of folk wisdom buried in the extant oral tradition of the peasants. Yet recent scholarship has seriously undermined the image of the Brothers Grimm traipsing across the countryside in search of *das Volk*. Rather, they collected stories from family friends—many of which were displaced French Huguenots living nearby—and from already published stories. From these the Brothers Grimm "reverse engineered" the material and, according to their own subjective desire, constructed fairy tales *that they believed* represented the true oral tradition of *das Volk*. The critical issue regarding the origins of the fairy tales thus has shifted from a question of the Grimm's historical accuracy as folklorists—complete with the idealized image of the field worker who unearths the gems of the oral tradition as he interviews peasants—to a more slippery, difficult image of individuals working at home, interviewing friends, reading previously published stories, sharing material with other scholars, and then presenting a construction of the oral tradition and an image of *das Volk* as if it were collected from the peasants themselves.

In attempting to elevate the ideological standing of the *Volk,* the Brothers Grimm served their own personal and professional ends, for as Hessians they were culturally stigmatized. If they could prove, on the other hand, that the Hessian *Volk* were true Germans, then two of their agendas might be served at the same time: the Hessian *Volk* as they were constructed by the Brothers Grimm in *Children's and Household Tales* might be understood as repositories of the Germanic tradition. From this an implicit argument for a unified German state based not on politics, but rather, on the ancient, yet simple folk wisdom of the German people might be made. Nationalism, then, according to the Brothers Grimm, might be understood not solely in political terms, but also in personal, familial terms. In other words, in the folk and fairy tales the Brothers Grimm constructed the German tradition in such a way that it did not appear to be nationalism, but instead served as an invisible frame inside which the simple folk wisdom of Hessian "family values" became all the more visible. In short, the Brothers Grimm were fighting a culture war. At stake was nothing less than ideological control over the meaning and significance of the German past and the German future. Zipes describes it this way:

> In seeking to establish its rightful and "righteous" position in German society, the bourgeoisie, due to its lack of actual military power and unified economic power, used its "culture" as a weapon to push through its demands and needs. In the process, the middle classes mediated between the peasants and the aristocracy and later between the aristocracy/high bourgeoisie and workers through institutions that were their own making and served their interests. One mode used by the bourgeoisie to create its own institutions and conventions was that of appropriation—taking over and assuming the property, goods, and cultural forms of lower classes and refining them to suit the sensibility and wants of bourgeois culture. . . . Such institutionalization was not really possible until the bourgeoisie needed it and had created the technology and other supporting institutions that would make the fairy tale a vital component in the socialization of children through literature.[6]

Though the child had always been the repository for adult culture, the Brothers Grimm understood—as did Napoléon—that if one wanted to have any impact on the shape of things to come, one must rigorously mold the child with that shape in mind. Ideological indoctrination of the child then became of paramount concern. This made sense to the Brothers Grimm, for they had been molded by the child-rearing traditions prevalent at the time, and would take this experience as a necessary and obvious reality as they shaped the image of the German oral tradition in the fairy tales. The point here is not an uncommon one, yet it bears repeating. There are those critics who maintain that in the fairy tales, "there is much less specific consciously cultural material" present, "and therefore they mirror the basic patterns of the psyche more clearly."[7] Critical assumptions about the mythic nature of the human psyche and its need to reproduce itself in symbol and story often lead to a dismissal of the psychosocial origins of the fairy tales. A critical approach that denies the fairy tale its ideological content denies the reader access to the psychosocial context at the moment of literary production, and so invites a reading of the tales that confuses ideological effects for universal, mythic realities. As ideological productions of the dominant culture, however, the fairy tales of the Brothers Grimm do not, in fact, record archetypal myths of the human psyche but rather, they reify cultural myth *as if* it were archetypal myth. Even so, the fact that so many readers have shared an identification with the fairy tales of the Brothers Grimm seems to speak to a universal nature that transcends culture and ideology. Rather, I believe that the fact that so many readers have shared an identification with the fairy tales speaks to the almost universal *nurture* of human relationship that the tales represent, reify, and reproduce.

Jack Zipes maintains a similar position regarding the psychosocial origins of the fairy tales when he writes:

> There is an interesting connection . . . between the Grimms' almost desperate search for a stable home, order, and cleanliness and their social concern for the welfare of Germany disturbed by war and French occupation. The personal becomes very much the political in their work, and their act of collecting folk tales and reconstituting them according to their needs and ethical notions of the "pure" German language and literature was essentially an act of compensation for the loss of father and homeland.[8]

Though I agree that the Brothers Grimm clung to the "paternal position" in their adult life, in part due to the early loss of their father, I believe that the psychosocial origins of the Grimms' fairy tales begin long before the death of Philip Grimm. Rather, the psychosocial origins of the fairy tales have no proper beginning, which is to say the origins of the fairy tales do not begin with the Brothers Grimm, but rather, with Philip Grimm and *his* childhood, for he parented his sons in the way that his father parented him. The grandfather, then, parents in the way *he* was parented, all of which produces and reproduces a child-rearing tradition so seemingly natural that the distinction between cultural tradition and biological necessity becomes lost in the fog of the dominant child-rearing ideology, so convinced as it is of its own rectitude, necessity, and obviousness.

Child-rearing pedagogies bent on the domination and the subjugation of the child were a direct appropriation of the Judeo-Christian child-rearing model as it was understood and adapted from the Bible, especially the Old Testament. For the Brothers Grimm this tradition existed in an intensified form, which, like the Puritans in America, drew on the Protestant Christianity of Calvinism, a theology defined by the doctrine of "original sin" first and last.

The childhood of the Brothers Grimm was characterized by a relationship with the adult structured by a number of conscious and unconscious ideological factors. First and foremost was the doctrine of "original sin" as espoused by the Reform Calvinist Protestantism of the Grimm family and of much of Germany. The doctrine of "original sin" cannot be overestimated, because with this doctrine in mind, any kind of violence and abuse is possible. From the point of view of the adult, the violence and cruelty practiced against the "willful" child is all "for the child's own good," since the child's soul is at stake. In other words, what is a little bit of pain and suffering now at the hands of the adult when all of eternity is at stake? The child's will must be *broken,* and it is the reformed adult's job to do it, always, of course, assuming that the adult is *reformed* and the child *wicked.* "Original sin" casts this specious assumption as an absolute truth. The adult need never question his or her treatment of the child, for it is ordained by Holy Scripture.

According to the Reform Calvinist perspective of the Brothers Grimm— and significantly, much of the otherwise disparate German people—work, cleanliness, orderliness, and above all, obedience were traits that, when adhered to passionately, would have "salvific" results for the depraved child. From the point of view of the dominant culture, the ideal child raised in this way is—or should be—tractable, obedient, and unobtrusive. These qualities lead to "success." Ironically, these qualities also lead later in life to the individual's experience of confusing and chronic depressions, ungoverned bouts of rage, addictions of all kinds, violence in human relationships, and, when widespread, enactments of cultural practices that offer themselves as "cure-alls" for what ails the individual and the society. Hitler's National Socialism represented just such a phenomenon. According to this kind of fascistic ideology, genocide is simply the price such a culture must pay to "right" itself and "rid" itself of its problems. Contemporary capitalism offers itself in a similar fashion to a population in so much unconscious need. Make no mistake: Western culture's consumption of the world's resources is an enactment of a genocidal practice largely unrecognized as such, yet when we consider habitat issues such as ozone depletion, global warming, population growth, mounting stockpiles of nuclear waste, over-fishing, poisoned oceans—the list goes on—future generations may very well label Western culture as a criminal culture engaged—largely unconsciously—in crimes against life.

Which brings us back to what Katharina Rutschky in 1977 called "schwarze pädogogile," or the *black pedagogy* of eighteenth- and nineteenth-century German child-rearing practices, which Alice Miller calls "poisonous pedagogy" in *For Your Own Good*. Whatever the child-rearing practices of the eighteenth and nineteenth centuries are named, the black pedagogy offers a way of seeing how violent child-rearing practices lead directly to the fascistic personality, or to what Theodor Adorno and Max Horkheimer describe in *The Authoritarian Personality* as the type of personality prone to passive acquiescence or, on the other hand, to the type of personality prone to domination and violence. These character types are two sides of the same cultural coin and, as such, complementary consequences of the same ideological antecedents.

Because the black pedagogy conceived the child as wicked, willful, and in need of "breaking," the child learns from the adult early and often that human relationships—and human love—are "naturally" invasive, often violent, and frequently humiliating. Human love so configured comes from the "outside" and manipulates the child's body so much so that the child loses direct access to the world of his physical body, including the emotions and intuition. The child of the black pedagogy learns early and often that the only way to ameliorate his suffering is to pretend that he is not suffering and so avoid adult interventions that are frequently hostile and violent. Pretending also requires the repression of emotion, for if the child cries, whines, or otherwise protests his treatment, recriminations—this time justified by the child's "misbehavior"—are often more severe and traumatizing because the adult's authority has been, according to the adult, questioned by the child. The hierarchy of authority must never be questioned; therefore the child who wishes to avoid violence, shame, and suffering learns early and often not to question the dominant social order. The very young child who cries, whines, or manifests other behaviors does so spontaneously in response to her emotional and physical environment. The child signals that her basic emotional needs are going unmet and that her experience at that particular moment is frightening, sickening, alienating, humiliating, painful, or lonely.

Dr. Schreber's child-rearing manuals of the nineteenth century went through forty printings and were translated into several languages. As Miller explains, "in these works it is stressed again and again that children should start being trained as soon as possible, even as early as their fifth month of life, if the soil is to be 'kept free of harmful weeds' " (*For Your Own Good*, p. 5). According to Dr. Schreber, the relationship between the child and the adult is adversarial and should be understood as such. The child will wait, like a cunning enemy, for her chance to usurp adult authority, even from the crib. When a child cries, and the adult has determined that the child's cries are without significance, the child's outburst should be treated as "the first appearance of willfulness." Dr. Schreber advises that the adult

> should no longer simply wait for it to pass . . . but should proceed in a somewhat more positive way: by quickly diverting its attention, by stern words, threatening gestures, rapping on the bed . . . or if none of this helps, by appropriately mild corporal admonitions repeated persistently at brief intervals until the child quiets down or falls asleep. . . . This procedure will be necessary only once or at most twice and then you will be master of the child forever. From now on a glance, a word, a single threatening gesture will be sufficient to control the child.[9]

Dr. Schreber's son grew up to be a paranoid hysteric and later a patient of Sigmund Freud.

In 1752 J. G. Kruger published "An Essay on the Education and Instruction of Children" in Germany. Like so many others, including Schreber's wildly popular child-rearing manuals of the nineteenth century—which were as popular as the Grimms' fairy tales and the Bible—they are part of the black pedagogy common in German child-rearing manuals of the eighteenth and nineteenth centuries.[10] The black pedagogy describes the relationship between adult and small child as a battle of good versus evil. When the child disobeys the adult, the hierarchical chain of obedience is threatened, and "such disobedience amounts to a declaration of war against you. Your son is trying to usurp your authority, and you are justified in answering force with force in order to insure his respect, without which you will be unable to train him. The blows you administer should not be merely playful ones but should convince him that you are his master."[11] The German child-rearing tradition of the eighteenth and nineteenth centuries has as its primary aim the control and domination of the child, all for the child's own good.[12] The child, according to the black pedagogy, comes into the world in desperate need of reform, and reform comes at the hands of the adult, often through violence. The violence is always the child's fault, however, for the child's willfulness, and not the adult's ideological assumptions about child-rearing, is the chief cause of it. Because the child is willful, stained by original sin, wayward, and destructive, the adult must enact decisive and punitive measures so that the child will not grow up "full of weeds." More importantly, however, the black pedagogy resulted in an obedient child, divided from himself and easily ruled by the adult.[13]

There is every reason to believe that what the Brothers Grimm describe as a "normal" childhood in their autobiographies was indeed ordinary *given the child-rearing traditions at the time* for the rising bourgeoisie. For instance, Zipes writes in *The Brothers Grimm*, "As soon as the children were of age, they were instructed in reading, writing, and mathematics by a private tutor and then sent to a local school, where they received a classical education. They were also given strict religious training in the Reform Calvinist Church and throughout their lives, Jacob and Wilhelm remained deeply religious and set high moral standards for themselves" (p. 2). "Normal" for the Brothers Grimm describes a childhood in which the maidservants and stern old Aunt Schlemmer raised the Grimm children and the father remained a distant, authoritarian figure. Philip Grimm died when Jacob and Wilhelm were eleven and ten years old. The unconscious need for a father shaped the brothers' relationship to each other, with Jacob freely acknowledging that he took on the father's role with his siblings, especially with Wilhelm. Jacob accepted the father's position with his siblings as it had been distantly modeled for him by Philip.

Philip Grimm was the town clerk of Hanau, a small town in the Kassel region. As town clerk, Philip Grimm was a central and respected figure who participated in or was secondarily related to most of Hanau's dominant culture. Philip's father had been the pastor of the Reformed Church in Steinau and his grandfather had also been an important clergyman in Hanau. It comes as little surprise, then, that the Grimm family organized itself as a "strict religious unit." The Grimm family took their religion seriously enough to consider Lutherans "foreigners," and Catholics as culturally backward because they lacked the enlightenment brought about by the Protestant Reformation.

Jacob believed sincerely that the modern German language was a product of Protestant thinking.

One key to a further understanding of the dominant ideology that informed the mind of the Grimm family—and of the Brothers Grimm as adults—is the nature of the family culture as it produced and reproduced the dominant culture and its prevailing ideology, marked as it was by religious and cultural "patriotism." Like many middle-class children of their day, the Grimm children were raised by maidservants and by their aunt. Philip Grimm remained a "magisterial" figure in his town clerk's uniform of blue coat, red collar, military-style leather breeches, and silver-spurred boots. "Even when not in uniform he appeared to the children in a kind of official capacity, escorting them to church on Sunday, reading prayers to the family, in general presenting a figure of authority."[14]

THE CHILD AS OCCUPIED TERRITORY

With the problem of French occupation clearly on his mind, while at the same time working for the occupying enemy, Jacob Grimm was torn. He admired French culture, and he had a deep need for a figure of authority to take him under wing and father him, for Jacob had been the father to his siblings since his father had died. It comes as no surprise, then, that Jacob admired the columns of French troops in their colorful French uniforms all serving *one man* in his deadly serious game of king-maker. For a time, French-occupied Kassel represented the possibilities of a massive military force used to bring order, control, and a bit of aesthetic style to a depressed population. Jacob Grimm loved the French, for they represented the kind of order he and his Germany had hardly known, except in the idealized past of an ancient, united, and sovereign German people. Yet, at the same time, the Brothers Grimm hated the idea of an occupied Germany.[15]

An occupied Germany was, for Jacob and Wilhelm, the direct result of Germany's fragmented political status, a status that changed little even after Napoléon's empire crumbled in 1813 and Jérôme Bonaparte, King of Westphalia, abandoned his throne and returned to France. Ironically, the French occupation of Kassel appears to have been the ideal political environment for the Brothers Grimm—especially Jacob—to pursue scholarly work, and it was at this time that the Brothers completed the majority of their collection, construction, and publication of *Children's and Household Tales*, published in 1812 more than a year before Kassel was returned to the hands of its German princes.

Jacob Grimm's years as Jérôme Bonaparte's Royal Librarian have been described as extraordinary, peaceful, stable, and secure. Finally the Grimms had access to the dominant culture, even if it was the culture of the occupying army. For once Jacob Grimm had access to a steady income along with time to pursue his scholarly activities. His duties as Royal Librarian were light, though Jacob impressed his employer and was rewarded with a position on the Kassel town council, one of the only Germans to be so honored. The motivations that drove Jacob to work so cooperatively with the French—and with King Jérôme—are unclear, yet it seems that, even as he disliked the idea of an occupied Germany, he enjoyed and freely mingled with the French. In short, Jacob was torn. He loved the German-Hessian tradition—so much of it informs the brothers' scholarship—while at the same time he embraced the French for their ideals of liberty, equality, and justice, even when they came in the form of an absolutistic, militaristic, totalitarian despot like Napoléon. Jacob's split character might be understood as, on the one hand, an acting out of his childhood needs for a father who lived up to his grandiose posturing. In this way, Napoléon—and his surrogate, Jérôme—might be understood as a kind of idealized image of Philip Grimm.[16]

The Brothers Grimm understood implicitly and explicitly—in part as a result of the French occupation—that a strong, centralized military government could subdue warring principalities, duchies, and other political factions *for a time,* but for lasting cultural hegemony something more than military power would be required. Stable political unification required the long-term institutionalization of the conquering culture's dominant ideology. This Napoléon understood as well, but his own grandiosity undid him and his attempt to institutionalize his empire—and thus make ideologically obvious the "rightness" of his conquest and his rule—failed, or so history records.[17]

The period of King Jérôme's rule was a brief, intense—though in no way unique—era of imperial power, totalitarian ambition, European infighting, and competing nationalisms made manifest with awe-inspiring violence unlike anything Europe had yet seen. It was, in short, a world in which the black pedagogy went continental with Napoléon attempting to *master* his unruly children *forever;* it was in this world that the Brothers Grimm sought their profession in life, and it was in this world that they began to collect, edit, and publish the first edition of one of the most popular books of the nineteenth century *Children's and Household Tales.* As folklorists, the Brothers Grimm worked to discover a German past embedded in the stories shared by the common people, or *das Volk,* that they hoped might lead to a remembering and an awakening of the German national spirit through an awareness of a national culture extant in the stories of the peasants. The Brothers Grimm believed literature to have a civilizing power of its own, "and were sincerely convinced of the moral as well as pedagogical value of their contributions."[18]

JACOB GRIMM AS MASOCHIST

In 1809 King Jérôme was so pleased with Jacob Grimm's services as Royal Librarian that he appointed him legal adviser to the city council. Jacob was

the only German to serve on the council, and he worked diligently, obedi-
ently, and happily to ensure the smooth operation of the occupying army's
government. And why not? The child trained to obey the authority figure
through the child-rearing process of the black pedagogy develops a character
structure dominated by masochistic traits in which submission to the authority figure becomes an unconscious and automatic act, growing as it does out
an of emotional need buried in the masochist's character structure. The
masochist organizes his life in such a way that he might fulfill an emotional
need that has been prohibited since childhood but remains chronic and pressing, although unconscious.

Ideological and emotional contradictions are easily ignored by the
masochistic character, which in part could explain why Jacob Grimm might
harbor "fierce Hessian patriotism," as one critic describes it, and yet at the
same time serve the occupying army, even gratefully. One way to explain this
is to understand Jacob Grimm's masochistic character structure, a common
personality type that results from child-rearing experiences at the hands of
adults who practice the black pedagogy. The masochistic character aims to
please the authority figure even when it means self-betrayal, for sacrificing
one's self is in fact no sacrifice for the masochist, since there really is no
sense of self that the masochist has access to in order to betray; as he betrays
himself, he feels the way he always did: numb. The reason for this is that the
child reared according to the black pedagogy has lost access to his intuitive
center in order to satisfy adult demands. The black pedagogy severs the biological connection between mother and infant, replacing it with cultural practices like wet-nursing, swaddling, or, later, bottle feeding, cribs, and day-care
centers for infants. Without a completed symbiotic relationship with the
mother signaled by child-led separation from the mother's breast and body,
the child is forever decentered from his body and vulnerable to cultural substitutes to chronic emotional longing.

The black pedagogy requires the child to repress longing, for according
to the adult, the behavior that manifests itself as a result of incomplete
mother-child symbiosis is merely "willfulness" and "misbehavior." The child
is encouraged through numerous implicit and explicit child-rearing experiences to deny and repress her longing or risk invasive attacks from the adult.
As a result she learns self-denial as a form of self-defense. In adulthood, however, self-denial becomes self-betrayal, an act of forgetting, an act of repression, and so the masochist might harbor rage and violence and not
consciously realize it. For her, betrayal is not betrayal, sacrifice is not sacrifice, since the state of contradiction and betrayal is how it always was—the
violence done to the self as a result of this unconscious process of self-
betrayal repeats the violence done to the child by the adult in the relationship
structured by the black pedagogy.

As an adult, therefore, the masochist remains vulnerable to beguiling ideologies—and vulnerable to unconsciously adopting them as his own—especially when they come from an authoritarian personality who claims paternal power, for the authority figure's ideology works on the masochist's unconscious and unrecognized needs, always promising the solution to a psychosocial problem that the masochist can never name yet remains defined by. The result is that the masochist often justifies in one sweeping moment of double-think the ideological contradictions—including political betrayals—of his life if it means the possibility of securing some escape from the stultifying emotional relationship with the father he never knew.

Child-rearing practices like the black pedagogy hold notions of personal sovereignty as the highest ideological good. The confusing irony for the child, is that the notion of "sovereign" becomes fused with the lived reality of intensive molding by the adult, including circumcision, swaddling, potty training, enemas, and other invasive techniques that interfere with the child's relationship to his or her own body. The masochist develops body armor—sometimes manifesting itself as intense physical rigidity or obesity—all as an expression of the child's need to hold off the invasive adult, while at the same time holding in feelings of pain, humiliation, and suffering so threatening to the adult.

When the adult violates the child's physical and psychic state *as a matter of course* and then calls it "love" or an important "lesson," the child's ego-consciousness develops along with the body. In the case of the black pedagogy, violence and love become fused and take on a particular cultural form in the child's mind: the child is encouraged to believe that the invasive cultural child-rearing practices of the adult are in fact the result of biological necessities brought on the child *as a result of her nature*. It follows, then, that when the adult's child-rearing pedagogy requires the child to repress strong affect in response to mistreatment, neglect, or violence, the cycle of cultural and ideological production and reproduction has come full circle. The cycle of violence and domination endemic to black pedagogy occurs as a result of the unconscious transmission not just of the adult's anger and rage, but of the dominant—yet unconscious—ideology that justifies and rationalizes the violent nature of the relationship between adult and child.

CHILDREN AND HOUSEHOLD TALES: HANSEL AND GRETEL

Though the fairy tales were not intended for children, it is important to realize that, on the other hand, the fairy tales were not intended for adults alone. Rather, the Brothers Grimm understood from the first edition of *Children's and Household Tales* that these stories were for everyone. "It is our firm intention," Jacob Grimm wrote, "that the book be regarded as an educational book" and that adults would read the tales to their children. Jacob warned, however, that the adult should not read "too much at once until the children could understand . . . but give them little by little another morsel of this sweet food."[19] Elsewhere he suggested that the tales were not for children, but rather, the brothers had "adults and serious people" in mind as their ideal reading audience, and that children were a secondary audience. Even so, children were always a part of the ideal audience the Brothers Grimm targeted.

The fairy tales of the Brothers Grimm represent a watershed moment in the production and reproduction of the dominant ideology that determined the relationship between the adult and the child. The Brothers Grimm recorded and collected the folk material with an eye towards finding the version of the fairy tale that felt "most true" to them. They felt that they had an intuitive understanding of how to discover the variant tale that reflected most clearly the peasant oral tradition.[20] Why is the peasant tradition as refracted by the Brothers Grimm so violent? Why is the child placed in so much danger so often in the tales? Why is the child so often abandoned, seduced, and devoured? Why is the child told time and again that the adult world cannot save children from the terror and trauma of their lives? In other words, why do so many of the tales—the most popular ones especially—revel in terror and the terrorization of the child? For the same reasons the black pedagogy used terror: a terrified child is easier for the adult to manipulate.

In *The Uses of Enchantment,* Bruno Bettelheim interprets the fairy tales of the Brothers Grimm from a classic psychoanalytic perspective and as such articulates one of the most famous ways of understanding the fairy tales and the terror they contain: the child needs terror. For Bettelheim, the fairy tale reflects something *essential* about the human experience, and in a way, he is right, yet in a significant way he is wrong. Bettelheim assumes that the tales come from an "anonymous oral tradition" and therefore the child recognizes in the tales her own inner world as it is reflected in them. We keep telling these stories, according to Bettelheim, because they deal with "universal human problems."[21]

The "anonymous oral tradition" Bettelheim finds in the tales is not anonymous and is not the oral tradition of *das Volk.* In a way, the tales do reflect a collection of "universal human problems," but not the ones Bettelheim finds significant. For instance, from Bettelheim's perspective, "Hansel and Gretel" represents the child's need to work through a necessary and inevitable developmental phase of what Freudian psychoanalysis identifies as "oral greed." Bettelheim's reading is typical inasmuch as he assumes that the children inadvertently call upon themselves the retributions of the witch in the forest whose house they devour.[22] The hunger of the child in "Hansel and Gretel," in other words, is not the depiction of real hunger, but rather, a depiction of psychosymbolic hunger. As a psychoanalytic critic indebted to Freud, Bettelheim reads with a set of assumptions regarding the child's nature indebted to the Oedipal theory and so he sees not terrifying cannibalistic human relationships depicted in "Hansel and Gretel," but rather a lesson that adults must teach to children: namely, that the child must learn to curb her appetites, for they are natural, yet *unnatural,* and when not mastered will lead to her destruction. Bettelheim, like Freud, reads the child's appetites not as *symptom,* but as *cause.* The psychoanalytic perspective thus allows—or encourages—the reader to ignore the obvious in "Hansel and Gretel": the desire on the part of the mother-as-step-mother-as-witch to eat her children. More than anything else Bettelheim's understanding of the fairy tale relies on a Freudian definition of the child's nature. Because of this, he inadvertently reproduces a familiar misreading—and a common one at that—and as such, *The Uses of Enchantment* represents a moment of unconscious reproduction of the ideological status quo.[23]

In *One Fairy Story Too Many,* John Ellis blasts the notion that the Brothers Grimm simply collected an "anonymous oral tradition." Rather, he argues that the Brothers Grimm themselves exerted considerable control over the content and form of the fairy tales as they were presented to the reading public in 1812, 1815, 1819, and subsequent editions. From the earliest preface, in which the Brothers claim fidelity to the peasant and folk tradition, Ellis shows that they consistently relied upon literate, middle-class sources for their fairy tales while, in effect, hiding this fact from their readers. The Brothers Grimm felt justified in this practice for they felt a keen sense of mission in their "folk" research. German culture was at stake and by dint of will and vision, the Grimms set out to collect, refract, and represent the German "oral" tradition to an audience in need of ideological unification. The tales—and much of their other scholarly work—represent the attempt of the Brothers Grimm to fashion a larger cultural story of a German people who were ancient and venerable and bound by something that transcended temporal political realities.

That the Brothers Grimm had in large part borrowed fragments from the literary tradition already established in France, especially in the case of "Little Red Riding Hood," in no way interfered with their larger mission. The Grimms had a broad reading of German culture, for in German culture existed the residue of European culture, and so a French tale served as well as a Hessian tale, since both tales represented something universal, something ultimately German—especially after the brothers finished reconstructing it for German consumption. Moreover, because sources for the fairy tales were frequently middle-class neighbors, family friends, and even family members, the Grimms inadvertently collected material from a layer of stratified ideology familiar and congenial to their overarching agenda. In other words, the sources for the much of the material that would become *Children's and Household Tales* were themselves the product of a childhood dominated by the black pedagogy of the German child-rearing tradition. In fact, the Hassenpflugs and Wilds, both middle-class sources for the Grimms' fairy tales, also provided "the future spouses of both Wilhelm and his sister Lotte."[24] In fact, far from a representative search for the authentic peasant voice in Germany, the Brothers Grimm collected nearly all of their tales from "just one Hessian city, Kassell."[25]

Ellis's analysis of the Grimms' source material for the fairy tales devastates the nostalgic myth of the Brothers Grimm as burgeoning folklorists working in the field, collecting the tales from the mouths of old peasants, presumably as the tales had been passed down from generation to generation of "*das Volk*." Ellis writes,

> The sources of the material the Grimms used were not older, untainted, and untutored German peasant transmitters of an indigenous oral tradition, but instead, literate, middle-class, and predominantly young people, probably influenced more by books than by oral tradition—and including a very significant presence of people who were either of French origin or actually French-speaking. . . . [The] Grimms deliberately deceived their public by concealing or actually misstating the facts, in order to give an impression of ancient German folk origin for their material which they knew was utterly false.[26]

Moreover, the Grimms, contrary to their statements in the prefaces to the tales, in many cases filled out, rewrote, and generally extended the tales to almost twice their original length from the 1810 manuscript to the 1812 publication. They justified this act because they considered their extended versions, revisions, and reconstructions of the source material as *more true* to the original spirit of the tales, which assumed that the tales in fact had an "original spirit" and that they, the Brothers Grimm, understood intuitively what the "original spirit" was. In short, the Grimms were awash in their own ideological assumptions, assumptions governed not so much by the universal spirit—or psyche—they appealed to and claimed to rely on in making their editorial decisions, as by their human ego, structured as it was by the dominant ideology of Hessian culture.

For instance, the "Hansel and Gretel" of the first edition is twice as long as the manuscript version, and the changes made by the Brothers Grimm suggest an unconscious need to idealize their own childhood and represent it as part of a universal German heritage. In the 1810 manuscript version of "Hansel and Gretel," the tale places responsibility for the abandonment of the children on both mother and father. By the time the Grimms had finished "revising" the tale, Hansel and Gretel have been abandoned by their stepmother and the father plays only a passive role, himself an implicit victim of the stepmother's character. The changes from the 1810 manuscript to the 1812 publication have, as Ellis describes it, the effect of reducing the emphasis on the conflict between parents and children and replacing conflict with an idealized moral frame that justifies, while at the same time dismisses, the latent violence as obvious and necessary. This is "a persistent tendency of the Grimms" and a hallmark of a mind trained by the black pedagogy.[27]

Though the surface features of "Hansel and Gretel" were modified and expanded by the Brothers Grimm from the manuscript version right up through the fifth edition, the latent and often manifest violence in the relationship between the adult and the child remains, though mystified and mythified by the Brothers Grimm. The 1810 manuscript version itself is no original peasant tale; rather, it is a tale retold to the Grimms by a middle-class friend in Kassel. In this early version Hansel and Gretel are abandoned by their mother and father in the woods; the father is aware of—though ambivalent about—his role. The children find a house made of bread and cake and sugar on their third day of starving in the forest. They then meet the owner of the house, an "old woman" who wants to fatten and eat the children. Gretel saves herself and her brother, when, instead of getting into the oven, she pushes in the old woman, "and the witch burned to death." They find jewels in the old woman's house and return home with them. The father becomes a rich man. The mother has mysteriously died.

The Grimms expand their source material for "Hansel and Gretel" to a tale almost twice the length of the 1810 manuscript version. In their revisions, the mother and father have dialogue about the mother's desire to abandon the children, a dialogue that, by the fifth edition, includes the father's feelings of regret and sorrow for his children, though he nevertheless agrees to take them out into the forest to starve. For, as the mother maintains, there is simply not enough food for all. She must separate from the children though they are not ready to separate from her. Though the father's protests grow increasingly more dramatic by the fifth edition of the fairy tale—as if he is powerless and a victim in his own right, even as he participates in the attempted murder of his children—no amount of softening here by the Brothers Grimm can conceal the fact that the adults—the father in particular—choose to abandon the children in the forest to die.

After walking for three days the children come upon "an old woman," described in later editions as "a wicked old witch." Here the Grimms have mystified the inherent murderous conflict between the adults and the children, and transformed it into a supernatural battle of good versus evil. No longer is the tale a question of the adult's responsibility to the child, nor is it a tale of the material conditions of the poor. Rather, the Grimms revise it so that the "original spirit" might be made more apparent, and for the Grimms this "original spirit" fashions a world in which human beings become symbols for the larger story of good versus evil, light versus dark.

Even so, the dominant, adult-centered ideology prevents many from seeing the obvious in "Hansel and Gretel," an obviousness that revisions, expansions, and mythifications do not fully conceal: "Hansel and Gretel" is a story of the adult's consumption of the child. It is a story of terror that, on the one hand, represents an all-too-common historical occurrence: adults eat their children, both literally and figuratively. Literally in that the old witch in the forest represents the mother, for both the mother and the witch would eat Hansel and Gretel. That is, when the mother denies food to her children in favor of her own needs, and so abandons them to die, she to live on food stolen from their mouths, she is quite literally eating her children every time she eats a bite of food that would have been theirs. The witch symbolizes the cannibalistic, narcissistic relationship the mother has with herself and with her children. The revisions, expansions, and mystifications of the Brothers Grimm not only fail to hide the narrative connection between the mother and the "wicked old witch," but in many ways draw attention to the mother's deadly narcissism.

As edition followed edition, the Brothers Grimm expanded the relationship between Hansel and Gretel, and as a result some critics have considered their relationship to represent the heart of the tale. Presenting the story as one of "oral greed" or "sibling rivalry" encourages the reader to miss the larger, more obvious story of the relationship between the adult and the child, and that the child's "oral greed" is, in fact, an adult-centered ideology that codes and thereby mystifies Hansel and Gretel's real conditions of existence: they are *starving*. The starving child needs to eat. The mother is responsible for withholding her ability to nourish the child, and for this, the tale punishes the mother, in the form of the wicked old witch. The father, too, is guilty, but as the tales progress from edition to edition, the father's crimes were exculpated by the Brothers Grimm. He was an unwilling participant and feels sorry for his actions. His passivity is rewarded and he is made rich by his children's canny survival skills.

Hansel and Gretel's dutiful return to their home manifests the dominant ideology's requirement for children: children must recognize the heavy burden they represent to the adult world and redress it. And so they return home hoping that with pockets filled with jewels their stepmother will be free to love them rather than eat them, content in the knowledge that they can pull their own weight and feed themselves and their family; all of this constructs an image of the child with a very short memory who has already forgotten the parents' betrayal. Hansel and Gretel return home and serve the betrayer because it is what children *must* do according to adult ideological hegemony.

The Brothers Grimm appear to have solved the problem of the murderous conflict between the adult and the child manifest in "Hansel and Gretel," for the triumphant ending of this tale has the children saving the poverty-stricken father. Everyone can finally eat. Yet the ending represents a regression rather than a progression from the tale's premise: the narcissistic adult eats the child one way or another. "Hansel and Gretel" is a tale of the cyclical nature of ideological reproduction. Consider where the children acquired their new wealth and their new-found ability to feed their starving parents. By vanquishing the old witch in the forest and thwarting her cannibalistic ways, the children free themselves and take her wealth. What do they do with the old witch's wealth? They eat it, forced to by cultural conditions that have driven them into poverty in the first place. In eating the witch's wealth, Hansel and Gretel become consumers of the witch—the mother—in much the same way she wanted to consume them. "Hansel and Gretel" is a story of a narcissistic—and violent—culture that reproduces itself in its children, and the Grimms were happy to reproduce this story, for it was *their story,* and in celebrating it, they celebrated themselves, idealized their own past, exacted unconscious revenge on the mother, and idealized and protected the father.

THE CHILD

Much of fairy tale scholarship accepts the specious notion that children need terror and traumatization to live a happy and well-adjusted life. Aside from the obvious contradiction that this way of thinking initially represents, the adult belief in the child's need for trauma suggests something of the cyclical nature of repressed childhood trauma and the unconscious need for the adult to relieve it by inflicting it on the child. The cycle of emotional and physical traumatization is justified by the notion that the adult has the duty to introduce the child to the hard, cold world so that the child might get used to it. Emotional and physical insecurity in the life of the child, in other words, somehow leads to an emotionally and physically secure adult.

The Grimms' additions to these tales are best described as conscious and unconscious ideological reshaping. Part of the reshaping process was, as Ellis and others have observed, conscious to the point of deception. On the other hand, much of what the Brothers Grimm added to the tales grew directly out of the ambient, dominant culture of conquest, violence, and nationalism in Europe at the time the Brothers Grimm assembled the first edition of *Children's and Household Tales.* The point is that the cultural and political events reflected and refracted the ideology already extant in the child-rearing traditions of the black pedagogy. Through child-rearing practices that relied on the violent domination and subjugation of the child the world is born, and it is a world all too ready to enact stories of violence, domination, and subjugation as an inevitable, invisible, and unconscious given.

Perhaps more important than any other aspect of the black pedagogy remains the cult of personality instituted by the father, in which the father by virtue of his god-like position as father is always right. Like the absolute dictator, the father has a divine right to rule made real by his use and misuse of sheer physical power. The emotional neglect inherent in the black pedagogy lies at the root of the adult's need to cathect and idealize a substitute father-figure. Miller describes it this way:

> Every ideology offers its adherents the opportunity to discharge their pent-up affect collectively while retaining the idealized primary object, which is transferred to new leader figures or to the group in order to make up for the lack of a satisfying symbiosis with the mother. Idealization of a narcissistically cathected group guarantees collective grandiosity. Since every ideology provides a scapegoat outside the confines of its own splendid group, the weak and scorned child who is part of the total self but has been split off and never acknowledged can now be openly scorned and assailed as this scapegoat.[28]

The black pedagogy assumes the child to be other, and as other, Miller argues, the child becomes the scapegoat or, as Lloyd DeMause argues in *The History of Childhood,* a "psychic toilet" for the adult's pent-up affect. As a result of the child's status as scapegoat, the child-cum-adult will later seek out a scapegoat—or a substitute "other"—to use as a site of projection for his own pent-up affect. The dominant ideology invites this cycle of violence to continue by enshrining nationalistic ideologies that rely on, rather than question, a world understood in terms of "us versus them." Intensified versions of this basic dualism are all forms of racism, homophobia, and sexism, and in its most intensified form, the combination of pent-up affect and the need for a scapegoat manifests itself as the genocidal practices of the dominant culture, as in the case of national socialism and anti-Semitism.

LITTLE RED RIDING HOOD

Consider the case of one of the most popular fairy tales of all time, "Little Red Riding Hood." The importance and the popularity of this tale, according to Zipes, are "impossible to exaggerate." What Zipes calls "the Little Red Riding Hood syndrome" represents "a dominant cultural pattern in Western societies."[29] What Zipes and others often forget to mention is that the Grimms' "Little Red Cap"—commonly known as "Little Red Riding Hood"—is an adult creation and projection, created and projected for the consumption of children and adults and as such represents a prototype literary event for the rise of children's literature. The rise of children's literature as a cultural and ideological commodity throughout the eighteenth and early nineteenth centuries was concomitant with the rise of what Philippe Aries describes as protomodern notions of childhood. Protomodern notions of childhood and the rise of children's literature run together and have served the dominant adult culture, for children's literature existed as a way of "civilizing children according to stringent codes of class behavior."[30] It should be remembered, however, that adults invented the stringent codes, and the source material for the invention of the adult world is the unconscious experiences of the child at the hands of the adult and the adult's culture. In this way, what Zipes describes as an "independent children's literature and children's culture" is not, in fact, independent of the dominant adult culture but rather is always a representation—and often a mere reproduction—of the dominant culture of the adult world, even if it manifests itself as an act of resistance. Resistance is not necessarily opposite to the dominant ideology. The two are simply the different sides of the same coin. This is nowhere more true than in the rise of children's culture in and through adult hegemony.

Charles Perrault's literary version of "Little Red Riding Hood" was published along with seven other tales in 1697. According to Zipes,

> Perrault was among the fortunate members of the haute bourgeoisie to be honored by the [French] court. He was a high royal civil servant, one of the first members of the *Academie Francaise*, a respected polemicist, and a significant figure in literary salons. Moreover, he endorsed the expansive political wars of Louis XIV, and believed in the exalted mission of the French absolutist regime to "civilize" Europe and the rest of the world. . . . he was also one of the first writers of children's books who explicitly sought to "colonize" the internal and external development of children in the mutual interests of a bourgeois-aristocratic elite.[31]

Thus Perrault, like the Brothers Grimm, sought to "colonize" the internal and external development of children in the interests of the dominant adult culture. For Perrault, like Napoléon after him—and like the Brothers Grimm themselves—believed in the myth of cultural superiority and nationalistic agendas.[32]

As a cautionary fairy tale, the Grimms' "Little Red Cap" deliberately leads the child into traumatic, primal suffering and then back again to life, consumed and regurgitated as a necessary step in the child's initiation into the dominant culture. As black pedagogy, "Little Red Cap" employed the familiar double-bind of the "impossible pedagogical situation" in which the adult leads the child into a pedagogical situation from which the child cannot find a way out, and so experiences extreme suffering, even death, and can only blame their own willfulness, ignorance, or naivete. The child suffers a profound defeat and so learns the lesson scripted by the adult: neurotic insecurity, self-doubt, and the need for adult control. The impossible pedagogical situation of the black pedagogy is always orchestrated by the adult so that it appears to be an inevitable, natural part of everyday life. The end result is the death of the child's spirit—or "willfulness"—and its resurrection at the hands of the god-like father who has power over the dominant culture—the wolf— in a way the child can barely comprehend. The child's trauma with the wolf is so great—and the attendant relief so palpable—that the child has no other course but to feel heartfelt gratitude for the adult's manipulations, for the child has been "saved" and yet remains unaware that the violence has been orchestrated by the adult, all "for the child's own good." In the Grimms' version of "Little Red Cap," the wolf represents an aspect of the dominant adult culture that the adult can unleash at will.[33]

Little Red Cap serves as a model for the ideal child of the black pedagogy in every way. She is dutiful and obedient. When the mother requires her to walk through the woods to her grandmother's, Little Red Cap does not hesitate. The mother invites her daughter. She says,

> Come, Little Red Cap, take this piece of cake and bottle of wine and bring them to your grandmother. She's sick and weak, and this will strengthen her. Get an early start, before it becomes hot, and when you're out in the woods, be nice and good and don't stray from the path, otherwise you'll fall and break the glass, and your grandmother will get nothing. And when you enter her room, don't forget to say good morning, and don't go peeping in all the corners.[34]

Little Red Cap responds, "I'll do just as you say." And it is important to remember that she does *exactly* as her mother commands, at least until the voice of the dominant culture accosts her while she is on her way to Grandmother's. It is important to note what the mother warns her daughter about: she reminds Little Red Cap of her filial duty to her grandmother. The primacy of family, of duty to family, and of the need for *unquestioned* filial loyalty are hallmarks of the black pedagogy that must be trained into the child "for the child's own good." In short, the mother expects unquestioning obedience from her daughter. Anything less, the tale cautions, will lead to the child's destruction by her own fault.

The mother is apparently too busy to accompany her daughter to Grandmother's. That Little Red Cap travels alone goes almost unquestioned, for if she does not travel alone she will not be so vulnerable to the predators in the forest. Making the child available to the predatory world, then, becomes a necessary component of teaching the child important lessons about obedience and adult authority. It should be noted that both the mother and the grandmother conspire to make Little Red Cap available to the predatory world. The mother, we are told in the Perrault version, was "excessively fond of her," and her grandmother "yet much more."[35] The Grimms state simply that Little Red Cap was a "sweet little maiden. Whoever laid eyes upon her could not help but love her. But it was her grandmother who loved her most. She could never give the child enough," and so, she made her a small, red velvet cap. The girl found it so becoming that she always wore it, and was recognized by all as Little Red Cap.

The unconscious competition between the mother and the grandmother for Little Red Cap's approval is almost universally recognized as a sign of the adult's love for the child. Rather, even in the modified Grimms' version the "love" of the adults for the child foreshadows the tale's trajectory. Adults want to consume the child, or costume the child, into a likeness that fits their conception of what they think the child should be. Yet Little Red Cap's costume *invites* the predator's gaze. That strangers should "love" Little Red Cap simply because of her appearance suggests that the tale idealizes the child, yet at the same time resents the child's beauty—a tension that will be developed in Victorian children's literature a half-century later. The child becomes a site for the projection of adult sexual desire; the red cap cries out to the adult predator: "feast your eyes!"

The black pedagogy and the story of "Little Red Cap" continue to unfold from the early nineteenth century until today. "Little Red Cap" is a story of the adult's unconscious sexual desire—pent-up affect in another form—projected onto the child. The story of JonBenet Ramsey's murder is one of the most popular contemporary versions of Little Red Cap: the adult costumes the child as a sexual object to be desired precisely to the degree that a child can be costumed as a woman and so confuse the adult's gaze and allow, for an instant at least, the child to be consumed by the adult not as a child, but as a consumable object that satisfies the adult's predatory needs.

As Little Red Cap's mother teaches her daughter what to do and what not to do on her journey to Grandmother's house, what she does not say is perhaps the most significant piece of information, and in her silence lies the latent power of adult black pedagogy. What she does say, however, is also significant. The mother is a careful woman who wants her daughter to act appropriately while at Grandmother's house. This means that Little Red Cap should curb her curiosity and not "go peeping" into all of the corners. Further, the child should remember her manners and say "good morning." Most important in what the mother does say is her admonition to "be nice and good and don't stray from the path."

More important, however, is the fact that the mother never informs her daughter of the danger of the wolf in the forest. Either the mother is stupid, and insensible, or she secretly manipulates her daughter so that she will confront the wolf. Or, perhaps the mother has simply been forced to repress the trauma of her own childhood experience with male predators and has been encouraged by the dominant adult culture to accept and celebrate what was done to her by the wolf, and so she unconsciously passes on the cruelty, suffering, and violence done to her onto her little daughter. In any case, the wolf as he appears in "Little Red Cap" appears as a fixture of the forest, a familiar and familial figure, and it is striking that the mother does not warn her daughter about this forthrightly. Rather, the mother sends Little Red Cap uninformed.

The tale continues: "Well, the grandmother lived out in the forest, half an hour from the village, and as soon as Little Red Cap entered the forest, she encountered the wolf. However, Little Red Cap did not know what a wicked sort of an animal he was and was not afraid of him." Little Red Cap's lack of fear suggests the naivete of the child, and echoes earlier oral versions in which the girl lacked an appropriate fear of the beast. But in the Grimms' version Little Red Cap's lack of fear implies the child's naive innocence and her extreme vulnerability. What happened to Little Red Cap's intuitive sense? Why does she not suspect that *something is not right*?

Little Red Cap cannot save herself because she has been trained to obey, and "to be nice and good." The child so trained splits from her body and its spontaneous intuitive responses to danger and instead becomes fused with the adult's idea of herself as an embodiment of adult pedagogy and adult ideology. Since infancy the child of the black pedagogy has been admonished to ignore her own body and her own feelings, and to project all of her attention onto the adult's requirements, even when they violate the child's intuitive sense of rightness.

The most significant moment in the mother's admonitions to her daughter is that she does not tell her, "*If there is a wolf, you will find him on the path even as you obey my admonitions.*" The path itself—and not the forest—holds the danger for Little Red Cap and this the mother fails to mention; the end result for Little Red Cap is an impossible pedagogical situation, a kind of narrative double-bind from which she has no escape. After all, Little Red Cap comes to bring health and well-being for which the child assumes the grandmother will be pleased, and so too the mother. In short, the wolf speaks the language of Little Red Cap's world. He too is an adult figure and Little Red Cap has been trained her entire life to obey and respect adults simply because they are adults. Moreover, the mother never warned her daughter about speaking to strangers, nor does she warn Little Red Cap about the predatory nature of wolves, and about their desire for women, young and old—especially a "young sweet morsel" like Little Red Cap. As a point of fact, the mother's warnings are so inadequate that she all but offers her daughter up to be consumed by the wolf. Little Red Cap is seduced from the path by the wolf—by the adult world of wolf, mother, and grandmother—and then and only then commits the transgression of leaving the path, a transgression for which she shall be sorely punished.

When Little Red Cap arrives at Grandmother's house, the wolf has already consumed the old woman and taken on her appearance. Now in the form of the Grandmother the wolf "satisfies his desires" by devouring Little Red Cap. Not long after the huntsman appears, he delivers Grandmother and Little Red Cap from the belly of the wolf and then dispatches the animal. The Brothers Grimm weave the moral of the story into the "first" ending of the tale and for almost two hundred years the dominant culture has been peddling its specious morality to children. It reads as follows: "Little Red Cap thought to herself, 'Never again will you stray from the path by yourself and go into the forest when your mother has forbidden it.' " From the belly of the wolf comes a reborn Little Red Cap whose rebirth is a birth into the world of adult ideology, adult contradiction, and self-recrimination. By tale's end Little Red Cap is convinced that she called her trauma upon herself, and the fairy tale encourages the audience to believe this as well. The narrative double-bind combined with the emotional and physical trauma of Little Red Cap's rape by the wolf serves adult hegemony, for the child in the tale—and the child who listens and tries to make sense of the tale's caustic logic and disingenuous morality—learns one thing: *to doubt herself.*

Psychoanalytic interpretations of this tale frequently blame the child for the mother's failure to provide the daughter with enough information. Bettelheim states flatly that Little Red Cap "is either stupid or wants to be seduced." In fact, Little Red Cap is not stupid, as the second ending of the tale suggests. Little Red Cap learns and so she locks the door, becomes suspicious of visitors, and protects herself from other wolves that would devour her. She does learn from experience. Little Red Cap was, however, uninformed and the responsibility for her ignorance lies with the mother. "Little Red Cap" is as old as human sexuality: it is the story of the adult's perverted desire to consume the innocent child and then justify the child's sufferings as a necessary consequence of misbehavior, all of which amounts to the dominant culture's ideological justification for the child's seduction by the adult. In short, it reads as follows: "She deserved it—or, she asked for it; if only she would have listened to her mother."

And so the child learns through a process of intellectual confusion and emotional traumatization to always obey the adult, even when the adult does not make sense; even when the adult sends you to your own death. Yet, "Little Red Cap" unraveled suggests the significance of a society dedicated to the black pedagogy in words and deeds: a society dominated by individuals with masochistic character structures amounting to a people obedient yet supremely angry underneath it all. The black pedagogy and the ideology it produces and reproduces represents the perfect soil for growing fascist culture.

"Little Red Cap" is black pedagogy. It is a tale of adult subversion and adult seduction. It teaches a morality of hyperobedience along with paralyzing self-consciousness. It is a tale that produces the child as a docile, confused automaton, but it is the docility of a deer caught in the oncoming headlights. Not knowing how much obedience is enough, the child is implicitly encouraged by the morality of the tale to abandon her own sense of rightness and intuitive sensibility in favor of the adult order, contradictory though it may be, for only the father can save her from herself and so from the wolf. When the impossible pedagogical situation has run its course—as it does in "Little Red Cap"—the adult is enthroned as the maker, shaper, and savior of the child—the adult order is to be obeyed. This serves the dominant ideological status quo. This serves the adult. This serves the totalitarian leader looking to replenish his dwindling ranks of infantry. Finally, the kind of hyperobedience, self-consciousness, and self-doubt inculcated by the confusing cautionary morality of "Little Red Cap" in no way protects the child-cum-adult from the murderous appetites of the wolf. The tale fails as a cautionary lesson because it refuses to caution the child about the real conditions of her existence: danger and destruction do not visit the child as a result of disobedient or transgressive acts; rather, the wolf claims the child as his own even as the child obeys and walks the path.

INSTITUTIONALIZATION COMPLETE

Near the end of his life in 1859, after his younger brother Wilhelm had died, Jacob Grimm wrote, "How often the sad fate of our fatherland keeps coming to my mind and makes my heart heavy and my life bitter. It is impossible to think about salvation without realizing that it will necessitate great dangers and revolts. . . . Only ruthless power can bring help."[36] Almost fifty years had passed since Napoléon's empire had crumbled, and Germany had yet to see political unification. This troubled Jacob Grimm. Even so, Grimm's plaintive plea for a "ruthless power" to unify Germany would be answered, only not in his lifetime—and he and his brother's cultural and ideological contributions cannot be underestimated if only for the sheer popularity of their fairy tales. Everyone knew them. Everyone loved them. By the 1870s the Grimms' fairy tales were incorporated into the teaching curriculum in Prussian and other German principalities, and some were also included in primers and anthologies for children throughout the Western world. By the beginning of the twentieth century the Grimms' *Children's and Household Tales* were second only to the Bible as a best-seller in Germany.[37] Running close in popularity to these were Dr. Schreber's manuals that espoused the child-rearing practices of the black pedagogy. After Hitler came to power in Germany in 1932—a macabre and horrifying answer to Jacob Grimm's prayer of 1859—the fairy tales of the Brothers Grimm remained a popular literary staple of the National Socialists, who apparently found in them something familiar, something familial—and above all, something useful for the forging of Hitler's "Teutonic Order."

According to Aimé Césaire, the grandiosity of Hitler's psychopathology should not be taken as an exception, but rather, as a perfect manifestation of the cultural and ideological conditions prevalent in Europe long before Hitler's rise to power. Hitler simply practiced on Europe what Europe had been practicing on the "other" all along in the form of colonialism.

> Yes, it would be worthwhile to study clinically, in detail, the steps taken by Hitler and Hitlerism and to reveal to the very distinguished, very humanis-

tic, very Christian bourgeoisie of the twentieth century that without his being aware of it, he has Hitler inside him, that Hitler *inhabits* him, that Hitler is his *demon,* that if he rails against him, he is being inconsistent and that, at bottom, what he cannot forgive Hitler for is not crime in itself, the crime against man, it is not the humiliation of man as such, it is the crime against the white man, the humiliation of the white man, and the fact that he applied to Europe colonialist procedures which until then had been reserved exclusively for the Arabs of Algeria, the coolies of India, and the blacks of Africa. (*Discourse on Colonialism,* p. 13)

For Césaire, Hitler "makes it possible to see things on a large scale," and that "whether one likes it or not, at the end of the blind alley" that is Western culture, "there is Hitler."[38] Rather than an exception, Hitler represents a cultural manifestation that proves the rule—he represents the outgrowth of, among other things, a Victorian Europe that nakedly "aspired not to equality but to domination" of races deemed inferior, degenerate, and incapable of navigating their own way—all of which justified and made necessary European colonization, domination, and subjugation.[39]

Foreign conquest of "the other" was part and parcel of the dominant ideology of Victorian Europe—especially of Victorian England—so it should come as no surprise that the Golden Age of Children's Literature should be thoroughly caught up in a dominant culture that constructed rhetorically the "savage" in terms of the child, and the child in terms of the "savage." The rhetoric of conquest was the same; who could doubt the outcome?

NOTES

[1]Hitler was so taken with Napoléon as a general and leader that he had Napoléon's only son's remains moved from Rome to Paris, so that the son's tomb might be near the conquering father's tomb. Napoléon's genius as a general should be mentioned here, for his ability to wield massive military force quickly and decisively —sometimes called Napoléon's "blitzkrieg"warfare—would influence Hitler's career of conquest profoundly.

[2]Edward Said, *Orientalism* (New York: Random House, 1998), and Ashish Nandy, *The Intimate Enemy: Loss and Recovery of Self under Colonialism* (Delhi: Oxford University Press, 1983) speak to the psychodynamic nature of the relationship between the colonizer and the colonized in terms of European colonialism in the nineteenth century, a subject that I will return to and expand on in relationship to children's literature, culture, and ideology in Chapter 4.

[3]Murray B. Peppard, *Paths through the Forest: A Biography of the Brothers Grimm* (New York: Holt, Rinehart and Winston, 1971), p. 2.

[4]Ibid., p. 2.

[5]For a more detailed look at Jérôme Bonaparte's monarchy, see Philip W. B. A. Sergeant, *The Burlesque Napoleon . . .* (London: T. Werner Laurie Clifford's Inn, 1905).

[6]Jack Zipes, *The Brothers Grimm: From Enchanted Forests to the Modern World* (New York: Routledge. 1988), pp. 21–23.

[7]Marie-Louis von Franz, *The Interpretations of Fairy Tales* (Boston: Shambhala, 1996), p. 1. Franz relies on a Jungian approach to the fairy tales, seeing in them a cross-section of the human psyche shared by all across time and space.

[8]Zipes, *Brothers Grimm*, p. 37.

[9]Quoted in Alice Miller, *For Your Own Good: Hidden Cruelty in Child-rearing and the Roots of Violence*, trans. Hildegarde and Hunter Hannum (New York: Farrar, Straus & Giroux, 1983), p. 5.

[10]Katharina Rutschky, *Schwärze Pädagogik* (Berlin, 1977). Other child-rearing experts in Germany of the eighteenth and nineteenth centuries include J. G. Kruger, C. G. Salzman, J. B. Basedow and D. G. M. Schreber.

[11]J. G. Kruger, "Gedanken von der Erziehung der Kinder" (Some Thoughts on the Education of Children). Quoted in Miller, *For Your Own Good*, p. xx.

[12]In *For Your Own Good*, Miller speaks to this point: "the conviction that parents are always right and that every act of cruelty, whether conscious or unconscious, is an expression of their love is so deeply rooted in human beings because it is based on the process of internalization that takes place during the first months of life" (p. 5).

[13]Why the adult enacted such harsh and punitive measures continues to be debated. Miller argues that it is a process of psychological projection. The adult uses the child to work out the pain, humiliation, and powerlessness experienced when she was a child and seeks to find the power lost as a child through the domination of her own children as an adult (*For Your Own Good*, pp. 3–63).

[14]Zipes. *Brothers Grimm*, p. 5.

[15]Ibid.

[16]The brothers lost their father when they were ten and eleven years old, a loss that informs consciously or unconsciously all of the Grimms' scholarship. Cf. Zipes, *Brothers Grimm*, pp. 3–27.

[17]Napoléon's ill-fated invasion of Russia in 1812—like Hitler 130 years later—stretched Napoléon's resources to the breaking point.

[18]Peppard, *Paths*, p. 30

[19]Quoted in Peppard, *Paths*, pp. 40–41.

[20]See John M. Ellis, *One Fairy Story Too Many: The Brothers Grimm and Their Tales* (Chicago: University of Chicago Press, 1983). In it, Ellis argues that the Brothers Grimm selected and edited their fairy tales along highly conservative ideological lines and deliberately misled the reading public into believing that they had "retrieved" the tales from the long-lost oral tradition extant in the peasant culture of Germay. Rather, Ellis argues, the Brothers Grimm invited friends and neighbors to their home to share stories they had heard as children, stories that were often of French origin, and frequently from the written tradition. The Grimms then took these tales and edited them to suit their conservative, Protestant, nationalistic agenda.

[21]See Bruno Bettelheim, *The Uses of Enchantment: The Meaning and Importance of Fairy Tales* (New York: Random House, 1975) for a classic Freudian reading in which he makes the children rather than the adult responsible for their plight. Also, see Perry Nodelman, *The Pleasures of Children's Literature* (White Plains, N.Y.: Longman, 1996), p. 254.

[22]Ibid.

[23]According to one biography of Bettelheim, his is a tragic story of unconscious ideological reproduction in the name of healing his patients. According to those patients he treated, Bettelheim frequently resorted to violent methods, striking them, yelling at them, and otherwise terrorizing them, all in the name of healing them. He was convinced that people needed terror and his readings of the fairy tales suggests that he was consistent in this way of seeing the child in the world. See Nina Sutton, *Bettelheim: A Life and a Legacy,* trans. David Sharp and Nina Sutton (Boulder, Colo.: Westview Press, 1996).

[24]Ellis, *One Fairy Story,* p. 26.

[25]Ibid., p. 27.

[26]Ibid., p. 36.

[27]Ibid., p. 66.

[28]Miller, *For Your Own Good,* p. 86.

[29]Jack Zipes, *The Trials and Tribulations of Little Red Riding Hood: Versions of the Tale in Sociocultural Context* (South Hadley, Mass.: Begin & Garvey, 1983), p. 3.

[30]Ibid., p. 10.

[31]Ibid., p. 11.

[32]Ibid., p. 53. By the time Charles Perrault and the Brothers Grimm adapted the fairy tale, all positive connotations of the wolf are lost, and instead, the wolf becomes something to fear and avoid, though the tale implies that avoiding the wolf is, ultimately, impossible. Yet the "animal nature" that the wolf represents is now, for the Brothers Grimm, ideologically one and the same with the child's "wild nature" from which only adult culture can save the child. Adult culture as it manifests itself in "Little Red Cap" aims at saving the child from its "wild nature" through intellectual confusion, emotional terror, and subsequent repression of the trauma of the tale, and of the trauma the tale evokes from the child's earliest experiences.

The Grimm version represents the unconscious projection of their child-rearing experiences. No longer is the child brave, awake, and aware of what is happening, as in the case of Paul Delarue's *The Story of Grandmother.* In Delarue's text, dating from the Middle Ages, the girl in the tale "does not have a special name, cap, or color. She is an average little girl visiting her grandmother. She is *not* afraid of the woods. She is *not* terrified by the wolf. She exposes herself but takes care of herself." From *The Borzoi Book of French Folk Tales, ed. Paul Delarue and trans. Austine E. Fife* (New York: Arno Press, 1980).

[33]The specific content of the wolf-as-metaphor has shifted over time. In oral variants of the tale dating from the Middle Ages, the wolf is cast as a werewolf. The werewolf is a human being who can dissolve the boundary between civilization and wilderness in himself and is capable of crossing over the fence that separates his "cilivized side" from his "wild side." A werewolf is a creature who looks "straight into the eyes" of his "animal nature," which is usually kept under lock and key by his culture. Consequently, this creature is the first to develop a consciousness of his "cultural nature." Charles Perrault published "Little Red Riding Hood" in 1697 and is the primary source for the Grimm's version. In the Perrault version the wolf still represents a liminal figure occupying both the cultural and animal world, but in French society, this is no longer an appropriate way of being, at least for the child. Perrault's wolf is a sexual predator living directly from his "animal nature," and the consequences for the unwary child are clear. The wolf represents a warning to the child—especially the girl

child—to eschew the animal and cling to the cultural world of the adult, in this case, as it is represented by the aristocratic excess of the court of Louis XIV. Ironically, like the later Grimms' version, the Perrault version deliberately misleads the child into the dominant culture of the adult world, and as such, into the wolf's culture where adults routinely prey on children. The wolf is the dominant culture and the child its unwilling victim.

[34]From Jack Zipes, ed. and trans, *The Complete Fairy Tales of the Brothers Grimm* (New York: Bantam, 1987), p. 110.

[35]From Iona and Peter Opie, *The Classic Fairy Tales* (New York: Oxford University Press, 1980), p. 122.

[36]Ibid., p. 9.

[37]Zipes. *Brothers Grimm*. p. 15.

[38]Aimé Césaire, *Discourse on Colonialism*, trans. Joan Pinkham (New York: Monthly Review Press, 1972), p. 14.

[39]Renan, *La Réforme intellectuelle et morale*, quoted in Césaire, *Discourse*, p. 14.

CHAPTER 4

Victorian Imperialism and the Golden Age of Children's Literature

*In reality power means relations, a more-or-less orga-
nized, hierarchical, coordinated cluster of relations.*

—MICHEL FOUCAULT, "The Confession of the Flesh"

THE IDEOLOGY OF THE OPPRESSOR

In 1910 Jules Harmand defended the colonist's right to dominate native peoples by invoking what was to him an obvious cultural and racial hierarchy.
For Harmand and countless others like him, colonial domination and subjugation of native peoples were, quite simply, a *moral* cause. European imperi-
alists—most notably Victorian England—believed it to be their *moral duty* to
dominate the less civilized, for in English culture the human species had
found its perfect form. Harmand's perspective remains remarkable for its
crystal-clear articulation of this ideology, an ideology that when practiced as
a pedagogy of oppression justified a racist and violent ideological hierarchy
upon the dominant culture's ability to institutionalize itself rhetorically.
Industrial powers—military and economic—were the concrete manifestations of Victorian "rhetorics of power" that made obvious and real the European right to dominate and subjugate the vast majority of the world's
population.[1] Harmand spoke for a dominant culture that believed itself to be
at its zenith when he wrote,

> It is necessary, then, to accept as a principle and point of departure the fact
> that there is a hierarchy of races and civilizations, and that we belong to the
> superior race and civilization, still recognizing that, while superiority con-
> fers rights, it imposes strict obligations in return. The basic legitimation of

conquest over native peoples is the conviction of our superiority, not merely our mechanical, economic, and military superiority, but our moral superiority. Our dignity rests on that quality, and it underlies our right to direct the rest of humanity. Material power is nothing but a means to that end.[2]

In *Culture and Imperialism,* Edward Said describes the ideological and epistemological underpinnings of European imperialism "as a Western style for dominating, restructuring, and having authority over the Orient." For the imperialist, the Orient represents the construction of an ideological idea as much as a reconstruction of the actual physical, geographical space of the colonized. The imperialist *invents* the colonized and then sells this ideological invention to them a product of an advanced civilization. Understanding the way in which Victorian culture dominated its empire requires an understanding of the ways in which the whole network of interests that Europeans invested in overseas represented an ideological discourse by which "European culture was able to manage—and even produce—the Orient politically, sociologically, militarily, ideologically, scientifically, and imaginatively during the post-Enlightenment period. . . . The Orient *was essentially* an idea."[3] Imperialism, therefore, is an entire fabric for which the weaving requires that "all kinds of preparations are made for it within a culture; then in turn imperialism acquires a kind of coherence, a set of experiences, and a presence of ruler and ruled alike within the culture."[4] Above all, imperialism and the ideology of empire begins at home.

Not surprisingly, the relationship between the parent and the child in Victorian England was precisely that of the relationship between colonizer and colonized, precisely that of the relationship between the physically dominant and the physically dominated. In 1834 the Reverend Jacob Abbot described the ideal relationship between the adult and the child in *Parental Duties in the Promotion of Early Piety,* one of many child-rearing texts of the Victorian period. The adult's job, first and foremost, is a *moral* one, and as such, any and all manipulations are therefore justified if it brings about the child's unqualified physical submission to the adult. Abbot wrote,

> I would also remark, that parents cannot take a single step to advantage in endeavoring to train up their children to piety, without first obtaining their *unlimited, unqualified, entire submission* to their authority. The *very first* lesson to be taught the child is to *submit, to obey.* There are various methods of obtaining this ascendancy. *In some way or other it* must be done. Your children must be habituated to do what you command, and to refrain from what you forbid; not because they can see the reason for it, but because you *command or forbid:* submission, not to your *reason,* but to your *authority* [remains vital]. . . . Be it remembered, insubordination is the essence of irreligion. I repeat it—insubordination is the essence of irreligion. (emphasis added)[5]

Once again it should be noted that Abbot's perspective on adult authority is remarkable only inasmuch as it is so thoroughly *ordinary*. In as stratified a culture as Victorian Europe—and especially Victorian England—ultimately nearly every class—from the working masses to the middle class, the bourgeoisie, and the aristocracy—believed in the hierarchy that Abbot articulates so plainly in the preceding passage. Victorian child-rearing pedagogy—a fully-fledged "black pedagogy" in its own right—reproduced imperialist ideology on an individual basis, one child at a time. From his or her earliest moments, the child was taught by the adult that those with power—especially physical and economic power—were *morally* superior. In other words, one's ability to buy and sell another, or to destroy the other when necessary, was a clear and present indication of one's individual and cultural superiority. Obviously, moral degradation followed the weak and the poor—and especially the child.[6]

"The basis of imperial authority," another historian writes, "was the mental attitude of the colonist. His acceptance of subordination—whether through a positive sense of common interest with the parent state, or through inability to conceive of any alternative—made empire durable."[7] Not unlike the relationship between master and slave, then, the durability of the imperialist relationship between colonizer and colonized required that the subordinated accept his or her subordination as inevitable, as an obviousness, as much a part of human nature as is, say, child-bearing.

The dominant culture's ideology of human relationship becomes of central concern when considering Victorian imperialism, for it is in the most basic nature of the human relationship—an ideological hierarchy of superiority that pitted us versus them—that imperial authority had its root and source. For domination and subjugation to be an unquestioned and even a celebrated way of life meant that the colonist's consciousness—and the consciousness of those masses of European people who passively acquiesced to the inherent violence of their culture—shared a basic assumption about the nature of relationships between cultures, races, and individuals. The church and the state supported the shared ideological belief in the racial, cultural, and ideological superiority of Victorian culture. Evolutionary science was used to "prove" the superiority and therefore the natural right of the European to dominate the global habitat. Nevertheless, church, states, and science did not invent this hierarchy. Rather, Victorian institutions merely refracted and intensified what most Victorians had been taught since birth and therefore accepted unquestioningly. From the cradle, the child learned that the world was divided between those who physically dominate and those who were dominated. Moreover, power—as in adult power—was always allied with moral authority. The child's power was allied with savagery, willfulness, indolence, wickedness, and immorality. Resistance to moral authority was a sign of one's otherness, and therefore justified even sterner "civilizing" measures.

Yet the resisting child was first the vulnerable infant and, as the infant of the Victorian middle or upper classes, was taught implicitly and explicitly that his inherent biological reality was incomplete and inadequate and only the adult—armed with the material expressions of the dominant child-rearing ideology—might complete what nature had left undone. These material expressions of the dominant child-rearing ideology include the child's nursery, a safe distance from the adult world; the baby's bottle, a safe distance from the mother's breast; the rubber nipple, another material substitute for the mother's breast; the bassinet; the crib; the nanny; and so on—all of which came to be understood as the child-rearing rule justified by the ideological belief that these practices were the hallmarks of a civilized race. All of these items share a common theme, they allow the mother to physically detach from the child long before the child seeks separation from her. The ensuing anxiety and emotional desperation of the child are then transformed by Victorian "black pedagogies" that require the unquestioned obedience of the child. The Victorian adult believed this to be necessary, for the child's "nature" made it obvious. Yet the child's "nature" was nothing more than the appropriate response to the nurturing she received, or failed to receive. The child's too early detachment from the mother is the moment in which a culture's ideological beliefs—and not human nature—shape human growth and development, for a child separated too soon from her mother will certainly manifest symptoms associated with "difficult" babies, including sleeplessness, colic, frequent infection, eating problems, and so on, all of which later justify even more cultural intervention by the adult in the form of child-rearing pedagogies that encourage parents to expect slave-like obedience from their children. "Teach them to obey you," one Victorian child-rearing expert writes, and children will be happy. "That one great lesson of all life, '*to submit.*' "[8] To ensure the child's submission, adult violence is necessary; however, according to the dominant child-rearing ideology, violence is always for the child's own good.

OF POWER, PUBLIC SCHOOL, AND PEDOPHILIA

Perhaps no author is more identified with the rise of children's literature than Lewis Carroll, whose *Alice* books inspired a generation of readers and writers. Lewis Carroll's *Alice's Adventures in Wonderland* came at a moment of cultural unrest when England "saw the recasting of British life" as the old order ostensibly gave way to the new. According to one social historian, "A distinctive English world view was being formed in the crucible of the mid-Victorian ferment of social ideas. . . . The central institution of the consolidation, the public school, came into its own in this period. . . . By Victoria's death, her nation possessed a remarkably homogeneous and cohesive elite, sharing to a high degree a common education and a common outlook and set of values."[9]

Even though only one in twenty Englishmen passed through the English public school, the public school nevertheless "became an archetypal national institution." Those who could afford it sent their sons to be molded into gentlemen; and those who could not afford the elite public schools sent their children to schools modeled after them. The public school and the dominant culture's ideology of class and power offered a way in which to inculcate "homogenous" ideological values, so much so that a cohesive elite—an educated, gentleman's class—would represent by their very existence the obvious rightness of the preexisting hierarchy inherent in the English class structure that came before the public school. The public school institutionalized the process of education more than it revolutionized it, for the public school reproduced the status quo and consolidated ideological and cultural power. The basic ideological assumptions from which the dominant culture, its institutions, and its enactments of the stories its institution teaches remained intact and were, in fact, intensified as a result of the public school's homogenizing ideological effects.

The class structure and the violence that reproduced it in the elite public schools of England were nothing new to those who attended them. Rather, the public school and its pedagogies of hierarchy and violence *confirmed* what the child always already understood about the world, for the child upon entering the public school would have already experienced years of domination and subjugation through child-rearing experiences at home while hearing ideological confirmation of the rightness of such a hierarchy from Sunday services at church. The public school consolidated the dominant ideology of hierarchy and violence through enactments of hierarchy and violence in the name of education, cultural progress, and, ultimately, moral superiority.

Common among the child's early lessons at home and at school was, according to Richard Wallace's study of Lewis Carroll, "that of self-control, more correctly emotional control to the point of constriction." Wallace notes that "psychological studies often refer to the Victorian period as "the Age of Anality," referring to a common Victorian "attitude of rigidity" and "self-control" that manifested itself in relationships of power and the need to control as the primary way of relating to others. Control also manifested itself as a desire to possess another, or to substitute objects that represent another and possess them. As a result, the pursuit, possession, and consumption of material things appeared as an obvious rightness in an age dominated by capitalism, a system that "rewards acquiring and having at the expense of giving and sharing."[10]

The chronic emotional anxiety and insecurity that informed the individual's need to control are, Alice Miller argues in *For Your Own Good*, learned as a result of the child's experience of emotional deprivation in childhood along with the attendant adult requirement for the child to repress emotional need as a sign of obedience, strength, and maturity. Chronic, unconscious *anxiety* is the common emotional and psychological legacy of the child raised according to repressive, controlling child-rearing pedagogies. Hierarchy and the violence that justified and maintained hierarchy were common not only between adults and young children, but also between teachers and students. Corporal punishment was the unquestioned manner in which adults maintained order in the public school, along with an unquestioned acceptance of the hierarchical imbalance of power between teachers and students. Students—especially young students—were degraded and incomplete "savages" who could be used as the senior classman or adult in authority saw fit. This included, apparently, sexual abuse, rape, and other forms of regular, ritualized violence. The hierarchy of Victorian culture, Victorian civilization, and Victorian moral superiority found its expression in the culture of the public school. One reformer of the period writes that the public school was "a life in which licensed barbarism was mingled with the daily and hourly study of the niceties of Ovidian verse. It was a life of freedom and terror, or prosody and rebellion or interminable floggings and appalling practical jokes." Public school was, in short, a life in which the students-as-siblings practiced a style of human relationship defined by the adults in "moral" authority over them and who maintained their moral authority through violence, domination, subjugation, and humiliation.[11]

Charles Dodgson came from just such an educational experience, first experienced at Richmond Grammar School and later at Rugby public school. The rigid hierarchies of domination and obedience between adults and students at these institutions represented almost exactly the hierarchical structure of human relationships he experienced as a child growing up. Dodgson was born in Daresbury, England, on January 27, 1832. His father's side of the family was dominated by churchmen, going back five generations. Dodgson was invented by his family even before birth, for if he was born a boy, he would be named Charles just as all the first-born men in the Dodgson family had been named for five generations. "Founded on the religious grounds, the Church of their time and Charles' parents believed that children arrived in a state of Original Sin, a concept their son would question later. . . . and were therefore beasts to be tamed, formed into the approved Christian and societal molds."[12] The result of the emotional and physical molding of the child by the parent in the early Victorian home of the Dodgson family was the child's early mastery of "self-control," treasured as it was by the dominant culture.

The senior Charles Dodgson exerted his control over his son in a manner consistent with his beliefs in the hierarchy of the church, the child's state of Original Sin, and the need to "reform" the child from birth so that he might enter into the dominant social order as a true Englishman. That the bourgeois adult culture believed they understood the most effective manner in which to rear the child reveals that the colonialist ideology is at one and the same time the dominant ideology of Victorian culture. The child was savage, the adult civilized. Fathering meant the exercise of godlike authority followed by the child's slavelike obedience.

Dodgson-as-Lewis Carroll-as-pedophiliac thus meant not merely a sexual desire for prepubescent girls. Rather, Dodgson's pedophilia is an expression of his felt sense of powerlessness as an adult, which he learned as a child in those relationships that required him to remain powerless and in which, as a result, he was frequently victimized by those who claimed adult authority over him.

The child's victimization came in the most ordinary of circumstances. Because the child-rearing pedagogies of Victorian England stressed that the child must exert "self-control" of his emotional outbursts of any kind, be they exuberance, sadness, or anger, the child repressed his emotional energy as a life-saving defense mechanism against the threatened humiliation, rejection, or physical "correction." One early symptom of Dodgson's repression was his well-documented stammering (a characteristic shared by his siblings). Pedophilia was another.

As an adult, the repressed and largely *unconscious* sense of powerlessness and rage Dodgson had internalized was transferred onto children who could serve as a mirror for his own narcissistic gratification. For Dodgson, prepubescent girls served this role exclusively. The prepubescent Alice Liddle—among others—attracted Dodgson because she represented a tabula rasa upon which he could write a story of his own desexualized idealization of his own sexuality, free from the problematic issues of homosexual longing, male masturbatory fantasy, and other disallowed sexual and emotional experiences Charles Dodgson experienced or was forced to experience while in public school. As an adult in pedophilic relationship with prepubescent girls, Dodgson has a "painless" relationship with a desexualized self that is highly charged with sexual energy despite the scrupulous—and public—manner in which Dodgson conducted his relationships with his victims.

Above all, Dodgson's concern in his relationships with girls and in his *Alice* books is one of *power*. The pedophile—like Dodgson the children's author—takes power over the child's body and especially her prepubescent sexuality in order to transfer onto her his need to consciously experience his adult sexuality, which for Dodgson required his absolute domination of the child. In the process of experiencing his own sexuality at the child's expense, Dodgson unconsciously acted out that part of his own emotional being that the authority figure shamed, denied, or abused when he was a child. Dodgson used young girls to feel his own power and take his own pleasure, and by doing so he inadvertently reproduced the very same relational hierarchy of power and domination that he experienced at home as a boy and at school as a student and satirized in *Alice's Adventures in Wonderland*. Yet even this book is an unconscious act of cultural reproduction, for in attempting to recover his own lost power through his manipulation of Alice's body Dodgson inadvertently produced and *intensified* the dominant culture's ideology of the child-as-fetish-object.

Dodgson's pedophilia as it manifested itself in his photography and his *Alice* books represents an ambiguous textual and cultural moment that defines pedophilia and sexual predation not as a sexual act, or as an act of overt violence, but rather, as a relationship of power of a very subtle kind. Coercion is a factor for the pedophile only inasmuch as he *never* appears to be coercing the child, but rather, he appears to be "loving" the child; he appears to be "relating" to the child; he appears to be "child-like" himself. The pedophile creates an atmospheric event in which his need for power and control over the child might be practiced, celebrated, and denied all at once. Dodgson's relationships with prepubescent girls—and his need to photograph them in the nude are infamous. Defenders of Dodgson have noted that the nude child's parent or guardian often observed the photography sessions without noting any inappropriate behavior on Dodgson's part. Nevertheless, Dodgson and the adults who witnessed his photography sessions were all members of a Victorian culture that, according to James Kincaid, accepted pedophilic practices as a matter of course, providing first that these pedophilic practices adhered to culturally sanctioned standards. Given the ideological climate of Dodgson's England, his behavior may have seemed to some to be odd, but certainly not criminal. He was simply a man who enjoyed photographing children, naked children, whenever he had the opportunity. Dodgson writes in a letter about his interest in photographing naked girls that he was simply "a great collector of those works of art," that is, of his own photographs of naked children. In other words, Dodsgon explains that he likes to photograph nude children because he likes to look at photographs of nude children.[13]

Dodgson had little trouble finding young girls to pose for him. Apparently, his behavior did not seem unusual to those adults Dodgson had to work with in order to gain access to their children. Dodgson undoubtedly appeared as the upright Oxford don in good standing with the intelligentsia of his culture, and *so he was*. He *was* the dominant culture, with its public schools, its church, its black regalia, its ancient universities. Dodgson represented the best and brightest of Victorian England and it was his culture that imperialism took to the four corners of the globe. And this is troubling.

Skeptics might argue that, if child-rearing techniques were as subtly violent as I have argued thus far, why was there only one Lewis Carroll, assuming of course that Charles Dodgson did in fact project his own pain and powerlessness into his *Alice* books? The point here is this: Dodgson was not alone. He was one manifestation of a cultural tapestry that told virtually the same story about the relationship between the adult and the child wherever one cared to look, at home or abroad. Hierarchy, power, domination, and subjugation were the order of the day.

For Dodgson, the idealized portrait of the child represented a symbol of an unrecoverable yet desirable childish innocence, fetishized by the author as the docile, prepubescent girl-child who would be used by the adult without realizing it and, most importantly, without ever resisting. She seems, in fact, to invite the "nonsense" the author constructs for her. Alice is the child Dodgson never was yet longs to be, an idealization of innocence that he desires and that he resents all at once; Alice is the idealized child that he releases into the world of Wonderland, into a chaotic, terrifying freedom from "sense," and yet, at the same time, the gamesmaster-and-wordsmith Dodgson retains ruthless control over all of the proceedings. Like his photography of nude little girls, then, Alice's adventures are a not-so-subtle power play of the adult at work in (and as) the mind of the child. Dodgson needs to exercise control, for the man who experiences himself as utterly out of control inadvertently finds himself playing the only game in town: hierarchical domination of the other in a culturally sanctioned form. Foucault calls this kind of rhetorical maneuver a "reverse discourse." The *Alice* stories might be understood in similar terms. A "reverse discourse" appears to speak on behalf of the persecuted group, say, in Dodgson's case, the child, for in the *Alice* books "Lewis Carroll" has articulated the magical, nonsensical world of the child's mind, or so the traditional wisdom of the dominant culture maintains. But as a "reverse discourse," *Alice* is in fact "a tactical element operating within the same field of force" that it questions, and it inadvertently employs the same vocabulary and the same hierarchical categorization of the world. "Under the guise of protest, this reverse discourse is worse than quiescent, since it is drawn into the service of the very master it hates."[14]

Power and relations of power produce reverse discourses as a conscious way of denying the game they are playing, while at the same time, unconsciously reproducing the dominant ideology that gave rise to them in the first place. Above all, Victorian culture represented a web of human and cultural relations that celebrated its power to dominate and remake the other in its own image—including, and especially, the child. This power went largely unquestioned by the status quo—and when it was considered by writers of the period it was more often than not reproduced as unconscious reverse discourses of adult domination over the child, or English domination over the other, as in the case of Charlotte Perkins Gilman, Frances Hodgson Burnett, Rudyard Kipling, Robert Louis Stevenson, and Kenneth Grahame, to name only a few. Power and the use of power defined the dominant ideology of Victorian England, and its practice—between the adults and the child or between

Mother England and her colonies—figured as a sign of the dominant culture's technological, cultural, and spiritual superiority. The use of power, in short, justified itself.

Not without individual and cultural consequences, however. On the one hand, most people choose to live lives of quiet desperation, quietly plagued by regular bouts with anxiety, loneliness, and anger. Most of us simply go on, and this serves the status quo. On the other hand, others choose to become violent and express their rage and powerlessness in extreme ways. Others still manipulate those that they can when they can, having been taught as children that power is the *nature* of the human relationship, and that taking power over others is the only real pleasure life offers. A felt sense of powerlessness— fueled and justified by unconscious rage at having been made powerless— motivates the individual who takes pleasure in his ability to dominate, subjugate, and use another for his own pleasure. Though rage often manifests itself through unpredictable violence, more often than not a sublimated version finds its truest expression in the hierarchical relation of power between the adult and the child. Here ambient and chronic rage can be expressed, denied, and sanctioned all at the same time; a violent culture unaware of its own roots of violence imbedded in the practice of its human relationships. All of this has led to a reproduction of the dominant culture in an ever-increasing spiral of intensification.

Extreme cases of rage and violence occur as a result of the experience of great emptiness and isolation in childhood, without any witness or transitional relationship of even the most moderate sort. In his study of Charles Dodgson, Wallace writes,

> Rage develops early from the frustration caused by a sense that needs are being neglected by those the child depends on, and then later either when as an adolescent or an adult he realizes the magnitude of how he has been cheated. Or, if he is faced with a traumatic emotional experience such as abandonment, fears of annihilation, or enormous loss it further destroys any sense of self that remains. For such a person may suddenly realize that primary caregivers or "society" as their surrogates are directly or indirectly responsible for his situation due to their failure to provide either coping skills or an environment in which the woefully inadequate learned skills "work." Rage expression can take many forms, including an explosive behavioral outburst, self-abuse, or a calculated vengeful act or series of acts executed with utmost cunning.[15]

According to Wallace, Dodgson was nothing if not cunning in his construction of the text. The nonsense of *Alice's Adventures in Wonderland* at every narrative moment has a shape and a structure. What concerns us here, however, is the nature of the relationships between Alice and the Wonderland characters, for they reveal a correspondence between the "real" world of Victorian England and the "dream" world of Wonderland, a correspondence that the "dream" cannot altogether mitigate, nor, I think, did Dodgson intend it to. That his "nonsense" was never seen for what it was in his lifetime was, according to his own diaries, a source of some anxiety for Dodgson, for even as he enjoyed his popularity as a writer he feared that at any time the nature of his venomous attack on Victorian culture—and the child—might be identified.[16]

ALICE'S ADVENTURES IN WONDERLAND

Having followed the White Rabbit down the rabbit hole in chapter 1, Alice finds herself in a room in Wonderland—there is a small table with a key on it, a small door with a keyhole, and a garden on the other side of the door. Alice wants to get through the door and into the garden, only she finds that she is too big. She finds a bottle marked "DRINK ME," and, of course, does so, for she is a curious child. Before she does so, however, she remembers a particular collection of rules that the "real" world taught her and so reasons that the drink must be safe:

> It was all very well to say "Drink me," but the wise little Alice was not going to do *that* in a hurry. "No, I'll look first," she said, "and see whether it's marked '*poison*' or not"; for she had read several nice little stories about children who had got burnt, and eaten up by wild beasts, and other unpleasant things, all because they *would* not remember the simple rules their friends had taught them: such as, that a red-hot poker will burn you if you hold it too long; and that, if you cut your finger very deeply with a knife, it usually bleeds; and she had never forgotten that, if you drink much from a bottle marked "poison," it is almost certain to disagree with you, sooner or later. (p. 11)[17]

The opening of Alice's journey is significant for as it introduces the terms of its oppositional discourse to adult culture, Dodgson cannot help but sow the seeds of his own—and his culture's—pedophilic desire for the child. The phallic imagery that Dodgson associates with Alice—bottles that read "DRINK ME," red-hot pokers, bleeding fingers, and knives—will be followed soon after by other phallic images, including Little Bill the Lizard, the Caterpillar, and, ultimately, *Alice herself.* Alice becomes Dodgson's primary phallus, for in manipulating her—as an objectification of his own rage and impotence—he enacts a relationship to the idealized child that unconsciously repeats the relationship his own parents had with him when he was a child. As a result, Dodgson's compulsion to repeat his past represents an unconscious grasping at the power stolen from him by the very adult world he satirizes in Wonderland. Alice's journey, then, is really a "reverse discourse" in which Dodgson draws himself into the service "of the very master he hates." *Alice's Adventures in Wonderland* is a chronicle of every child lost in the adult world, caught in the liminal moment between herself as a physical body and the adult's requirement that she conform herself to the ideological identity given to her. Alice—and every child—will emerge, ultimately, as the properly cultivated Victorian adult—represented by the image of Alice's older sister, who frames the narrative.

Alice's journey truly begins in chapter 1, when she decides that the bottle is not marked poison and so quickly finishes it off. She rapidly shrinks and realizes that now she cannot reach the key that opens the door to the garden. Soon after, she finds a cake marked "EAT ME." She obeys, as all good girls do, and grows to an enormous size. Alice begins to wonder aloud about her identity, for her trip underground is an un-birth through the "birth canal" of the rabbit hole. Alice desires to go even further *backward*, however, into the Queen of Hearts' garden, which, by the story's end represents a rebirth into the true emotional reality of the Victorian world of the child. Through "nonsense," Dodgson represents the world the child had lived in all along without questioning it.

The process of un-birthing herself from her cultural and ideological reality is unsettling and Alice asks herself the question every pilgrim asks at the beginning of a journey: who am I? "I'm sure I'm not Ada," she says, "and I'm sure I can't be Mabel, for, *she's* she, and *I'm* I, and—oh, dear, and oh dear, how puzzling it all is!" (pp. 15–16). Alice's dream is, after all, a *nightmare* of undermined identity. When Alice attempts to soothe herself and win her identity back by reciting all that she has been taught at school, she fails, for she cannot remember the words to the poem she attempts to recite, and so she believes herself to be Mabel—for Mabel is a failure at school. Alice resigns herself to her condition: alone, confused, and terrified. Then, suddenly she bursts into tears and cries: "I do wish they *would* put their heads down! I am so *very* tired of being all alone here!" (p. xxx).

Like Dodgson, Alice needs to know if her identity is one and the same with her physical body, for if this is the case, her entire self has been distorted as a result of her physical transformation. Or, perhaps her identity remains separate from the physical body, and as such, her idea of herself may remain intact even though her body has changed. Having lost touch with the body she took for granted, Alice attempts to find herself in her mind by recounting the "lessons" stored there, lessons that she learned at school and that make up her identity in the world. "I'm sure those are not the right words," she says, and her eyes fill with tears again as she goes on, eventually she finds herself floating in a liminal sea of her own tears. When Alice almost drowns as a result she berates herself: "You ought to be ashamed of yourself," said Alice, "A great girl like you . . . to go on crying in this way. Stop this moment, I tell you!" (p. 18). Alice needs no adult with her to remind her of the shamefulness of her feelings and her expression of them. She flagellates herself, but to no avail. The voice of adult culture does nothing to stop her tears, and she fills up the room with them.

Chapters 1 and 2 function neatly as Dodgson's oppositional discourse to the adult order. Alice articulates the child's condition as Dodgson understands it. Here Dodgson speaks for the child—and for himself as a child—through Alice. And her concerns are not for nothing. She asks precisely the same kinds of questions Dodgson himself asked as a bright, precocious child: Who am I? The intensity of this question for Dodgson should not be underestimated, for he felt keenly his differences from other children, other boys especially, and strove to conform to his father's strict Victorian ideal even as his experiences at public school impressed upon him the obscene hypocrisy of the adult order. Dodgson would suffer his entire life from anxiety and its physical symptoms, including stammering, sleeplessness, and migraine.[18]

As the idealized portrait of the Victorian girl-child, Alice recovers quickly from her identity crisis and seems to remember little of it as she proceeds. Dodgson's idealization of the resilient child, however, is a plot device necessary for Dodgson's pedophilic fantasy, for the girl-child remains simply "curious" about what is happening to her and as such, she implicitly invites the power that toys with her to continue on.

Alice's journey is really a quest. The garden that entices Alice with its bright flowers and cool fountains is, of course, the Queen of Hearts' garden, and in her garden madness and violence reign. Yet Alice desires it nonetheless, for she only knows her longing and her need to see the garden, and Dodgson will lead her there after a torturous journey. On the way Dodgson mocks the absurd moralizing of eighteenth- and nineteenth-century texts for children that contain the "simple rules" all children should obey, and that when broken lead to disastrous and often mortal consequences for the child. Alice's own adventure is in part a response to this kind of condescending manipulation of the child's fears. Yet Dodgson is not immune from the dominant culture's manipulation of the child, but rather, his *Alice* texts rely on an ideological hierarchy that justifies adult power and adult manipulation of the child's body even as it scrutinizes it.

When Alice gains entrance to the Duchess's house in chapter 6 and finally gains entrance into a conversation—and feels pleased with herself—she is met by an insult meant to keep her in her place: "You don't know much," said the Duchess to Alice, "and that's a fact" (p. 48). Alice attempts to change the subject when insulted by the Duchess, as she does routinely throughout her journey. Alice believes that she has no right to defend herself, for she is just a child, and as a child she ranks very low indeed on the chain of signifiers that reveal the ideological source of the adult's power over the child. The monarch, the aristocrat, and the newly rich industrialist each maintain their hierarchical position over the underclasses in the same way the adult maintains power over the child: those in power are in power because they are closer to God, see His plan more clearly, and as a result of their exalted status on the ideological hierarchy must help others *submit* to His will.[19] The savage, the poor, and the child *need* to be civilized according to the dominant hierarchical class structure of Victorian England, and it is this ideological hierarchy that informs *Alice*.

Consider how Dodgson's representation of the Duchess's violent madness speaks implicitly to the relationship between political hierarchy and family hierarchy. As Alice continues her bizarre conversation with the Duchess in chapter 6 the Cook begins showering the Duchess with saucepans, plates, and dishes for no apparent reason. "The Duchess took no notice of them even when they hit her; *and the baby was howling so much already, that it was quite impossible to say whether the blows hurt it or not*" (p. 48, emphasis added). For a moment Alice recognizes the chronically violent situation as mad and cries out in defense of the baby, the other, the vulnerable, or, by extension, herself:

"Oh please mind what you're doing!"

The Duchess will have none of Alice's interventions, for another child's welfare is none of Alice's concern. "If everybody minded their own business," the Duchess said, in a hoarse growl, "the world would go round a good deal faster than it does." This was one of Dodgson's mother's favorite phrases.[20]

The Duchess's chronic anger is met by the Cook's violence; she continues to accost the Duchess with saucepans and fire-irons. Finally, the Duchess cries out, "Oh, don't bother me!" She begins singing a lullaby to the baby and gives it a violent shake at the end of every line. The Duchess then flings the baby at Alice, who is encouraged to nurse the child.

> As soon as she had made out the proper way of nursing it (which was to twist it up into a sort of knot, and then keep tight hold of its right ear and left foot, so as to prevent its undoing itself), she carried it out into the open air. "If I don't take this child away with me," thought Alice, "they're sure to kill it in a day or two. Wouldn't it be murder to leave it behind?" She said that last word out loud, and the little thing grunted in reply.

"Don't grunt," said Alice; "that's not at all a proper way of expressing yourself" (p. 49). Alice attempts to address the baby's condition, but as she plays the role of mother in the relationship she immediately finds herself teaching "proper expression." Anything else would be to "coddle" the child and risk "spoiling" it. Alice understands her job as "adult" to be one in which she immediately offers the baby not comfort or emotional support, but rather, lessons in etiquette and demands of obedience.

"If you're going to turn into a pig, my dear," said Alice seriously, "I'll have nothing more to do with you. Mind now!" (p. xxx). Like the Victorian parent Dodgson was familiar with, Alice's parenting is contingent on the baby conforming to her ideas of how it should be. Dodgson hints that the end result of a child-rearing ideology that demands submission and obedience at the risk of violent punishment or physical abandonment, does not produce a proper gentleman or lady, but rather, disagreeable animals.

Finally Alice decides to release the pig and it trots into the woods. " 'If it had grown up,' she said to herself, 'it would have made a dreadfully ugly child; but it makes rather a handsome pig, I think.' And she began thinking over other children she knew, who might do very well as pigs. The ironic implication is, of course, that Alice herself—and everyone else in Wonderland—is a pig. The Chesire Cat describes it to Alice this way:

> "We're all mad here. I'm mad. You're mad."
> "How do you know I'm mad?" said Alice.
> "You must be," said the Cat, "or you wouldn't have come here" (p. 51).

In other words, Dodgson reminds his readers, if one exists in the dominant culture, one is part and parcel of the madness that defines the dominant culture. But the Duchess, the Cook, and the baby suggest that madness in *Alice's Adventures in Wonderland* is not strictly a psychological state, but rather, a state of relational chaos. In such a state a constant power struggle exists over who has the right to make meaning and so define and control the nature of human relations. In other words, to be mad is to seek power and to seek power is to seek the unilateral right to define and enact the dominant ideology of domination and subjugation and so justify one's claim to power— and it is precisely this kind of terrifying madness that Dodgson foregrounds when Alice visits the Mad Hatter's Tea Party.

When Alice finally enters the garden and meets the Queen of Hearts she has come to the "heart" of the madness that defines Wonderland. It is no surprise that the Queen and King have very much the same relationship as the Duchess and the Cook and that the Queen treats her subjects in much the same manner as the Duchess treats her baby. The Queen asks Alice, "What's your name, child?"

> "My name is Alice, so please your Majesty," said Alice very politely; but she added to herself, "Why, they're only a pack of cards, after all. I needn't be afraid of them!"
> "And who are *these*," the Queen then wants to know, "pointing to the three gardeners who were lying round the rose-tree. . . . she could not tell whether they were gardeners, or soldiers, or courtiers, *or three of her own children*" (italics added here).
> "How should *I* know?" said Alice, surprised at her own courage. "It's no business of *mine*." The Queen turned crimson with fury, and, after glaring at her for a moment like a wild beast, began screaming "Off with her head! Off—." (p. 63)

Dodgson is unsparing in his attacks of the notion of "mother love." The Queen is more than willing to execute all of those under her charge. As comical, nonsensical, and surreal as the Queen's threats seem to be, she also represents the absolute, capricious, and terrifying power the adult has over the child. Anything can happen at any time, and it is at the pleasure of the adult to determine right from wrong, up from down, and any other rules of any other game in order to preserve and defend the status quo. The child, Dodgson insists, must simply play along by virtue of her size and her apparent lack of power even though she suspects that the adults in charge are nothing but a "pack of cards," or, perhaps, a "pack of liars."

Dodgson allows Alice one final confrontation with the Queen in which she might be able to announce what she has come to understand: adult power over the child—and any and all relation of power—is nothing but a card game with rules written by those in power to defend and maintain their position. It is not for nothing that Alice's final words while still in Wonderland are words meant to topple the oppressive social order:

> "Who cares for you? said Alice (she had grown to her full size this time). You're nothing but a pack of cards!"
>
> At this the whole pack rose up into the air, and came flying down upon her; she gave a little scream, half of fright and half of anger, and tried to beat them off, and found herself lying on the bank, with her head in the lap of her sister, who was gently brushing away some dead leaves that had fluttered down from the trees upon her face. (p. 98)

Alice's attempt to expose the Queen and her queendom for what it is, represents Dodgson's attempt to expose the hypocrisy, violence, and nonsense with which the "real" world maintains itself through its domination of the child. At this point Alice wakes up and recounts her "curious" dream to her sister.

No sooner does Alice awake from her dream in Wonderland than "she got up and ran off, thinking while she ran, as well she might, what a wonderful dream it had been" (p. 98). As if Dodgson understood that Alice's final interpretation of her dream as "wonderful" might not be enough to idealize and soften the terrifying elements of the story, he includes a brief reprisal of Alice's journey told by the older sister. Her version backgrounds the violence of Alice's dream and in one paragraph foreshadows the interpretive strategy that readers take up and practice for generations. Alice's older sister does not see Alice's dream as a nightmare, but rather idealizes Alice's journey as having something to do with "the simple and loving heart of her childhood." In short, Dodgson obfuscates the truth of his narrative when he has Alice's older sister consider how

> this same little sister of hers would, in the aftertime, be herself a grown woman; and how she would keep, through all her riper years, the simple and loving heart of her childhood; and how she would gather about her other little children, and make *their* eyes bright and eager with many a strange tale, perhaps even with the dream of Wonderland of long ago; and how she would feel with all their simple sorrows, and find a pleasure in all their sim-

ple joys, remembering her own child life, and the happy summer days. (p. 99)

Though Dodgson claims otherwise, there appears little of happy summer days, simple sorrows, or innocent pleasures in the course Alice's journey. Rather, the relationships between Alice and the other characters are complicated, frequently dark, and often violent, especially Alice's relationships with authority figures like the Duchess and the Queen of Hearts. The adults in *Alice* are predictable only in their tendency for unpredictable violence. They are driven by rage to threaten and to do violence. Even Alice, when playing the role of adult, enacts the very same adult pedagogy that threatens her throughout her journey.

What accounts for the popularity of this "enduring classic?" In *Child-Loving: The Erotic Child and Victorian Culture,* James Kincaid explains our fascination with the eroticized child in Victorian culture—and the tendency we have for obfuscating the true nature of the adult appropriation of the child. He writes that

> we have looked to power for a solution to the mess it has gotten us into; and power has provided us with a story, wherein the effects of power's working on children are presumably undone. It is a story told to exonerate power. It looks like a story told to help children, but it is not. In this story, we are cast as attractive characters entirely free from desire, children are free from sexual attraction or from any desires of their own, and a few—but not too few—sociopathic people are possessed of needs that they then enact in terrible ways. Power has told us that if we rely on this story we cannot go wrong, so long as we repeat it often and loudly enough. Whether we now tell this tale because we need it for reassurance, because it provides us with easy access to the unthinkable ourselves, or both, there seems to no end to our capacity to find in it charm and gladness.[21]

We need to believe in fantasy, in other words, even when that fantasy tells an accurate story about the "real" world. What is the "real" world? It is, as Foucault and others have argued, a world defined by power and by the relations of power that produce and reproduce ideological reality. The personal consequences of relations of power are manifold and complicated, as in the case of Charles Dodgson and his *Alice* narrative, for it appears to be an oppositional discourse that speaks to the child's place in a mad, violent, hierarchical world while it remains, at the same time, a story of Dodgson's pedophilic manipulations of the image of the child. In the end this is no contradiction, but rather two sides of the same ideological coin; Victorian culture appropriated the idealized image of the child for its own purposes, namely, to support the ideological and cultural status quo, for empire meant wealth and power, and power meant wealth and empire. For empire to succeed, it must begin at home.

It seems obvious now that Dodgson himself was of two minds about the dominant culture, for as Charles Dodgson he was a tortured, alienated man who believed himself to be a hypocrite that might at any time be exposed. For while he wore the robes of the Oxford don and an unordained Anglican priest, he created and collected what today might be considered a hoard of child pornography. The Lewis Carroll persona gave Dodgson the opportunity to expose his secret pedophilic life for all to see without anyone really seeing, for in publishing *Alice* he took revenge on a hypocritical adult culture that had betrayed him as a child. And yet Dodgson *was* that culture, for if nothing else, he was a man of his times, and *Alice* makes this clear. Even as he attacked the dominant culture's misuse of power as hypocritical madness in the narrative, he did so by drawing on his own unconscious beliefs internalized as a child, beliefs that were fused with repressed feelings of rage, loss, and sadness combined with a sense of powerlessness. As a result, Dodgson's attack on Victorian culture reproduced the ideological hierarchy of his own mind—which was the dominant culture's mind—fused as it was with the repressed suffering of his childhood that he could never openly acknowledge. The result of Dodgson's experiences was one of the most famous children's books to come out of the "golden age" of children's literature, *Alice's Adventures in Wonderland,* a narrative that explicitly attacks—and yet quietly celebrates—the corrosive pleasures of the adult's manipulations of the child.

THE WIND IN THE WILLOWS

Coming some forty-three years after *Alice's Adventures in Wonderland,* Kenneth Grahame's *The Wind in the Willows* was published in 1908 near the end of what has been called the "golden age" of Children's Literature.[22] Though Grahame was only one of a great many adults writing for children in the late Victorian period—a period that included writers such as Mark Twain, Rudyard Kipling, L. M. Montgomery, Frances Hodgson Burnett, J. M. Barrie, L. Frank Baum, and Beatrix Potter—his *Wind in the Willows* continues to be considered a classic of the period.

It came at a time when the dominant Victorian culture was beginning to display a mistrust of its own material progress. The literature produced for children in this period frequently contains powerful, unconscious appeals for the status quo and for the "rightness" of the spirit of progress, civilization, and empire as the English conceived of it. One might consider Kipling's *Jungle Book* and even Burnett's *A Little Princess* as works that explicitly or implicitly rely on unquestioned notions of English imperialism to frame and justify their narratives. Yet even as the wealthy and elite in England grew ever wealthier and ever more powerful at home and abroad, English culture registered a hesitation and, in part, articulated a resistance to its obsession with wealth, progress, and empire. One social historian describes the moment this way:

It is a historic irony that the nation that gave birth to the industrial revolution, and exported it throughout the world, should have become embarrassed at the measure of its success. The English nation even became ill at ease enough with its prodigal progeny to deny its legitimacy by adopting a conception of Englishness that virtually excluded industrialism. . . . . The idealization of material growth and technical innovation that had been emerging received a check, and was more and more pushed back by the contrary ideals of stability, tranquillity, closeness to the past, and "non-materialism."[23]

And according to Charles Dickens, the status quo of English industry and English empire "could be created at much too high a price." Indeed, the creation of wealth—economic growth—as a social goal increasingly appeared to him to be a moral cancer, claiming—and promising—ever more life, poisoning natural and essential human values.[24] The true spirit of the English was not, according to men like Dickens, industrial or progressive, but rather, *conservative*. The social and spiritual qualities of the "true" English way of life—a conservative way of life that looked to the best in the pastoral English past—would and should recover its rightful place as the leading edge of English society. English society must, according to the conservative side, civilize its progressive side or else run the risk of losing forever a chance to recultivate the Arcadian garden that England was thought to be according to the myth of preindustrial England popular at the time.[25]

Should England be an industrial workhouse or a pastoral garden? *The Wind in the Willows* is a story that takes up this question implicitly in its quest to articulate the mystical feelings Grahame associated both with childhood and the idyllic English past that childhood represented. For Grahame, the chaotic energies of too much leisure, too much wealth, and too much technological innovation must be controlled—repressed violently if necessary—if England were to retain any of its original pastoral tranquillity. A rebellion against the status quo must take place if England were to rediscover anything of its preindustrial spirit. Grahame's rebellious attitude expressed itself as a celebration of an Arcadian English past that, ironically, he structured according to the patriarchal hierarchies of race and class that lay behind the industrial threat from which his book attempts to offer an escape.

In *The Wind in the Willows,* Grahame draws on images of an idealized pastoral English past—the animal world of the River Bank, the Wild Wood, and the rest—caught up in and in conflict with the forces of wealth and technology of its own making that ostensibly threatened the social order. In the book this takes the form of Mr. Toad and his spendthrift love for every new invention, especially the automobile. Yet there is a more important story of social disorder than the threat Mr. Toad represents to the innerworkings of Arcadia, and it comes from the bottom of the social hierarchy in the form of the Weasels and Stoats, a racially segregated "other" that represents the true threat to the social order.

The wistfulness of *The Wind in the Willows* only thinly masks the ideology of Victorian imperialism that drives the story, for in the longing of each character for one's "true home"—and the longing of the reader as well—Grahame offers, in an ideological sleight-of-hand, English imperialism and its ideology of racial ideology as succor. This destabilizing contradiction in *The Wind in the Willows* exists in almost every children's book somehow or other, because literature for children is by definition written by the adult for the consumption of the child. The adult's conscious and unconscious experiences as a child *always* figure into the content, structure, and ideological awareness of the adult who constructs a children's text.

This is true for Grahame as well. His inability to honestly address and process the emotional confusion brought on by the loss of both of his parents—the death of his mother and, soon after, the desertion of his father—serves as the unconscious emotional material that informs *The Wind in the Willows*. For even as the novel unites the diverse expressions of Victorian class culture, it does so under the sign of shared delusion about racist hierarchy, about superior and inferior people, about domination, subjugation, power, and the security of economic privilege. Because Grahame remains steadfast in his own delusions about his own personal past, the ideological content of his repressed unconscious mind dominates the latent structure of *The Wind in the Willows*. The characters of the novel remain unable to see that the power and violence that determine their relationships structure their world as an ideological hierarchy that justifies cultural domination and subjugation. Grahame remains blind to this because ideology has constructed for him a "reality" upon which his eyes—and thus his characters' eyes—rest with complacent comfort, finding a reassuring reflection of their own essential innocence in the ideological status quo.

Grahame's attachment to the status quo is not surprising, given the unrest and insecurity that defined his childhood. Grahame lost his mother in 1864 to scarlet fever when he was

> barely five. . . . Kenneth too caught scarlet fever. His maternal grandmother, Granny Ingles, arrived to nurse him and to help her stricken son-in-law, who never recovered from the loss of his wife and did virtually nothing to help his children recover from it. What James Grahame did do was to shift all of the burden of caretaking and much of the financial responsibility as well onto the shoulders of Granny Ingles . . . Kenneth's father seems to have sunk into both depression and alcoholism.[26]

Moreover, Grahame "did not form a strong attachment to his grandmother, who is reputed to have treated [him] . . . coldly" (p. 3).[27] And by 1866—only two years after the death of his mother—his father abandoned Grahame and his siblings and never returned. Two years later, Grahame left for St. Edward's School in Oxford, one of the elite public schools of Victorian England. Like Charles Dodgson, Grahame spent the better part of his later childhood in the English public school, where Victorian culture subsumed him and offered itself as the shaping ideological event of his young life. Where there was emotional longing, need and, perhaps, desperation, the public school offered structure, hierarchy, and obedience.

It comes as no surprise, then, that *The Wind in the Willows* combines an emotional wistfulness with a conservative ideological agenda. Chapter 1 begins with the Mole's longing to be free of his present condition. "The Mole had been working," Grahame writes, when suddenly the Mole feels a sudden sense of claustrophobia and simultaneously feels himself caught up in a wave of longing to be out, above ground, and in the open air. Mole responds to his need and "bolts out of the house without even waiting to put on his coat" (p. 1). Mole's abandonment of his house represents in part a desire to abandon his station in life, for as a Mole in Grahame's animal world, he has a station, and changing one's station in life is as difficult a task as changing one's class in Victorian England. Climbing from the lower class to the middle might be possible if one had the intelligence, the opportunity, and the luck to secure the economic resources necessary, for class, Grahame will subtly remind the reader throughout the story, is a matter of economics as much as friendship, and beyond these, the reader is assured, the hierarchical world of *Willows* is controlled by something far more mysterious than economics. Behind the hierarchical world of race and class are the forces that bless the status quo and help it along, represented in the text by the mystical and mythic Piper at the Gates of Dawn. In spite of all this, however, Mole is allowed his transgression and he "moves up" suddenly and spontaneously to a new, more civilized world; thus the story begins.

The Water Rat befriends Mole as a superior might befriend a newcomer who needs to be educated about his station in life. As gentle and generous as Water Rat is with Mole—Rat's patience is enviable at times—it is the gentleness and generosity of the condescending parent to his amiable child. Water Rat is an ideal and as such he justifies the social hierarchy, for as a man of tweed and pipe tobacco he stoops and so gives a leg up to the slightly musky muckworker who appears on his doorstep. As the socially civilized member of the pair, it is the Water Rat's moral duty to introduce the Mole to the world above ground properly, which means that Rat introduces Mole to the ideological, socially hierarchized space of his world, which is, of course, *the* world. Mole's reality—for the time being—*does not exist* except as a bothersome behavior or two to be dislodged by Water Rat's modeling of his superior ways.

At the top of Water Rat's world is the aristocrat, Mr. Toad, the superior figure who occupies his position not so much for his high ideals or his civility as for his birth into wealth. This alone proves his superiority, though his behavior troubles all those who know him. At the ideological center of the Water Rat's society—and somewhere off the social hierarchy, or so it seems, lives the Badger. The Badger lives among the denizens of the Wild Wood and quietly rules them as the plantation owner rules his enlightened slaves, while physically dominating those who will not be wooed by his quiet power. Badger might be understood as a kind of "gentleman" figure, someone who can move up and down the social hierarchy with ease and grace because he knows it so well, and because he believes in it completely. He is the social hierarchy's chief guardian. Badger is a kind of concrete embodiment of the mystical Piper at the Gates of Dawn—and he represents a character of considerable cultural and ideological power, namely, his ability to organize and wield physical power. Water Rat fears him, for Water Rat is essentially insecure about his position. Mole is mysteriously drawn to him and will be rewarded by Badger for his courage.

Badger understands implicitly that it is his job to maintain the status quo of the animal world, and so, by story's end, he is responsible for leading the Mole, the Water Rat, and the Otter on an attack to roust the upstart Stoats and Weasels who have stepped out of their station in life and taken up residence in Toad Hall while Mr. Toad sits in jail. As already noted, the Weasels and Stoats represent the marginalized "other" that threatens the stability of the animal class hierarchy. When the "other" attempts to usurp the position of someone "above" them and therefore "superior" to them, the "other" needs—in fact deserves—to be annihilated for the good of the social order, whether they accept the dominant culture's ideological reality or not. In fact, when the "other" resists the dominant social order, this resistance represents not a moment to reconsider the cultural and ideological order of things, but rather, the resistance of the "other" to domination merely *confirms* their backward and benighted state.

Water Rat teaches Mole about the order of things in the world above ground, and his racist taxonomy represents Victorian class consciousness perfectly. Water Rat explains to Mole that there is a ghetto out there that the civilized are best to avoid, known as the Wild Wood:

> The weasels and stoats live in the "Wild Wood." "We don't go there very much, we river bankers," the Water Rat says to the Mole. "Aren't they—aren't they very *nice* people in there?" said the Mole a trifle nervously.
>
> "W-e-ll," replied the Rat, "let me see. The squirrels are all right, and the rabbits—some of 'em, but rabbits are a mixed lot. . . . there are others," explained the Rat in a hesitating sort of way. "Weasels—and stoats—and foxes—and so on. They're all right in a way—I'm very good friends with them—pass the time of day when we meet, and all that—but they break out sometimes, there's no denying it, and then—well, you can't really trust them, and that's the fact. (p. 11)

Even as maintaining one's station in life is of paramount concern in *The Wind in the Willows,* the Water Rat tolerates the Mole's need to discover a new way of life above ground, and so it seems *some* social climbing is acceptable for Grahame while some is not.

When the Water Rat meets the Sea Rat he hears a tale of travel, adventure, and romance that puts him into a kind of trance. He, like the Mole before him, longs to find a different life. In fact, he decides to leave the River and his friends to "go south." The Mole is deeply disturbed by his friend's need to make a change and see the world, and so feels absolutely no qualms in physically restraining Water Rat in his home until the "fit" passes. The Mole distracts the Water Rat with idle chatter, and then with pencil and paper, enticing the Water Rat with the possibility of writing some poetry. Finally, the Water Rat picks up the pencil and began scribbling and "it was a joy to the Mole to know that the cure had at least begun" (p. 18).

Ironically, the Mole is unable to see his own experience in Water Rat's longing. Mole can only understand Rat's desire to pursue his longings as a kind of disease for which he must restrain him and administer a "cure." The longing for something unnamable serves as both a source of resistance to the status quo—Mole's adventure above ground—while at the same time, providing an unconscious justification for defending it through subtle, or even violent, means. Mole restrains Rat gently, and later, together they will more violently restrain Mr. Toad from pursuing his own life, all for his—and the dominant culture's—own good. Relations, it seems, are sites of power, and as such, sites of cultural and ideological reproduction.

When the Badger, Water Rat, Mole, and Otter restrain Mr. Toad from driving his beloved automobile, violence is justified yet again, for Mr. Toad represents a threat to the social order. "Apparently, friends may behave violently toward each other in order to keep one of their number within the confines of the felicitous space established by Rat at the Beginning."[28]

Kincaid notes how prevalent ritualized violence was in Victorian England. Adults beat their children "to save their souls," and

> far from being unnecessary, the rod is God's major tool for fashioning the world just the way he likes it. Those who do not want God playing a part in all this often evoke a more general concept of correction: that it is being done for the child's own good, good that will be available for use in this life, as the habits or ideas absorbed in the beating will make one rich, happy, or something equally satisfactory. The parent is doing, if not God's work, then, at least moral work—as in a *good* spanking—and also hygienic work—as in a *sound* or *healthy* spanking. Often it is felt to be imperative, a duty performed to save, if not souls, then lives. Better pain now than pain or death later.[29]

Badger's relationship to Mr. Toad in chapter 6 is precisely that of a morally indignant parent to his recalcitrant and mischievous child. Mr. Badger, the

Mole, and the Rat set out to find Mr. Toad in order to set him straight. Grahame describes it as "a mission of mercy." The Badger demands that Mr. Toad take off his driving clothes, and when he does not, Badger commands,

> "Take them off him, then, you two."
>
> They had to lay Toad out on the floor, kicking and calling all sorts of names, before they could get to work properly. Then the Rat sat on him, and the Mole got his motor-clothes off him bit by bit, and they stood him up on his legs again. A good deal of his blustering spirit seemed to have evaporated with the removal of his fine panoply.

Badger defends his actions by accusing Mr. Toad of having caused them. "Independence is all very well, but we animals never allow our friends to make fools of themselves beyond a certain limit" (p. 108). What Grahame is in fact saying through Badger is what countless adults have said to the child to justify violence. The child asks for violence simply by being a curious, spirited child. The adult fears looking like a fool, and projects this onto the child in the form of concern for the *child's* reputation.

When the Badger's words fail, the animals decide to "try what force can do." The animals take Mr. Toad upstairs and lock him in his bedroom. As conservative a text as *Willows* is, the characters of the Mole and Mr. Toad nevertheless suggest an incongruous element in Grahame's unconscious literary reproduction of the ideological status quo. Though he is overpowered by force for a moment, Mr. Toad resists the force of his friends, escapes through his window, and lives to drive another day. For this he is punished by the human world, however, when he is thrown into prison from where he must make yet another narrow escape. Nevertheless, though promising reform, Mr. Toad remains to the end a character of mischief, a trickster, a force that represents a destabilizing of the status quo at every turn. Or does he?

The English gentleman was, according to Bertrand Russell, "invented by the aristocracy to keep the middle classes in order," and this is the role the Badger plays in maintaining and preserving the ideological status quo of *The Wind in the Willows*. This was necessary because class distinction intensified as a response to the economic and technological pressure of the industrial revolution. Mr. Toad's profligate ways might, quite literally, end in social revolution. Mr. Toad must be kept in check if the wealthy elite were to maintain their claim to moral and cultural superiority. In this way, Mr. Toad's antics—like adolescent behavior—might in fact be coopted by the dominant social order as a necessary demonstration of tacitly allowed resistance that ultimately serves in maintaining the dominant social order by suggesting that there are margins, places to escape to, modes of behavior that are not controlled by the dominant culture. The dominant culture adopts the trickster for its own purposes and harnesses anarchic force to the social enterprise. Dissent is welcomed, for it represents an opportunity for the need for socialization, just as the rebellion of the Stoats and Weasels justifies the rightness of status quo and the violence used to maintain it.

And so Badger, the gentleman of the Wild Wood, facilitates Mr. Toad's return to his rightful place at the top of the social hierarchy. The absent father *must* return—like Odysseus from his travels—and he will be revealed, finally, as the hero who in his person reproduces and so justifies the rightness of the dominant the social order—even if he requires help to do so, even if he is a misfit. Badger, too, figures importantly as a father figure who "cares" enough to take control of the wayward Mr. Toad—prodigal son in some respects—though Toad remains "superior" by virtue of his wealth and aristocratic position in the social hierarchy. Badger's authority comes precisely from the fact that he does not question Mr. Toad's ideological place above him, only the fact that Mr. Toad's behavior threatens to bring it *all* down, and this would directly impact Badger. In saving Mr. Toad, in other words, Badger saves himself. He protects Mr. Toad's material and ideological existence though he has little respect for Toad as a *toad*.

Even so, Badger's responsibility is to the social order, and so he leads the attack on Toad Hall and drives out the destabilizing, lower-class Weasels and Stoats. The cultural revolution is ended and all is right with the world. Beyond and behind Badger's moral and ideological authority lies the mysterious, ever-watchful Piper at the Gates of Dawn who also preserves and protects the status quo—and who spiritualizes the father's authority. For though the Piper passively looks on from a distance, he remains aware of all of the animals' travails and implicitly blesses the dominant, hierarchical culture as a design sent from heaven for the society's own good.

Badger represents the father figure Grahame unconsciously longed for his entire life. Mole's triumph is not so much his move up the social ladder, for he moves only very little. Rather, Mole's triumph in *The Wind in the Willows* is also his destruction, for he abandons the status quo of his own life and finds a father figure who takes him under his guidance. The end result is simply that Mole becomes a more active force in maintaining the very social hierarchy that kept him "down" in the first place. From this perspective Mole and Grahame become one character. Grahame's own longing and need for a father gather in Badger as a character that represents the contradictory nature of this story, fusing as it does violence with love and social *oppression* with social *restoration*. In the final triumph over the denizens of the Wild Wood, Grahame explicitly invites the reader to fall in with the "winners" on the one side of the ideological divide, for falling in with the Weasels and Stoats is simply not an ideological option. Ideology makes it clear: they are *born* losers. Yet on the other hand to fall in with Badger and Mole is to fall in with an idealized representation of a pastoral space that offers violence and hierarchy as the stuff of dreams and fantasy. When power is rightly wielded,

Grahame reminds his readers, all is right with the world, and all the world recognizes the right of the powerful to wield their power.

> Sometimes, in the course of long summer evenings, the friends would take a stroll together in the Wild Wood, now successfully tamed so far as they were concerned; and it was pleasing to see how respectfully they were greeted by the inhabitants . . . but when the infants were fractious and quite beyond control, [the adults] would quiet them by telling how, if they didn't hush them and not fret them, the terrible grey Badger would up and get them. [The threat] never failed to have its full effect. (p. 259)

This final paragraph of *The Wind in the Willows* waxes poetic about the establishment and perpetuation of the status quo while noting that those dominated are, in effect, *grateful* for their taming. And yet, when all is said and done, Grahame understands that the story of power and domination embedded in *The Wind in the Willows* is above all a story of taming with violence and with threats of violence, and it is a story best told to the child by the adult.

COLONIZING THE CHILD

The picture book *The Story of Babar* was first published in France in 1931 and then in English two years later. Along with picture books like H. A. Rey's *Curious George,* Jean de Brunhoff's *Babar* is a twentieth-century text that tells the story of Western colonialism and its "obvious" right to appropriate the African continent and its resources in the name of Western civilization. The colonizer's power to dominate and subjugate the African population is justified in both Rey and Brunhoff's picture book narratives by appeals to the "obviousness" of the superior civilization's right to manifests its superiority in, among other ways, its ability to deface and destroy in the name of cultural "rehabilitation." Babar is rehabilitated by his French education, French technology, and French materialism—and so he becomes a French colonialist. Colonialism—and the benefits it brings to the native—is so "obviously" good for all concerned that when Babar returns to Africa his elephant community immediately crown's him king. The natives, apparently, intuitively understand when a superior is among them and so subject themselves to him without question. *Babar* is a French invention that represents an idealized fantasy of French power, French colonialism, and French absolute monarchism—it is a paean to the divine right of kings and the willing subjects who cannot wait to be dominated by such an enlightened monarch. That the French Monarchy was long gone in 1931 when *Babar* was first published in France is beside the point—this is a story that the adult tells to himself about his culture and invites the child to consume along with him. [30]

George, on the other hand, is kidnapped from his African tree and forcibly relocated to a zoo in America. The narrative recounts George's journey from wild monkey to civilized, not-so-obedient child. George *needs* to be punished along the way for being himself, a spirited, willful child who simply will not learn how to behave. Like *Babar,* the end of *George* reproduces imperialist ideology *and* the dominant child-rearing ideology in one fell swoop: George needs—even *wants*—to be properly subjugated by the dominant adult culture, and in George's case his prison is not the result of ideological indoctrination like Babar's education, but rather, George's rehabilitation takes another, more literal course: when he is finally placed in the Zoo by the Man in the Yellow Hat at the end of the text, the illustrations and narrative explicitly and forcefully maintain that George has found his true home and his true happiness.

Western culture can fabricate a reality more suited to George's needs than nature itself, or at least that is one of the implicit messages of *Curious George.* This might be restated in the following terms: the adult knows what's best for the child, for the child is, after all, just a little monkey, or an ignorant savage, and cannot possibly understand what he needs. The logic that underscores George's relationship to the adult is one and the same with ideological justifications common to the American slave owner's discourse about the African slave. Yet in *Curious George* it becomes more obvious that the captivity narrative of the slave and the captivity narrative of the child draw on the same ideological assumptions about the nature of power as a biological right, whether it be grounded in assumptions about race or assumptions about physical size: in either case the superiority that results is the ground for the colonialist rights afforded to the dominant power.

The ideological construction of an ideal "childhood-as-Zoo" in *Curious George* reproduces the slave-owner's logic while anticipating later twentieth-century culture as well: for at the end of *Curious George* the Zoo becomes a representation of the dominant culture's institution-par-excellence and is "obviously" superior to the native jungles of George's African home. H. A. Rey reproduces what most assumed to be true—and what many still assume to be true today: human culture can do nature better than nature can do itself. That nature often dies as a result of the dominant lockstep march of "technological progress" is, according to the dominant ideology, merely one of the bugs yet to be worked out of the system. According to *Curious George,* the child is happy in his new home—yet this claims rings hollow and false, though Rey depicts George with a balloon in hand and a smile on his face. For even as the text makes claims to George's happiness, it reproduces the logic of the slave owner who, in defending the harsh conditions of plantation life, maintained that the African was unfit for his African home *in the first place* and that plantation life allowed the slave to "make something" of his life. In short, the slave was "better off" in chains in South Carolina than free in the Congo. So too George, according to Rey.

Curious George reproduces the dominant ideology of the child-as-slave by depicting George as an inchoate and incomplete creature emotionally befuddled and in need of domination. Rey's inconsistent handling of George's emotional life in the story offers a way of seeing George and the claims to George's final happiness in the Zoo as specious and, ultimately, adult projections of a child invented for the adult by the adult. Consider the many instances when the text of the picture book describes George as sad, scared, or, in fact, almost drowned. The accompanying illustrations almost always depict George with an enormous smile on his face; even as George is "struggling in the water" and near drowning, Rey depicts George smiling, at ease, and seemingly enjoying himself at a most dire time. When George is hauled out of the ocean Rey depicts him vomiting fish and sea water, yet his smile remains unaffected. The message is clear: George is a happy monkey *no matter what is happening to him.* The depiction of George's emotional life confirms what the dominant ideology teaches about the child: the child has no real emotional subjectivity and so can be—and *must* be—subjugated and made a subject of adult power or risk remaining in a primitive state.

That the Man in the Yellow Hat is, in fact, *selling* George to the Zoo is never an issue in the story. That these issues are, in fact, behind this story is beyond doubt. Whatever form imperialism takes, be it educational reform, economic reform, technologic reform, political reform, or countless other manifold ways that adult culture demands the "other" to submit to reform, these demands always serves the dominant power, and the subjugated other must be convinced, through indoctrination or, if this is not successful, through force, to accept the dominant power's enactment of their cultural story as the real and the only destiny of human life.

The Story of Babar and *Curious George* are more than stories of Western colonialism. These two picture books are representative examples of the ways in which adult culture in the form of "literature for children" represents itself to itself through the stories it tells about "reality," especially as that reality is enacted through a lived relation of power between the adult and the child. The depiction of relations of power in these stories comes with an ideological bullet that, like Tom Sawyer's dream in *Huckleberry Finn*, penetrates flesh in the same way "real" bullets do.

Like the idyllic illustration that opens *Curious George,* Brunhoff too depicts the original, undisturbed jungle home of Babar as an unspoiled Eden where the ideological hierarchy between adult and child appears to be nonexistent. Babar's mother gently rocks her baby in a hammock as butterflies gently flutter overhead. She sings softly to him. The following double-page spread portrays the young elephants of the jungle playing together as an idealized community without conflict, and without *perspective.* Brunhoff's double-page illustration represents the elephants in such a way that the reader's eye can locate no "center," no vanishing point, no "back or front" to the elephants activities. All seems to be going on at the same time in the same way everywhere. Everything in the elephants' world is, in other words, happening *now* everywhere the reader's eye gazes. No one part of the page is any more important than any other part of the page. Babar is just one of many elephants.

This lack of perspective in the illustration style suggests the elephants' lack of political or cultural perspective. As a result, they cannot defend themselves. They *need* a more advanced culture, a political hierarchy, and the power that comes with it in order to protect and preserve what they have. That the elephants will *lose* their Eden in order to protect it is the conundrum of modern civilization, but no matter. Brunhoff plunges ahead with his narrative, yet remains caught between the rock and the ideological hard place that the story of colonialism represents, for into the Eden of the elephants' playground comes "a wicked hunter" who shoots and kills Babar's mother even as Babar rides on her back. Babar cries over the body of his dead mother while the hunter approaches. Babar flees. "The hunter," Brunhoff writes, wanted "to catch poor Babar." Like the Man in the Yellow Hat, the hunter is out for pleasure, for sport, and for economic gain. Fortunately, it seems, Babar escapes the hunter and avoids an early death or years of imprisonment in a French zoo or a display case in a world's fair.

Though Babar flees, his escape is only apparent, for he unknowingly flees directly into the arms of the French culture that produced the hunter, his pith helmets, his safari outfits, and his mighty elephant gun. Babar's French education thus represents a moment of ideological reproduction and cultural intensification, for the story implicitly suggests that if you kill an elephant, it dies only once. If you teach an elephant about an ideology of death and domination and then send it back to convince others that a culture grounded in an ideology of death and domination, is a preferable way to live, the culture of death and destruction is reproduced exponentially. The hunter has succeeded in either case.

When Babar loses his mother his shock and sadness rings true, unlike the way in which Rey depicts George's emotional response to his captivity. French civilization offers Babar a surrogate mother—a better mother, in many respects, than his own, for as an African elephant Babar was doomed to live his life in obscurity, but as a Frenchman he has been unknowingly prepared to become king of the elephants, all thanks to the rich old lady's omniscient largess and, of course, the "wicked hunter." Here is the work of ideology at its most intense moment of inventing the nature of human relationship. Babar-as-child is traumatized in the story by the loss of his mother. The picture book invites the child to identify with Babar and if the child does so, the child will identify in part, unconsciously and emotionally, with the loss of the mother, for the child subjected to the detached parenting of Victorian child-rearing ideology will have a keen emotional awareness of what it feels like to be abandoned. The trauma now refreshed by the picture book's narrative, Brunhoff offers the cold solace of ideology in the place of the mother: French clothes, French food, French cars, French dinner parties, and French education. Babar needs a mother and instead he gets the rich old lady, an idealized figuration of the dominant culture who, like the ideal mother, knows just what he needs without him even having to ask. She "has always been fond of little elephants," Brunhoff writes, and "understands right away that he is longing for *a fine suit*" (emphasis added).

Yet "mother culture" in the figure of the rich old lady does not, in fact, know what Babar is longing for; she does not understand, surfeited as she is on wealth and luxury and power. Babar has just lost his mother. The last thing he needs is a suit. Yet, having no emotional support to offer Babar, instead she gives him money. Desperate for something, and isolated as he is from what he knows, Babar-as-child accepts the old lady's proffered adult substitutes—in this case, money and the cultural power money brings with it—as "real coin." What Babar learns from the rich old lady will define him for the rest of his life, for the child separated prematurely from the mother's body is first and foremost emotionally and therefore ideologically vulnerable. He will experience chronic emotional need as the defining aspect of his unconscious life and his conscious life will be spent in the *hunt* for fulfilling substitutes. The dominant ideology coopts and structures the child's desire and so uses his need as a way of reproducing the dominant culture, which in Babar's case, becomes the need for material possession enacted on a grand scale as a need to control and dominate nature and so create "civilization." In short, Babar will transform his native lands by bringing an intensified and "improved" political hierarchy to the jungle and so remake Africa. All of this appears as only "child's play" in Brunhoff's picture book, yet behind it all is a story of the death of the child's soul and the rightness of adult exploitation of the child's vulnerability.

When Babar takes the colonizer's culture as his own and returns with Céleste, his sometime cousin and now his queen, he does more than a thousand poachers could do in exterminating his native community. Yet according to the text, Babar must be king, for he wears clothes, wears a hat, drives a car, and *packs* his trunk. Moreover, just before Babar returns triumphantly to the jungle, the elephant king dies from eating a poison mushroom. This not only makes room for Babar's ascendance to the throne, but it also points to the native's inability to exist in their own land, for the aged, experienced elephant—a king no less—still cannot see the difference between food and poison. How unfit these elephants are to rule themselves! And make no mistake—Babar is no longer an elephant, for in Babar's rule it is not the elephants ruling themselves, but rather, the colonial power ruling through Babar. That this is "right" the picture book assumes as *obvious,* given the *obviousness* of the dominant culture's technological—and therefore moral—superiority.

When Babar returns to the jungle, he brings with him French ideology in the form of "civilization" expanded on by Brunhoff in the third book in the series, *Babar the King*. In this story King Babar puts an end to the spontaneous living that characterized jungle existence in the first pages of *The Story of Babar*. Instead, Babar rules over a world in which spontaneity must be exchanged for the regimentation of work and the need to produce "civilization," not because it is demonstrably better than the spontaneous life of the jungle, but rather, because French civilization is, in the world of Brunhoff, *an absolute good*. The playfulness of the elephant community, especially the children from the opening pages, becomes a way of life lost to the past. Work is the proper relationship of the elephant to his land, "sweetened" by the king's gift-giving largess, learned from the rich old lady. Even so, there is no mistaking the fact that the elephant works for work's sake, not to gain anything, for there is nothing to gain. The elephants had it all long before they were convinced to build Celestville. The elephants lost their access to the means of production of their own lives for a few beads and shiny trinkets. "Work will make you free," King Babar informs his subjects.

MOVING PICTURES

The rise of film at the end of the Victorian period provided the means by which the dominant ideology might more effectively deliver its story to its children. As consumer culture intensified near the end of the Victorian period, one man would emerge to become one of America's great propagandists and ideological heroes. Walt Disney understood as only a few individuals did in his time the power of a shared story and what that meant for the man who could effectively deliver it to a wide audience. Disney perfected the full-length animated feature and in the process perfected a means of reproducing the dominant ideology in terms of a shared story that at once idealized and commodified the violent nature of the dominant culture's lived relations and made the consumption of this story a source of national pride.

NOTES

[1]See Edward Said, *Culture and Imperialism* (New York: Knopf, 1993). Also, cf. Frantz Fanon, *The Wretched of the Earth,* trans. Constance Farrington (New York: Grove Weidenfeld, 1963).

[2]Quoted in Philip D. Curtin, ed., *Imperialism* (New York: Walker, 1971), pp. 294–95.

[3]From Edward Said, *Orientalism* (New York: Random House, 1978), pp. 2–3.

[4]From Said, *Culture and Imperialism*, p. 11.

[5]Jacob Abbot, *Parental Duties in the Promotion of Early Piety* (London: Thomas Ward, 1834), p. 37.

[6]The successful colonist demonstrates through ambient, invisible force whenever possible and through visible, monstrous force when necessary that an advancement of colonization represents an advancement of the entire human species, for the colonizer teaches that the dominant culture embodies the vanguard of human evolution—or spiritual understanding—as the case may be. Successful colonization causes the colonized to recognize their "natural" self as lacking and incomplete, while at the same time they recognize their essential inability to add anything substantive to their material and cultural condition, mistaken as their "natural" self. First and last, however, it should be noted that colonization occurs individually through shared cultural practices of the colonizer's dominant ideology of cultural superiority through child-rearing pedagogies of domination and subjugation. See Ariel Dorfman, *The Empire's Old Clothes: What the Lone Ranger, Babar, and Other Innocent Heroes Do to Our Minds,* trans. Clark Hansen (New York: Pantheon, 1983).

[7]David Kenneth Fieldhouse, *The Colonial Empires: A Comparative Survey from the Eighteenth Century* (1965, reprint, Houndmills: Macmillan, 1991), p. 103.

[8]Ellice Hopkins, *On the Early Training of Girls and Boys: An Appeal to Working Women* (London: Hatchards, 1882), p. 343.

[9]Martin J. Wiener, *English Culture and the Decline of the Industrial Spirit: 1850–1980* (Cambridge: Cambridge University Press, 1981), p. 158.

[10]Richard Wallace, *The Agony of Lewis Carroll* Melrose: Gemini Press, 1990), p. 94.

[11]See Lytton Strachey, *Eminent Victorians* (New York and London: G. P. Putnam's Sons, 1918), p. 5.

[12]Wallace, *Agony,* p. 92.

[13]See Humphrey Carpenter, *Secret Gardens: A Study of the Golden Age of Children's Literature,* (Boston: Houghton Mifflin, 1985), p. 51.

[14]James Kincaid, *Child-Loving: The Erotic Child and Victorian Culture* (New York: Routledge, 1992), pp. 21–22.

[15]From Wallace, *Agony,* p. 11.

[16]Ibid.

[17]All quotes are from Lewis Carroll, *Alice in Wonderland,* Norton Critical Edition, ed. Donald Gray (New York: W. W. Norton, 1998).

[18]See Wallace, *Agony,* pp. 171–96.

[19]Or, the same ideological hierarchy results when examined from a Darwinian perspective: those in authority have a biological right as a result of their more "evolved" condition—those in power are in power because they are the "fittest" and as the "fittest" they have proven their right to control.

[20]See Wallace, *Agony,* p.118 .

[21]Kincaid, *Child-Loving,* pp. 360–61.

[22]The "golden age" of children's literature has different beginning and ending dates, depending on one's point of view. Generally speaking, however, the "golden age" of children's literature runs from around the middle of the nineteenth century and ends around the beginning of World War I. Some say it began with *Alice in Wonderland* in 1865. This is a date that informs my own point of view.

[23]From Martin Wiener, *English Culture and the Decline of the Industrial Spirit: 1850–1980* (Cambridge: Cambridge University Press, 1981), p. 6.

[24]Charles Dickens, quoted in Ibid., p. 34.

[25]Wiener describes the tension between the machine and the garden as a signal cultural conflict in England. America had its own cultural conflict between the pastoral and the industrial. "In England, the symbols of Machine and Garden, Workshop and Shire, were in more direct opposition. These symbols embodied a tension that had become implanted deep within middle-and upper-class culture over at least the previous century. Much of the peculiar character of English domestic history over this period was the result of a nation, or at least an elite, *at war with itself*" (p. 7, emphasis added).

[26]Ibid., pp. 2–3.

[27]Kenneth Grahame, *The Wind in the Willows* (New York: Macmillan, 1950).

[28]Lois Kuznets, *Kenneth Grahame: Twayne's English Authors Series* (Boston: Twayne, 1987).

[29]Kincaid, *Child-Loving*, p. 250.

[30]Jean de Brunhoff, author and illustrator of *The Story of Babar,* was born in 1899 in Paris. He died of tuberculosis in 1937 having completed four *Babar* stories. His son, Laurent de Brunhoff, picked up in 1938 where his father left off and so *Babar* and his legacy live on in a continuing series of picture book sequels, television adaptations, and ongoing merchandising campaigns. For other arguments regarding *Babar's* colonialist leanings see Herbert Kohl, *Should We Burn Babar? Essays on Children's Literature and the Power of Stories* (New York: New Press, 1995). Also, see Stephen O'Harrow, "Babar and the *Mission Civilisatrice:* Colonialism and the Biography of a Mythical Elephant," *Biography* 22, no. 1 (Winter 1999): 87–103.

CHAPTER 5

Walt Disney, Ideological Transposition, and the Child

*Under monopoly all mass culture is identical, and the
lines of its artificial framework begin to show through.*

—MAX HORKHEIMER AND THEODOR ADORNO,
Dialectic of Enlightenment

THE BIRTH OF THE DISNEY MYTH

As economic depression ran rampant in Chicago and the rest of the United
States in 1893, Elias Disney—Walt Disney's father—took a job as a carpenter
and helped to construct the World's Columbian Exposition. The exposition
celebrated four hundred years of European conquest in America and was
hailed by some at the time as "the third greatest event in American history"
behind only the American Revolution and the Civil War. As a particularly
intense—yet in many ways ordinary—moment of cultural and ideological
reproduction, the exposition aggressively announced the meaning of four
hundred years of European domination of the New World. The story that the
World's Columbian Exposition told American culture about itself to itself
was unequivocal: the past four hundred years of European expansion, and the
American experiment itself, was nothing less than an unbridled and unqualified triumph of a superior race that had taken a continent and proceeded to
capture it with all of the force that industry, agriculture and science could
muster. Though the American desire to move west and conquer so-called savage and untamed land was the manifest ideological theme of the day, few
middle-class Americans questioned the dominant culture's desire to take,
deface, and destroy what stood in its way. Yet this is not a condemnation so

much as an observation regarding the power of ideology and its ability to code even the most horrific violence as a story of progress and civilization.

The Chicago exposition offered its visitors the chance to forget themselves and so bask in the glory of the collective life of the nation and its manifest destiny. Events like the exposition in Chicago confirmed and intensified what most Americans already assumed to be true about the inevitable destiny of the American experiment. Its nature and meaning was on display and it amounted to nothing less than a tour de force of American technological power at its zenith. The individual visitor was implicitly and explicitly invited to contextualize his or her own suffering in light of the larger associative life of the nation and the shared story that foretold its promising future.

As all stories of power do, this one had its downside. The Native American occupied a lowly place as sideshow freak that confirmed the idealized West depicted in Buffalo Bill's hugely popular "Wild West" shows, while African-Americans were all but disallowed from participating in the exposition either as employees or as exhibitors. The dominance of white European conquest in American history was refracted through the dominant imperialist ideology of 1893 and made real and made *right* as an obvious reality and, implicitly, as an obvious cultural *necessity*. The Chicago exposition did not sell imperialist ideology to its visitors so much as it assumed it to be true and relied upon it to construct an American cultural myth that fervently believed in its special mission, justified as it was by the assumed racial superiority of white, middle-class Americans.[1]

The Columbian Exposition displayed a particularly aggressive kind of cultural salesmanship. The ideology at work in Chicago implicitly and explicitly formed a seamless, ambient atmosphere that made obvious the way in which patriotism, racism, and consumerism defined the Ideal American and so defined the nature of his triumph through tough times. The Ideal American visitor to the Exposition was fresh from the conquest of the American continent—though he had never been an actual participant—and ready to enjoy the material fruits of his conquest, in spite of the transient economic hardships of the present moment. The exposition celebrated the future of America as an extrapolation of an idealized American past and so it functioned, at least in part, as a distraction from the contemporary cultural unrest, for in 1893 economic depression raged. One of the nation's worst depressions to date "deepened owing to the era's continuing boom-bust business cycles. Wall Street stocks plunged on May 5, with the market all but collapsing on June 27. Six hundred banks closed their doors, thousands of business firms failed, and seventy-four railroads went into receivership." The depression continued through 1897 and brought with it labor unrest, unemployment, farm foreclosures, and widespread bankruptcies.[2]

In spite of economic depression, the Columbian Exposition promised a brighter tomorrow through the acquisition of things. Materialism and the selling of materialism were coming of age, and the exposition as a "quintessential Victorian artifact" represented a significant and unprecedented way to reach millions of people with a vision of the future, dominated as it was by consumer goods that would make life easy, provided one could afford them.[3] Many of the displays offered a compelling, seductive logic that would become a refrain in later consumer capitalism of the twentieth century: one could spend oneself into prosperity. Displays at the exposition were didactic to a fault in teaching their innocent viewers about how far their dollar could take them towards affording the good life on display there. The good life *could* be afforded even in tough times, provided one knew how to spend wisely. "New York constructed an actual residence," one social historian writes, as a way of modeling an affordable middle-class lifestyle, all based on the wise consumption of domestic goods:

> Katherine Davis, a Rochester social reformer, coordinated the designing and furnishing of the Workingman's Model Home. She imagined a young engaged couple—a laboring man earning $500 a year and a woman, a domestic servant, making $156 a year plus board—as its prospective buyers. Their house, a two-story, wood-frame dwelling, built at a cost not to exceed $1,000, contained a front parlor, a front bedroom and two smaller children's bedrooms. A range and room stoves heated the house. In the two-year engagement Davis conjectured for her hypothetical couple, she calculated that the two could amass $400, of which $100 would be kept as savings, leaving $300 for furnishing their mortgaged dwelling.[4]

The New York display provided long lists of household items and their costs throughout the exhibit, as well as providing detailed cost estimates that listed the way a family of five might live in such a dwelling on what at first appeared to be an insufficient income. Katherine Davis's goal was nothing less than "social reform," however, and her administrative plan for the new American family demonstrated that American values such as thrift, frugality, hard work, and careful planning might make the good life available to those that could spend their way into prosperity. On the surface this meant that *everyone* would be able to afford the good life. Yet the good life as it was displayed in Chicago was defined by domestic product manufacturers who wanted to make American families *consuming* families in order to sell products. Like any and all ideological events, then, the Columbian Exposition of 1893 catered to the perceived tastes of the middle class with dazzling displays even as it shaped and directed those tastes with a particular agenda in mind. In short, exhibits were used to expand consumer markets. The degree to which notions of egalitarian economic reform facilitated the expansion of consumer markets was the degree to which egalitarian economic reform functioned as a part of the ideological status quo. In other words, consumption was represented as a decidedly American thing to do.

If the exhibits celebrating American ingenuity and its technological superiority were not enough to convince fairgoers of America's inevitable right to cultural dominance in the "new world," the midway's ethnological exhibits documented the obvious "rightness" of American cultural hegemony in another way, depicting peoples of other cultures as curiosities, such as the Javanese, or as trophies, such as the Sioux. The exhibitors staged "living ethnological displays of nonwhite cultures. These exhibits of people . . . appeared on the midway, juxtaposed with wild-animal acts, joyrides and other side shows." The ethnological display was ordered according to imperialist Victorian ideology, or what was then called the "sliding scale of humanity." The "sliding scale of humanity" physically displayed the racist Victorian ideology that justified colonial imperialism as a given good and a moral duty. On the "sliding scale" the European was placed at the apex, while

> nearest to the White City were the Teutonic and Celtic races, represented by the two German and two Irish enclaves. The midway's middle contained the Muhammadan and Asian worlds. Then, continued the observer, "we descend to the savage races, the African of Dahomey and the North American Indian, each of which has its place" at the remotest end of the midway.[5]

Cultural domination and the right to economic expansion were, according to the dominant ideology, a biological right as manifested by the "sliding scale of humanity," a hierarchy of power and conquest that at the exposition represented not a genocidal culture run amuck, but rather a dominant *race* that dominated its world as a God-given right, or perhaps as a right accorded to it by natural selection. However average Americans justified their belief in their own racial superiority, they did so with an ideology firmly yet unconsciously grounded in their own physical and emotional experience of having been dominated as a child at the hands of the adult. A world of hierarchy, domination, and power made obvious sense to the average individual who visited, or perhaps helped to construct, the World's Columbian Exposition of 1893. For the exposition—and others just like it—was simply a continuation, a confirmation of an already extant ideology of power and conquest learned in school, learned at church, and practiced in almost every home of Victorian America. Elias Disney's home was no exception, for he, too, had internalized the dominant ideology of Victorian America and transmitted its legacy of power, violence, and suffering to all of his sons, including his youngest, Walter Elias Disney.

WALT DISNEY AND IDEOLOGICAL TRANSMISSION

Ideology is transmitted generationally through the practice of lived relations, and this is nowhere more true than in the generational transmission of ideology between the adult and the child. Whereas the adult practices the dominant culture's child-rearing ideology as an ideology enacted—as a practice recommended by others, by experts, by texts—and converts this information into a lived relation between adult and child, for the child the nature of the lived relation with the adult is an obvious reality. The very young child can only accept the circumstances of her birth and the relationships that inform her as real and inevitable. If the pedagogical nature of the relationship between the adult and the child is one of power, domination, and control, as was commonly espoused by Victorian child-rearing experts, the emotional and physical affects of child-rearing relationships determined by the adult's need for power and control intensify the process by which the child's self—and her idea of herself—is taken up and determined by the dominant ideology that informs the adult world and so informs the way in which the adult relates to the child.

All of this describes what Judith Kestenberg calls "transposition," the phenomenon whereby "the wishes, desires, fantasies, ideals and experiences of a parent are unconsciously transmitted to a child." Though transposition technically refers only to the transmission of massive trauma, it can be used "to describe the reciprocal dialogue between every child and his parent."[6] Louise Kaplan describes transposition this way:

> Whereas any parent will consciously encourage a child to imitate and identify with her courage, virtues, and ideas, she will do everything in her power to block the transmission of terror, shame, and guilt. Yet when it comes to the transmission of massive trauma, the parent's conscious desires to protect her child seem to count for very little. The child suckles "the black milk". . . . of trauma, relishes and absorbs it, cultivates its bitter taste as if it were vital sustenance—as if it were existence itself. The transposition of trauma. . . . originates in the parent's unconscious needs and wishes must rely on and exploit the child's happier susceptibilities—to be at one with the parent, to be close to the parent, to partake in the parent's power, to be like the parent, to be loved and admired by the parent, to maintain a dialogue with the parent. The psychological process that comes from the child is normal. What the child is absorbing is abnormal.[7]

Ideological transposition might thus be understood as the psychodynamic process by which a traumatic and violent culture reproduces itself first and foremost in the lived relations between the adult and the child. Ideological transposition might be further understood as an intensification and refraction of the ordinary generational transmission of the adults' beliefs, values, and desires. In fact, ideological transposition suggests that there is no "ordinary" generational transmission of ideology, for ideology is always transmitted traumatically from the adult to the child. Nevertheless, ideology's function is to code the violence inherent in ideological transposition not as a lived relation of violence and power, but rather, as a relation of suffering made necessary by the adult's love for the child. From this early trauma and confusion the child learns to cultivate an *idea* about his traumatic experiences as a defense against them, or as a justification for them, or both. In the end the child invents his idea of himself from the ideas about "the child" that circulate in the dominant ideology of the adult world. In this way, the child becomes taken up by ideology and, as Althusser describes it, becomes caught up in "an imaginary relationship to the actual conditions of his existence" (p. 164).

Even after the parent is no longer a significant relationship in the child's later life, the child-now-adult has, if an unconscious victim of traumatic child-rearing experiences, relinquished an existence in the present and instead strives to live out an idealized version of what the child believes to be the parent's past. Ideology codes this unconscious dream life as the "real" thing, when in fact it represents the endless psychological return of a poisonous cycle that involves the individual's unconscious need to vent rage at the adult for the adult's violence. Appropriate expressions of rage and anger are rare, however (though inappropriate ones are common), because ideology offers the individual countless reasons to deny the violence experienced as a child, claiming among other things that the violence never occurred, or, on the other hand, that the violence was deserved, and quite frequently, both at the same time. All of this amounts to an intellectual clinging to an idea of the adult self and of the child the adult once was that remains caught up in and determined by ideology. The result is an adult who remains perpetually fused to an imaginary relationship that offers intellectual denials and justifications that serve to repeat the past and repress the actual experiences of his emotional condition in the present moment.

The child so raised grows up with an unquenchable need for power and control. Elias Disney's parenting suggests that he, like so many adults of his time, practiced child-rearing techniques that consciously justified adult violence as a moral and religious necessity. Elias Disney was a particularly violent man, however, and Walt Disney's experiences as a child at the hands of his father were particularly and chronically violent. Ideological transposition offers itself as a way of understanding how Walt Disney internalized his father's Victorian ideology—manifested so neatly at the Chicago World's Columbian Exposition of 1893—and then came to commodify it and reproduce it for mass consumption in his films and theme parks.

WALT DISNEY-AS-CHILD

Walter Elias Disney was born in Chicago in 1901; he was named after the Reverend Walter Parr, a minister of St. Paul Congregational Church and close friend of Elias Disney.[8] Elias Disney was a staunch believer in what might today be called "Christian family values." Hard work, Elias Disney believed, would lead his lower-middle-class family to the life of leisure and ease of the wealthy bourgeoisie. Unfortunately, wealth and leisure eluded Elias Disney even as bad debts and a racially mixed neighborhood in Chicago persuaded him to "rear his five children in a wholesome Christian atmosphere."[9] In 1906 he bought a forty-eight-acre farm and moved his family from Chicago to Marceline, Missouri.

Elias Disney's get-tough farming philosophy, like his child-rearing pedagogy, demonstrated his rejection of cause and effect in favor of what could only be called an irrational belief in his own *will*. According to Elias Disney, "putting fertilizer on plants is like giving whiskey to a man. He'll feel better for a while, but afterward he'll be worse off than he was before."[10] The metaphor Elias Disney employs here is suggestive, for it informs his Victorian child-rearing ideologies as much as it explains his struggles as a farmer. It followed for Elias Disney from his tortured reasoning that "feeding" one's crops might "spoil" them, and so make them "weak." Elias Disney was, in short, confused. Apparently his neighbors convinced him that he should, in fact, fertilize his corn. No one persuaded him to stop beating his children.

According to both the unauthorized *and* the authorized Walt Disney biographies, Elias Disney beat his children regularly. Described by his friends as "dour" and "gloomy," and by his critics as "violent" and an "autocratic martinet," Elias Disney failed at almost all that he attempted to do, including farming in Marceline and a newspaper delivery franchise in Kansas City, enterprises that occupied much of Walt Disney's years as a child. Elias Disney failed in part because he relied on the exploited labor of his sons and paid them little or nothing for their efforts, expecting instead that they would serve him day in and day out from an inborn sense of filial love and loyalty. Rather, when it became possible to fend for themselves, three out of his four sons ran away from home.

Yet Elias Disney's parenting was, in most ways, ordinary, for violence was a common tool used to keep the willful and potentially rebellious child in his place. Without violence, so the dominant child-rearing story intoned, the child might go to hell, or perhaps worse for the father-farmer who needed farm hands, the child might become shiftless and lazy. Violence was a necessary motivating force, for it served to "correct" the child whenever he strayed from the path and desired to experience himself on his own terms. For Walt Disney this meant doodling and sketching, not farming or delivering papers. It was a given, of course, that the adult always had this path in clear view whereas the child remained blind to it. Given this, it was the adult's moral and spiritual duty to "correct" the child violently when necessary; to do anything less was to spoil the child and make him soft. Walt Disney was only five years old when his family moved to the farm in Marceline and nine years old when the family left for Kansas City. As short as those years were for Walt Disney, they came at a formative time in his psychological development. In his authorized biography, Walt Disney explains that Marceline "left more of an impression than any other time in his life. Forty years later when he built a barn for a workshop on his estate in California, it was an exact replica of the one he had known in Marceline."[11]

The violence Elias Disney served his sons on a daily basis came with the same Protestant ideology so common to the dominant Victorian child-rearing ideology—as well as to the Monroe Doctrine and Manifest Destiny—steeped as it all was in notions of autocratic authority justified by a morality grounded in Protestant Christianity. The human relationships that developed between father and son as a result amounted to a horror story of violence and humiliation for Walt Disney, though so ordinary at the time as to seem meaningless and not worth noting. According to Marc Eliot's unauthorized biography of Walt Disney, Elias Disney's punishments were frequent and brutal. He "used corporal punishment to enforce maximum productivity and thought nothing of taking a switch to his sons, or the fat part of his leather belt, to administer the "corrective" beatings that became a daily part of the boys' routine. At the slightest provocation, real or imagined, Elias would march Roy and Walt to the woodshed and dispense his brutal punishments."[12] Walt Disney's older brother, Roy, and his mother, Flora, offered little protection to the youngest son, Walt. According to Eliot, Walt Disney's mother was a passive woman who, like her children, submitted herself to her husband's "moral" authority, and so she could offer only scant comfort to her sons.

According to the authorized biography, Elias Disney flew into rages at the slightest provocation, and when he did he "struck out with whatever was in his hand—a length of board, the handle of a hammer. Walt learned to run when he saw such outbursts coming."[13] Walt Disney remembers that the beatings he received from his father stopped when he was fourteen. His authorized biography recounts,

> One day Elias upbraided Walt for not handing him a tool fast enough. Walt's temper was as hot as his father's, and he replied sharply. Elias accused him of impertinence and ordered him to the basement for a thrashing. . . . When Walt reached the basement, his father was still in a rage, and he swung a hammer handle. Walt grabbed it away. Elias raised his hand to strike the boy. Walt held him by both wrists, and his father could not escape. Tears began to appear in Elias's eyes. Walt loosened his grip and climbed the stairs. His father never tried to thrash him again.[14]

As heroic as young Walt Disney's behavior is in the above passage—he becomes his own hero, a self-made man who makes himself by standing up to the father's violence, a common theme in the Disney myth—something else about the anecdote remains chilling. The anecdote innocently reveals the nature of the relationship between Elias Disney and his son. The father has, up until the son's fourteenth year, beat his son for "impertinence." Just what amounts to impertinence is, for the child, undoubtedly a mystery and more often than not a fairly relative matter. In other words, the adult decides when and where an offense has been committed. Furthermore, the anecdote recounts the nature of the thrashing—far from a "corrective" encounter between adult and wayward child, the anecdote reveals that Elias Disney flew into towering rages that justified not just spankings, but brutalizations with the *handle of the hammer.* There is every reason to believe that, except for the son's resistance in the above passage, the anecdote represents one of the many ways in which the father used the child to exercise his fear, rage, and desire for power, all because he detected a disrespectful tone in the voice of his son. Again, the anecdote informs indirectly that what Elias Disney heard in his son's voice was *the father's anger,* for "Walt's temper was as hot as his father's." Rage transmits itself generationally through relationships of violence and oppression. Ironically, one of Elias Disney's ostensible motives in beating his sons was to secure the respect "due" the father.

Walt Disney's experience of violence at the hands of his father was nothing less than the traumatizing effort of ideology as it ploughed itself into his body via the lived relationship between the adult and the child. The ideological justification for Elias Disney's child-rearing practices—filled as they were with the unconscious rage from his *own* violent experiences as the "other" while a child—was all around him in his culture, in its celebrated history, and in the story the dominant culture told to itself about itself in places like the Chicago World's Columbian Exposition of 1893: power is order, violence is progress, domination is civilization.

Because ritualized child abuse always comes with adult ideological justification, Walt Disney, like every abused child, had a vested interest in learning the ways and means of adult violence if only to defend him against it. And because he was taught explicitly and implicitly that his behavior specifically set in motion the events that led up to his pain and suffering, Disney frequently worked all the harder to learn the required "proper" behavior—usually amounting to absolute submission as a slave submits to his master—and so avoid the need for more adult "correction."

In this way Disney learned the father's ideology and at the same time learned its existential nature, for rage rarely follows a set pattern, at least not for the young victim, since the causes of the adult's rage lie beneath the adult's level of awareness and so remain unavailable to the awareness of the child. Even the child's emotional release—so crucial for healthy development—when faced with violence quite often represents for the adult a sign of willfulness, so the child learns to swallow it and save his life for the moment, for the adult promises to "give the child something to cry about" if the crying does not cease. The autocratic adult often takes as much pleasure in the ability to control the child's internal, emotional life as he does in his ability to manipulate and terrorize the child's body.

Walt Disney would never completely escape from the physical and emotional trauma of his childhood. Rather, he would revisit it time and again as a young adult and later in his idealization of his childhood in his films, his theme parks, and his own California estate. Even so, Walt Disney's work in the entertainment industry remained unconscious of its psychodynamic origins. He preferred to idealize the past rather than understand it. As a result, a large portion of adult culture and the stories adult culture tells itself about the child are devoted to the concretization of the anger and powerlessness adult expresses through his lived relation with the child.[15]

The point that bears repeating is this: ideological transposition takes place as a lived relation first and foremost between the adult and the child, even in the most mundane acts of parenting. When this relationship is a lived relation of violence—and given the dominant ideology that informs child-rearing practices, child-rearing is essentially a lived relation of violence—ideology interpolates the child's body and the child's mind simultaneously. Paulo Freire speaks to the ubiquitous and therefore invisible nature of violence in *The Pedagogy of the Oppressed*. His definition of violence and oppressive relationships informs my argument. Freire writes,

> Any situation in which "A" objectively exploits "B" or hinders his and her pursuit of self-affirmation as a responsible person is one of oppression. Such a situation in itself constitutes violence, even when sweetened by false generosity, because it interferes with the individual's ontological and historical vocation to be more fully human. With the establishment of a relationship of oppression, violence has *already* begun. Never in history has violence been initiated by the oppressed. How could they be the initiators, if they themselves are the result of violence? How could they be the sponsors of something whose objective inauguration called forth their existence as oppressed? There would be no oppressed had there been no prior situation of violence to establish their subjugation.[16]

He goes on to explain that violence is initiated by those who oppress, by those who fail to recognize others as persons. Elias Disney took power over his child's body and in the process implicitly said, "this violence is right, this violence is good. My right to use you to vent my rage is complete." The child's spontaneous response of fear, outrage, and shame often makes no difference to the hierarchical structure of the relationship between adult and child, and in fact, the child suspects, the child's emotional responses to the adult's rage are in part the *cause* of his treatment, or so the adult encourages the child to believe. In this way, then, the adult effectively thwarts the child's vocation to become more fully human and encourages the child to believe that he has, in fact, initiated the violence through, say, his "impertinence." Long before the first beating, then, violence has already begun between Elias Disney and his child, for the adult has already been interpolated by an ideology of oppression in which, as Freire says, "to be is to be like the oppressor." In other words, to be an effective parent one must oppress one's children and call it something else and sweeten the child's submission with rewards that identify it as "good behavior."

DISNEY AS IDEOLOGICAL TRANSPOSITION

When the "golden era" of Disney full-length animated films came to an end in 1942 with the release of *Bambi,* it did so in part because of the enormous costs involved in animating full-length feature films and in part because the government had impressed the Disney studios into wartime service. Though Disney initially chafed at the government's request, his ability to produce propaganda on time and under budget led to steady income. Steady income was important for Disney studios, for though Walt Disney had found popular fame as a cartoonist and film-maker, financial security continued to elude him. Costs and cost overruns plagued the studio and hampered his efforts to realize his "artistic" vision. For instance, when it was released in February 1940 at a cost of three million dollars, *Pinocchio* was the most expensive animated film ever made. As such, the film was an enormous risk for Disney and the Disney studios, which could ill afford a box office flop.

The production costs of *Pinocchio* were, for Disney, labor costs, and because Disney was unwilling to pay his animators according to Hollywood scale, or in many cases give them artistic credit for their work, 293 animators finally went on strike late in May 1941. After months of bitter negotiation and ill will, Roy Disney finally settled the strike by agreeing to binding arbitration in the matter. Yet for Walt Disney things were not so easily settled because for him the strike had been a personal act of betrayal by disloyal and ungrateful "children." Soon after the strike Disney fired the ringleaders of the walkout and then contacted the chairman of the Joint Fact-Finding Committee on Un-American Activities. Disney urged him to investigate the other strikers of the studio. Apparently the desire for decent labor conditions and fair wages was, according to Disney, simply "un-American."

Walt Disney's management style reproduced the domineering relationship he had come to understand as the norm between the authority and those that served "under" him. According to Friz Freleng, a one-time employee of Disney studios, Walt Disney understood that invoking ideas like "family" and "loyalty" in his relationship to his staff helped to offset the hard work, long hours, and low pay that he offered. Yet, in spite of Disney's insistence that everybody on the staff was one big, happy, loyal family, according to Freleng, Disney was in reality a "harsh taskmaster, severe and not always reasonable in his criticism. The many early defections were the result of his highstrung temperament and his inability to work harmoniously with his men."[17] Disney's management style lead to frequent labor defections, including the famous labor stoppage at Disney studios in 1941. When repeatedly prevented by Walt Disney from organizing as a collective bargaining unit, the studio's animation team—the most successful artists in the studio's history, having produced the critically well-received full-length animated films *Snow White, Pinocchio, Bambi, Dumbo,* and *Fantasia*—were attacked publicly and privately by Walt Disney as disloyal to him and, by extension, to their country. Even before a strike settlement was reached Walt Disney publicly accused each of being a Communist. For the next several years those responsible for organizing the work stoppage at the studio "were subjected to relentless investigation by the FBI and suffered irreparable damage to both their reputations and careers."[18] Marc Eliot, Disney's unauthorized biographer, describes Disney's state of mind this way:

> Walt Disney believed the strike leaders had committed a profoundly immoral act against the studio. His Midwest Fundamentalist father had brought him up to believe that loyalty to the head of a family was the truest test of one's character. To disobey one's father was an act of immorality that brought disgrace upon the head of the family.[19]

Walt Disney's animators were his "boys" and he was the paterfamilias. When they dared to question his treatment of them, rather than look at their claims, he reacted as an outraged and betrayed father, visiting upon them the institutional vengeance that he knew would destroy them. Arthur Babbitt and Dave Hilberman, both reputed to be the most talented animators in Hollywood at the time, were chiefly responsible for the work stoppage of 1941. After the labor conflict, Babbitt and Hilberman were fired and their names stricken from studio histories, as an example of what happens to those accused of disloyalty: annihilation. Yet this was nothing new for Walt Disney, because this kind of behavior was what those in authority did to their "children." In firing Babbitt and Hilberman and declaring them nonpersons, Walt Disney reproduced what his father had done to his children decades before.

The oldest Disney brothers, Herbert and Raymond, disappeared one night from the family farm, tired of the overwork required by their father. Rather than simply announce their decision to move out and move on, however, they felt it necessary to escape in the night out their bedroom window. Perhaps this was a display of histrionics on their part, or perhaps it reflects the degree to which the two brothers felt imprisoned by a power greater than themselves. In any event, when Elias Disney discovered that his two farm hands had abandoned him and their family, he decreed that their names should never be spoken again in the Disney home. Herbert and Raymond Disney became nonpersons by protesting with their actions the treatment they received from their father. When Babbitt and Hilberman protested Walt Disney's autocratic management style, Walt Disney unconsciously reproduced what he had witnessed as a boy regarding power, authority, and reality. The father decides who exists and who does not.

Disney's need to control all of those around him is legendary. He felt it his moral obligation to help "clean up" Hollywood and offered himself as a domestic spy to the FBI in 1940. Disney was angered by what he considered Hollywood's dismissal of his success up to 1940, and he blamed this in part on those he believed to be in control of Hollywood: Jews. Disney's assignment as a domestic spy "was to report on the activities of Hollywood actors, writers, producers, directors, technicians, and union activists the FBI suspected of political subversion. Disney perceived his FBI commission not only as his patriotic duty but as his high moral obligation."[20]

In 1938 *Pinocchio* was in production, and the high cost of producing full-length animated features continued to threaten the long-term security of Disney studios. Moreover, the severely depressed economic climate of the country had taken a heavy toll on labor morale, both at Disney studios and elsewhere. The political and ideological status quo was being seriously questioned. Labor unrest was common. Some even feared political collapse. It was in this climate that some powerful Americans found Hitler's fascism and his anti-Semitism appealing. The social order might be restored, Hitler promised, if the root cause of the social problem was addressed, and this made sense to Disney, for Disney believed himself to be on the losing end of a Jewish conspiracy to keep him from success in Hollywood. One critic writes that during the months of production on *Pinocchio,*

> Uncle Walt regularly attended meetings of the American Nazi Party in Hollywood, where *Mein Kampf* sold like hotcakes at corner newsstands. It comes as no surprise that Nazism resonated with Disney: he shared its conceit of white supremacy, its antagonism towards independent organized labor, its abhorrence of urbanism, and, above all, its hatred of Jews. He regarded himself as a bastion of Protestant morality in an industry dominated by Jew-spawned frivolity and lewdness.[21]

The point here is that the economic and cultural unrest of the Great Depression intensified already existing racist ideologies that had been generationally transmitted from the Victorian era to the period of the Great Depression. Fascism was in the air because it had *always* been in the air. To the conservative business owner, like Henry Ford, the Jews represented a constant threat to the ideological notion of Anglo-Saxon cultural and racial superiority. Henry Ford's publications, including The *International Jew,* and his newspaper, the *Dearborn Gazette,* were dedicated to, among other things, anti-Semitic propaganda. In *Explaining Hitler,* Ron Rosenbaum argues that Henry Ford's anti-Semitism, and perhaps his financial backing, helped Hitler come to power in Germany. Rosenbaum writes that,

> it's remarkable how easily—or conveniently—Ford's contribution to Hitler's success has been lost to memory in America. It wasn't lost to Hitler, who demonstrated his gratitude by placing a life-size oil portrait of the American carmaker on the wall of his personal office in party headquarters in Munich and by offering, in the twenties, to send storm troopers to America to help Ford's proposed campaigning for the presidency. The worldwide publication of Ford's vicious anti-Semitic tract, *The International Jew,* which Hitler and the Nazis rhapsodically read, promoted, and distributed in Germany, the influence of Ford's work and fame—he was an icon of the Modern Age in Germany—helped validate for a gullible German public Hitler's malignant vision of the sinister "Elders of Zion" Jewish conspiracy.[22]

Anti-Semitism was alive and well in the twenties and thirties in America as well as Germany, and it comes as no surprise that a man like Disney might seek a moral scapegoat for the nation's—and for his studio's—troubles. In fact, the motion picture industry in Hollywood had from its beginning been marred by the anti-Semitism of other famous Americans, including Thomas Edison, who orchestrated anti-Semitic pogroms against Jewish-owned nickelodeons in 1912 because they threatened his monopolistic control over the means of film production. Like Ford, Edison characterized his hatred of Jews as a love for America.[23]

When *Fantasia* was in production in 1940, Walt Disney had an opportunity to ask one of the most successful businessmen of his day, Henry Ford, whether he should sell public stock in his studio. Disney worried about losing control to countless stockholders, and the thought of losing total control made him uneasy. Ford admired both Mickey Mouse and his creator. Walt held Ford in equally high esteem, and the two men developed a lasting friendship. Ford admired Disney because he was a successful self-made Protestant in a field dominated by Jews. Still, Ford explained, because the stock market, like the film business, was controlled by Jews, Disney ought to sell his entire company outright before losing it to "them," piece by piece. Disney took Ford's advice quite seriously and thanked him for his words of wisdom.

Pinocchio represents Walt Disney's own conscious racism combined with the own unconscious internalization of the ideological social order of Elias Disney's Victorian America—that is, of the dominant culture—all of which had been intensified and popularized indirectly by the social unrest of the Great Depression. The fascist agenda of *Pinocchio* should come as no surprise, though for many it does, simply because of the ideological static that interferes when one attempts to seriously consider a "children's" film as a product of cultural and ideological processes. Even a cursory examination, however, reveals stereotypes at work that were, for Disney and many others, central to the idea of a Christian and wholesome nation.

The moral forces that conspire against Pinocchio are, among other things, a short list of the enemies of Hitler's Germany. Consider the "mannered, effeminate, urbane" theater-loving Fox. He is a dissolute and immoral character of the theater, and with his partner, the Cat, who "constantly slithers around him and through his legs," represents the stereotype of the theater-loving homosexual, a danger to the child and to the state. Stromboli, who buys Pinocchio, is the most obvious racial stereotype in the film. He represents the "Gypsy," and as such he is inhumane, greedy, dishonest, and violent. Finally, there is the stereotype of the Jew, who appears as a "cruel businessman who deals from a shadowy corner of a restaurant on a dark and foggy city street— so greedy and evil that he scares even The Fox and The Cat" (Roth, p. 18). Homosexuals, gypsies, and Jews lead the naive, vulnerable, and *incompletely invented* Pinocchio away from his proper vocation—school—and instead, lead him and other foolish children to possible destruction by tempting them with *pleasure*. Pleasure is wrong. Suffering is right. So, Disney makes sure that Pleasure Island appears as a kind of nightmare world:

> The atmosphere is dark and crowded, dense and full of movement—in short, city-like. The urban vice is there: Pinocchio and a pug-faced boy hang out in a pool hall. The Communism is there: the main attraction is a mansion that the boys are allowed to demolish in an orgiastic attack on private property. The degradation follows: the boys, having made asses of themselves figuratively, become literal donkeys. . . . That *Pinocchio* could, nonetheless, very well have served as a Hitler Youth training film is not simply a reflection of Uncle Walt's devotion to National Socialism. Rather, he and Hitler— as well as countless other corporate leaders, government planners, architects, cultural purveyors and social thinkers in Europe and America— shared an overall social vision. They dreamed of a dispersed post-urban society, with a population—kept in line by a strong domestic realm instilling a keen sense of blood loyalty and "family values"—that could be efficiently mobilized to serve either the military needs of the state or the labor needs of industry.[24]

When *Pinocchio* evokes its intended emotional response, it does so by drawing on the child's—or the child within the adult's—fear of having failed the adult and the dominant culture, and of becoming an ass as a result of "childish" greed. There is no appropriate emotional need in *Pinocchio* except the need of the child to save the father. Pinocchio's incomplete status as a construction of his father's lonely imagination can only be completed by a show of obsequious submission to Gepetto, after which the world is set aright and the puppet becomes a real boy. Yet, ironically, the story presents growing up as a process by which the child learns to submit to the dominant ideology even as the dominant ideology interpolates the child. This, and only this, is how one becomes "real."

"Indeed," one critic writes, "when projected through the lens of Disney's psyche, Pinocchio reveals a powerful Fundamentalist underpinning: the quest for self-redemption and the hellish fate that awaits those who lack the inner strength to resist the inherent evils of pleasure." *Pinocchio* represented Walt Disney's most primal Fundamentalist belief in the need for the individual will to triumph over itself and become one with the dominant ideology. For this sacrifice of pleasure, "one will be rewarded in the next life for the abstinence, hard work, and loyal devotion in this one." As much as *Pinocchio* represented Walt Disney's own personal journey through his childhood, it also reflects the anxiety brought about by the cultural events of the 1930s. As a story of childhood that resonates with the fear of the times, Walt Disney's version of *Pinocchio* had been so changed from Carlo Lorenzini's original text—an already problematic narrative—that when Lorenzini's surviving nephew saw the three-million-dollar blockbuster, he "tried and failed to sue the studio for libel."[25]

Propaganda, it seems, was well suited to Walt Disney and his creative process. Even before World War II, he, his wife, and a large entourage made a trip to South America to gather the material required to complete a government propaganda project inspired by the "Good Neighbor Policy," a foreign policy intent on wooing the loyalty of the Western Hemisphere even as Europe began to tumble towards chaos in 1940 and early 1941. The propaganda films commissioned by the Coordinator of Inter-American Affairs would "carry the message of democracy and friendship below the Rio Grande" in an attempt to address "any remaining tensions with South American governments in order to maintain hemispheric unity as a bulwark against foreign invasion."[26] Disney had already distinguished himself as a producer of government propaganda "couched in the simplicity of the animation medium," and so he seemed the logical choice to show the "truth of the American way" to South America."[27] The material Disney and his staff collected south of the border "was eventually rendered into nearly two dozen films, both shorts and features, both educational and escapist, both—in the prevailing terminology—"direct and indirect propaganda." There are three films that represent Disney's cross-cultural experience: *South of the Border with Disney* (1941), *Saludos Amigos* (1943), and, in particular, *The Three Caballeros* (1945).[28]

When World War II began, the military commandeered Disney studios as a munitions dump and west-coast defense post. Soon after, Disney shifted production to wartime propaganda, although a third of his artists had been drafted. Even so, he managed to produce ten times as much film footage during the war years as he did prior to 1941. He did this by working his employees six days a week, ten and twelve hours a day. Alcoholism, apparently, was common among his employees. Moreover, many of Disney's artists report that they feared for their livelihoods when they heard Walt Disney approach them as they worked.[29] He was quixotic, sullen, and unpredictable, according to those who worked for him, and if he felt personally challenged or slighted by an employee's competing vision for a project—manifested by an off-hand or otherwise professional remark about a story board or a design layout— Disney would end his personal and professional association with that artist. Disney expected loyal, obedient, submissive employees and he employed only those men who would follow his vision to the letter.

The financial risks of running his studio as a military dictatorship constantly threatened its solvency. For example, in 1942, the studio worked to complete an animated film version of Alexander de Seversky's *Victory through Air Power* at a tremendous pace, for Disney had to produce and release the movie in record time if he was to successfully influence war policy. To do so, Disney personally financed the animated feature. The movie failed to return a profit. "The curious appeal," Richard Schickel writes,

> of strategic air power to people of rightist political leanings has never been analyzed, though it is perhaps not amiss to note that any philosophy that views the human aggregate as a mob incapable of choosing its own destiny and therefore in need of totalitarian leadership can easily be stretched to accommodate a certain indifference to massive, unselective destruction of that inconvenient mob . . . Peremptory aggressiveness at long range and in a manner that spares one the sight of the suffering it causes is a way of "getting the boys back home" quickly.[30]

Disney's obsession with the notion of air power and the long-range bombing that air power provided for was the perfect expression of technological innovation: efficient war. "Air power was, to him, efficient . . . Disney loved efficiency."[31] *Victory through Air Power* was an homage to the technological progress Western culture had made—for it documented the ever increasing efficiency of aircraft to carry bombs. Walt Disney was excited about dramatizing Seversky's book, for like Seversky, Disney recognized that "every thing advances in wartime."[32] War forces technological innovations. Or, in more accurate terms, wars of conquest and destruction spawn more efficient means of conquest and destruction. This cycle thrilled Disney, though he understood the cycle differently. For him, war was a given, and to win, advanced weapons of mass destruction were required. The most efficient means to kill was the surest way to peace, or at least that was Disney's thinking, and the fact that Disney's thinking continues to remain an established "fact" in the dominant political culture of American foreign policy speaks to the enduring influence of his *Victory through Air Power*. It might be said, then, that though Disney lost close to a half-million dollars of his own money financing the production of the film, his investment paid off over the long run, for *Victory through Air Power* represented the story of air power as the story of war and the many military technological innovations that it gives rise to. Like so many Disney films, *Victory through Air Power* is the story of power and the need to constantly reproduce the cultural conditions that would lead to technological innovations. *Victory through Air Power* is the quintessential arms-race propaganda film, for in it Disney depicts war as a *felix culpa,* since war results in the ever-more-efficient means to wage war, and this, for Disney, is worth celebrating.

Wartime production of propaganda films began when the U.S. Naval Bureau of Aeronautics asked Walt Disney to make twenty animated training films. The films taught audiences how to kill mosquitoes, how to pay their taxes, how to rivet sheet metal, how to fire an antitank gun, how to spot an enemy plane, and how to think about the Germans. Anti-Nazi propaganda was a common theme in Disney animated shorts. They included lessons in the evils of mass hysteria, the brainwashing tactics used by Germans to convert their youth into Nazis, and, most famous of all, how to laugh at the Fuehrer's face. Disney managed to profit from government contracts, though only barely, because he brought most of his wartime films in on time and under budget. Disney accepted his role as wartime propagandist with a patriotic élan, believing on the one hand that it was his duty to serve his country. Yet, on the other hand, the studio's mounting debt almost certainly motivated him as well, for government contracts represented a fairly steady, if marginal, profit. After the war some accused Disney of profiting from it which, in relative terms, remains accurate; whereas Disney complained of the government's invasion of his studio in 1941, his was one of the few studios in Hollywood at the time to receive compensation for its war time efforts.[33] His efforts were further rewarded when the 1943 release of the Donald Duck cartoon, "Der Fuehrer's Face," quickly won an Academy Award and propelled Walt Disney into the public eye as a true wartime patriot.

At the same time, Disney identified himself as a Hollywood conservative to be feared when he became vice president and one of the founding members of the Motion Picture Alliance for the Preservation of American Ideals. In one of his first acts for the organization, Disney wrote a letter to North Carolina Senator Robert R. Reynolds, urging the House Un-American Activities Committee to intensify its presence in Hollywood.

THE MAGIC KINGDOM

Even though Disney Studios was, for some, a sweatshop, and even though Walt Disney's politics were quasi-fascist, and even though a film like *Pinocchio* said as much, audiences remained captivated by Disney animation, though not enough to secure the studio a sure financial footing until well after the war years. In 1940 a writer for the *Atlantic Monthly* visited Disney studios and wrote a story that represented an idealized portrait of both the audience and the movie maker. In "Genius at Work: Walt Disney," Paul Hollister takes the reader on a tour of Disney's animation studio on an average day.[34] More than anything else, Hollister is grateful for Mickey Mouse. From his first appearance in the 1928 *Steamboat Willie* to his most recent animated short in 1940, Mickey Mouse had been a loyal and optimistic companion through the Great Depression; for this, and really for this alone, Hollister implies Disney should be canonized. The story of Mickey Mouse is, according to Hollister, the story of Disney's creative brilliance. In reality, Hollister's story is the story Disney promoted about himself to himself and to anyone else who cared to listen. As a result, Hollister's history of Disney leaves out the brilliant men, including Ub Iwerks and Arthur Babbitt who were largely responsible for Disney animation, Disney music, and many of the Disney characters, *including Mickey Mouse.* According to Hollister, however, Disney created Mickey Mouse "just as you would create Niagara Falls, the Tehachapi Mountains, the Panama Canal, or the Hope Diamond" (p. 40). In short, Mickey Mouse—and by extension, Walt Disney—is a kind of creative God, reigning over one of the great wonders of the world. Hollister's article represents what would come to characterize the Disney myth through the century, and at its most intense it remains nothing short of a cult of personality. And this is how Walt Disney would have it.

Iwerks's surviving relatives, however, tell a different story. Fresh from losing his first animated cartoon character, Oswald the Lucky Rabbit, to his eastcoast distributor, Charlie Mintz, in 1928, Disney returned to Los Angeles in need of a new cartoon character. Iwerks, a long-time partner, friend, and associate of Disney, immediately came up with a mouse character. Disney's wife named him "Mickey." Nevertheless, in the making of the Disney story, Disney cast himself as the grandiose hero of his own cosmic drama, and the Disney story informs Hollister's story. Consider the rhetoric of the following passage. Hollister writes,

> Up around Disney's place, it is only a stone's throw from *Steamboat Willie* to Leopold Stokowski, Deams [sic] Taylor, Ludwig van Beethoven, Johann Sebastian Bach, and Creation. Mickey's first sound voice in *Steamboat Willie* was Walt Disney's voice, and so it is as Mickey plays the Sorcerer's Apprentice in *Fantasia*, and so it has always been and, please God, may it always be. (p. 26)

Hollister's unqualified praise might be explained as the effusive bombast of a more "innocent" time, but characterizing Hollister's "past" as innocent and naive suggests that later audiences have become more critical, less trusting, and more aware. Though intellectual inquiry into Disney past and present has increased over the past two decades of the twentieth century, so, too, have the Disney corporation's profits, its theme parks, and its continuing vision to build a new world order according to Walt Disney's original suburban, Victorian vision. Celebration, Florida, a Disney-owned development, is one of the most blatant—yet seemingly invisible—examples of Disney quasi-fascist culture manifesting itself as the "American Dream" to date. Even so, there appears to be no end to some consumers' need to revere Disney (the man and the corporation) as a cultural icon, as a reproductive site of the moral and the good, and as a teacher of children. Nevertheless, Disney's rise to icon status represents, among other things, the ongoing, deep-seated emotional need so many Americans continue to have for an idealized childhood, complete with an idealized father figure to call their own. When all is said and done, Disney and Disney films—both yesterday and today—remind us of how wonderful it was to be dominated, and how, after all, the domination of the weak is an obvious and necessary fact of life.

The Disney myth softens the naked violence of the predatory relationship yet retains its basic structure, for in their attempt to keep the audience "Mickey Minded," Roy and Walt Disney inadvertently stumbled across the formula for economic success that would come to dominate children's culture through television and film in the latter half of the twentieth century. The formula goes something like this: if the child can be made to understand that his emotional need is not a symptom of incomplete human relationship, but rather represents an a priori psychological state, and if the child's emotional needs can be coded as a *cause* to consume, and if consumption can be dramatized as an obvious and appropriate way of meeting emotional need, and if the dominant culture represents Disney and consumption and childhood as one cultural event, then the child's consumer needs—and those of the adults that children bring with them—might be manipulated accordingly. The most effective means of assuring a Disney future lay in the idealization of the past, both historic and personal. For when the child is separated from his or her own emotional process by child-rearing techniques that prevail in the dominant culture, and when the dominant culture then celebrates the psychological consequences of those techniques as inevitable "facts of life," the child is vulnerable to ideological lessons that fuse consumption, patriotism, and emotional need into an imaginary—ideologically determined—self. Disney theme parks enact this story seamlessly.

Disneyland is a manifestation of the power of "a small number of cynical men who base their domination and exploitation of the 'people' on a falsified representation of the world which they have imagined in order to enslave other minds by dominating their imaginations." In other words, Disneyland offers a nostalgic, unreal reality that confirms the "real" reality outside of the park. Yet this "real" reality outside of the park is no more real than Sleeping

Beauty's castle. All are products of the dominant culture, the one giving rise to the other in a mutually reinforcing process that reproduces ad infinitum the imaginary nature of the relationship between the adult and the child as an idealized and peaceful story of domination, subjugation, and consumption. As such, the imaginary relationship in and out of the park "underlies all the imaginary distortion that we can observe."[35]

Consider a specific example of how ideology functions to confirm itself: Robert De Roos wrote about a 1963 visit to Disneyland in a *National Geographic* article entitled, "The Magic Worlds of Walt Disney." Like Paul Hollister's, De Roos's article is an homage to the innocent genius of Walt Disney. In an especially revealing moment, De Roos describes his visit to Main Street, USA, misnaming it the "Town Square." Clearly, De Roos has his own unconscious agenda. He sees what he needs to see. His visit to the "town square" of Disneyland is, according to De Roos, a step "right into Walt Disney's childhood: the square with its redbrick Victorian elegances is a distillation of Walt's early memories of Chicago and Marceline and Kansas City shortly after the turn of the century."[36] De Roos forgets to mention that Walt Disney was not born until 1901 and could not consciously remember Victorian America at the turn of the century. Yet, in one way De Roos is absolutely correct. Disneyland's Main Street, USA represents a moment of *transposition* in which Walt Disney's father's idealized past—witnessed by Elias Disney at the 1893 World's Columbian Exposition—and re-presented by Walt Disney as his and the consumer's need to remember a more "innocent " time, if only for the price of admission.

Though De Roos represents Main Street as the heart and soul of Disneyland, nevertheless, he remains unable to recognize Main Street's chief end—merchandising—as significant. Rather, Main Street "is a place for strolling. People stop to peer into the windows of the apothecary shop and the old-time general store, and to look over the shoulder of a sidewalk artist as he sketches a portrait." Almost thirty years later in *Inside the Mouse,* Susan Willis and Jane Kuenz documented their experience at Walt Disney World, Florida's bigger, more aggressive reproduction of Southern California's Disneyland. Unlike De Roos's celebratory article from 1963, Kuenz and Willis bring a resistant awareness to their visit to the theme park. What they discover, to their surprise, is the park's hypnotic power that directs all activities towards one end: consumption. Willis writes,

> Imagine my surprise—resolute antishopper that I am—when I found myself hypnotically drawn into Disney World's gigantic shopping mecca. Armed with notepad and pen, I had set out to research the tourists: follow them, watch them, record their conversations. But here I was handling the merchandise. And in so doing, I was actively participating in the construction of one of Disney's themed environments. I might have shopped all day had I

not run into my companion in research. We had separated earlier: she to take
photos and me to take notes, only to find ourselves staring at each other
across a rack of Colombian textiles. (p. 40)[37]

Willis and Kuenz observe that in Walt Disney World "every item of merchandise is equally and simultaneously a stage prop whose combined effect is the
creation of a themed environment more total than anything one finds in a
[retail clothing store] but equally vague in its references to real places and
cultures" (p. 40).

The Disney theme parks represent sites of cultural reproduction in that
the wildly successful merchandising that goes on at the parks can only
succeed if the visitor recognizes, albeit unconsciously, the cultural codes
deployed in the park. The magic of the Magic Kingdom then "depends on the
baggage of ideological assumptions the visitor brings into the park and finds
activated in Disney's display of merchandise. . . . These shoppers fully participate in the ideology of global capitalism, for which the duties of citizenship
are equated with the practice of shopping" (pp. 40–43). The Magic Kingdoms
in California and Florida—and Japan and France—reproduce an intensified
representation of the dominant culture as an all-out passionate orgy of consumption, justified in the name of "vacation," "leisure," and "family." Using
these familiar and ostensibly innocent signifiers, the Magic Kingdom celebrates the practice of consumerism by emotional appeals to cultural, historical, and *personal* nostalgia for the "lost" innocence of "childhood" made real
again for the price of admission, for the price of Disney merchandise. To own
a Disney toy is to claim the right "to be a kid again," but not just any kid in
any childhood story. To own a Disney toy is to own a cultural artifact that
trails clouds of ideological fog that allows the visitor to consume and forget
the real conditions of existence for an idealized past that never existed.

Ironically, in buying and owning a piece of Disney merchandise, say, for
instance, a Mickey Mouse pencil, a Donald Duck bank, a Goofy hat, or a
Minnie Mouse shirt, one holds the material consequence of the real conditions of existence in one's hands. At the same time, however, the consumer
bears unconscious testimony to the blinding power of ideology, for in holding
Disney merchandise one holds the story of labor exploitation—often
exploitation of child labor—in one's hands. Consumer capitalism as the Disney corporation currently practices it cannot function without cheap,
exploited overseas labor, labor that frequently amounts to indentured slavery
justified by "market" forces, forces that Disney gladly exploits and reproduces. Ideology makes this story unavailable to the consumer who loves all
things Disney. Disney's ideal consumer remains caught up in the "magic" of
childhood, intent on the need to forget and, like Disney himself, intent on
tranquilizing his own suffering through the consumption of merchandise.

Disney has become the dominant ideology and so when Disney invites the consumer to indulge his need to tranquilize unconscious emotional suffering through consumption, it seems as though the entire world offers the same invitation. Although the consumption of Disney merchandise—say, a McDonald's "Happy Meal" that comes with a "free" Disney toy—is coded as innocent childhood fun, it nevertheless amounts to using and reproducing the suffering of others to assuage one's own suffering. For example, a lifetime of mindless consumption of McDonald's beef is, of course, deadly to Brazilian rain forests, the long-range Brazilian economy, and the global habitat, as well as the human coronary system. The Disney toy that so often accompanies the child's hamburger, fries, and soda makes the meal "happy," or so the child is told in a continuous barrage of ideological indoctrination. Consumption leads to happiness, or so Disney, McDonald's, and other multinational corporations would have the child believe.

Disney consumerism rather than overt signs of militarism, signals the continued existence of colonialism's hierarchical relationship in terms of economic domination and economic subjugation, all in the name of childhood. As Willis and Kuenz note, "While Disney's one world consumerist mall depicts a globe depeopled of producers, it sports an abundant population of first world shoppers, who . . . find ourselves free to trade in the signs of multiculturalism" (p. 43), in reality, trade is economic and cultural hegemony of a particularly domineering sort, for consumerism becomes, as Henry Giroux describes it, "the unifying force through which families organize themselves and their relations to others."[38] To remain in relationship to one another in the "spirit" of Disneyland requires the consumer to look no further than the merchandise on the display shelf, for the abundance of consumer goods in the theme parks—and outside the theme parks in the dominant culture that gives rise to and maintains Disney as Disney maintains the cultural status quo—relies increasingly on cultural domination and human exploitation of vulnerable peoples in "undeveloped" societies around the world, many of which serve as labor workhouses that support the ideology of leisure so important to Walt Disney in his vision of a new world order. From this perspective, Disney's Magic Kingdom represents an intensification of the cultural hegemony of the kind manifested in the World's Columbian Exposition of 1893, and made palatable by Disney's specious appeals to the consumer's unconscious emotional longings for more. As such, consumerism becomes the practice of cultural hegemony in the guise of an innocent desire to recover and relive for a moment the spirit of childhood. It should be noted that ideology informs the consumer's relationship to the terms "spirit" and "childhood" so that in purchasing Disney merchandise one reproduces reality itself, albeit a decidedly ideological reality. In the end, say Willis and Kuenz, the consumer participates unconsciously in the practice and the reproduction of "unexamined nationalism and a system of social relations based on consumption. These combine with lesser capitalist virtues conducive to 'progress' and designed to encourage the reproduction of subjects for life in what we are continually told is our future" (pp. 56–57).

The future for Disney lies in the past, but not in just any past. Rather, the future as Disney envisioned it lies in the unreal, idealized past of Victorian America. Walt and Roy Disney fused the dominant culture's rising belief in materialism and helped to teach a generation of children that consumption represented a kind of civic duty and, ultimately, the most salient expression of one's patriotic spirit. Consumption of Disney culture and Disney product's has become an expression of one's love not just for Mickey Mouse, but rather, for Disney's idea of family and for Disney's idea of America, its past, and its future. The technological innovation of Disney full-length films with their dazzling and labor-intensive multiplane animation sequences, and the corresponding technological innovation of Disneyland's world-within-a-world ambience, represent manifestations of American culture which, from the perspective of Walt Disney's mind, constructed as it was from the ideology and child-rearing pedagogy of Victorian America, represents racial and cultural superiority, leading to the inevitable conclusion learned from his father and his father's Victorian culture: the "superior" have a right, even an obligation, to dominate the "inferior" as a latter-day expression of "manifest destiny" and cultural hegemony. Disney's cultural hegemony produces and reproduces itself through a subtle but chronic emotional appeal to the child, invoking the child's unconscious need for adult acceptance and support. The Disney myth coopts the child's needs and offers a simulacrum of emotional acceptance in which the child's unconscious human needs are met with intellectual ideologies that seduce the child into the adult's culture. In the Disney myth the child's happiness remains contingent upon the child's willingness to obey and fulfill his or her duty as described by adult culture, usually figured in Disney films as inexorable forces of nature, as in *The Lion King's* reactionary appeal to the dominant status quo that exists not as an ideology of the father to be resisted, but rather, as an inevitable turning of the "circle of life" that rolls through all things. Simba "grows up" and learns that disobeying the father is *always wrong*. The child must always follow the father's orders or risk excommunication from the community. Simba learns to obey—and the child learns as well—through a narrative that dramatizes how all of the forces of nature conspire—the good guys *and* the bad guys—to teach the child to always obey the father's commands.[39]

THE "NEW" DISNEY

After years of family feuding and financial frailty, Disney Studios shuffled its top management and in 1985 brought in, among others, Jeffrey Katzenberg and Michael Eisner. Soon after, Eisner "revamped the Disney studio's entire operation," and fell back on a formula that had launched Walt Disney fifty years before: full-length animated adaptations of classic fairy tales. Under Eisner's leadership the studio adapted Hans Christian Andersen's fairy tale, "The Little Mermaid," as its signal return to high-quality animated feature film. *The Little Mermaid* was released in 1989, following closely upon the heels of the financially successful *Who Framed Roger Rabbit* in 1988. Though some complained that the studio had "abandoned its creative heritage" with the "new" Disney films of the late 1980s, others pointed at the continuity between the Walt Disney years and Michael Eisner's stewardship. *Roger Rabbit* represented a return to one of Walt Disney's favorite mediums, the mixture of live-action and animation. "A veteran storyman suggested the character of Roger Rabbit looked an awful lot like Walt's original Oswald the Lucky Rabbit. Even Katzenberg couldn't resist telling interviewers how much *Beauty and the Beast* 'owed' to the look, style and approach of *Pinocchio*."[40]

The Disney corporation was, after much negotiation and bitter feuding, officially renamed "The Walt Disney Company," finally settling once and for all the family feud over who was the real motivating force behind the birth and rise of the studio and its entertainment empire. Roy Disney and his heirs had fought aggressively for recognition before and after Walt Disney's death. The company pursued an aggressive program of ideological reclamation, drawing on the mythologized history of Walt Disney and the "golden era" as the source for its "new" identity, and because the public had always identified Walt Disney as the "genius at work," the financially prudent decision was to reify the public myth as a corporate reality. Along with superficial changes to the company's identity, the "new" Disney branched out into retail markets with the Disney Store in 1988 while staking the financial future of its Anaheim park, Disneyland, on a new thrill ride, Splash Mountain. Splash Mountain opened on July 17, 1989, just weeks after *The Little Mermaid* opened in theaters nationwide.[41]

Splash Mountain represents a signal example of ideological transposition, for in Splash Mountain, Disney's 1946 full-length feature, *The Song of the South*, rides again. Even before its release, the film was objected to by minority groups who feared—rightly—that the film would present a callous and backward depiction of African-Americans. As production began in 1943 on *The Song of the South,* Walt Disney announced that his version of Joel Chandler Harris's Uncle Remus tales "would be an epochal event in screen history."[42] Following Walt Disney's announcement, "a newly formed Hollywood organization, the Interracial Film and Radio Guild, expressed concern that the film might portray blacks in a degrading fashion." Angered, Walt Disney declared that the film would be "'a monument to the Negro race' with as much historical impact as *Gone With the Wind*."[43] Objections to the film's depiction of African-Americans continued in 1946 and "at every one of its re-releases in 1956 and 1972." Objections to racial stereotyping in *The Song of the South* have continued since 1946 and the studio has removed the movie from circulation, vowing never to rerelease the film to theaters or on video. Shelving *The Song of the South* presumably represented the Disney Company's acknowledgment that its idealized depiction of the slave-holding American South obfuscated the real conditions of existence for African-Americans both in the South of the nineteenth century and the mid-twentieth century. Moreover, the studio's decision to remove the film from circulation seemed to have been tacit acknowledgment that *The Song of the South* was indeed offensive, though innocent in its offense because Uncle Walt did not, in fact, intend to offend anyone.[44]

The Song of the South was released in Atlanta "four years after *Gone With the Wind*, surely riding that blockbuster's breeze," write Susan Miller and Greg Rode. The movie was publicized exactly as Walt Disney desired, as a "cultural retrieval of important American 'folk literature,' the late nineteenth-century stories of Joel Chandler Harris." The movie opens with a small family—

> a mother, father, and son—in a carriage riding to visit Grandmother, somewhere near Atlanta. Father is teaching the sounds of frogs, and the joy of listening to Uncle Remus's stories, which Son will soon be hearing. But there is clearly tension between Mother and Father, who evidently is in trouble for writing about cotton mills and other political issues in the Atlanta paper.
>
> This "evidently" is important. We cannot, that is, exactly hear the garbled interplay between Mother and Father, presented *sotto voce* to keep it from son Johnny, but simultaneously to mystify and distance adults' troubles from us all. And we never will understand it fully—Father and Mother are simply having trouble, despite their responding to Johnny's "are you mad at each other?" with "of course not's" that were the middle-class norm before family therapy informed such scenes. [45]

The housekeeper at Grandmother's evokes a more benevolent slave-owning era, though Tempy the housekeeper is one of many African-American "retainers of now indeterminate status" in the film, evoking in their metaphoric ambiguity the world of antebellum mansions of *Gone with the Wind*. The "indeterminate" African-American retainers enter periodically to surround the porch of the Big House when its white owners gather and enact a tableau of white, bourgeois benevolence.

The family story of Johnny and his misguided Mother, who desires that he dress, act and play "appropriately," frames the stories told by Uncle Remus to Johnny and his "servant," Toby. The African-Americans "appear more at home out in the surrounding woods, gathered around a communal fire to sing after equally theatrical coming-in-from-the-fields scenes. The African-Americans in *Song of the South* are, precisely, 'happy campers.'"[46] The tales told by Uncle Remus in *The Song of the South* echo Johnny's desire to escape Mother and reflect the larger frame narrative seamlessly: *African-Americans and children are much happier when they know and accept their place in the world.* Appearing only three years after *Pinocchio* and immediately after Walt Disney's propaganda work for the U.S. government, it comes as no surprise that *Song of the South* represents the hierarchical, racist agenda that Walt Disney unconsciously mistook for Protestant largess.

All of this brings us back to Michael Eisner, Splash Mountain, and the "new" Disney. When it came time to design and build a new roller coaster in the Anaheim theme park, Disney Imagineers returned to the Disney archives to locate a narrative that would structure the ride thematically and would at the same time reproduce the so-called magic of Walt Disney's original vision of family entertainment. Designers chose *The Song of the South* as their classic Disney text. The legacy and the narrative of *The Song of the South* live on in Splash Mountain:

> A tour through Splash Mountain is a study in the creation of . . . curtains of fantasy [and] how such curtains serve to shroud from our view the distasteful, brutal, often racist implications that are an inescapable feature of their construction. Such implications are the unavoidable but invisible back weave of the [ideological] fabric.[47]

Inadvertently (or inevitably), Splash Mountain functions as a chronic, ambient site of ideological reproduction and remains a striking representation of the power of ideological transposition. Except present-day "reality" in Disneyland is, as Splash Mountain reveals, nothing more than a collection of past ideologies reified and made "real" through the dazzling technical innovation that codes the subsequent emotional traumatization of the experience as innocent fun. The bitterness of the story is made palatable and ultimately invisible through the theme park's "sweet atmosphere," which serves to make invisible the consumer's indirect participation in what amounts to a celebration of the slave-holding agrarian society of the Deep South. Animatronic characters sing "Zip-a-Dee-Do-Dah" while riding the cutting-edge technology of the nineteenth century, the Mississippi steamboat.[48] It should be noted that the figure of the steamboat includes no animatronic slaves chained on the deck. How could it? The Magic Kingdom is about fun, and reality is simply not "fun." And so, with this specious justification, Splash Mountain makes invisible the real conditions of racial hegemony both in the slave-holding past of the South and in the present, which is a consequence of America's slave-holding past. Splash Mountain—like the Magic Kingdom itself—represents a seemingly innocent example of ideological transposition that codes the ideological hegemony of a culture's racist past as the stuff of innocent family entertainment.

Just as Splash Mountain was drawing record lines in the Magic Kingdom, *The Little Mermaid* announced the return of Disney animation to commercial success with one of its most popular and financially successful feature-length animated films ever. The film is an adaptation of Hans Christian Andersen's literary fairy tale of the same name. And no wonder. Andersen, like Disney, infused his fairy tales "with general notions of the Protestant ethic and essentialist ideas" that confused ideologically determined hierarchy as a "natural biological order." Because Andersen (like Disney) desired nothing more than to be recognized and so receive the bourgeois seal of approval, Andersen wrote fairy tales that flattered the status quo. As a result, his tales were "deemed useful and worthy enough for rearing children of all classes," for the stories implicitly and explicitly teach the inevitable and inexorable "rightness" of hierarchy, class, and the natural superiority of some over others. The dominant, essentialist ideology stands as an invisible justification for the misuse of adult power to maintain, first, adult hegemony over the child and then as a cultural consequence, the misuse of power to maintain subsequent hegemonies of race, class, and gender.[49]

"The Little Mermaid" is typical Hans Christian Andersen, for it preaches to children a lesson of servile obedience, a lesson made real by invoking an emotional trauma related to the child's already unacknowledged state of fear and insecurity, which the tale promises to extend if the child is not "good."[50] The intellectual confusion—and so the splitting of the child's intellect from her body—occurs in part as a result of Andersen's rejection of the body and its pleasures and his celebration of suffering, humiliation, and subjugation as a "blessing" from God. According to Jack Zipes, "desirous of indicating the way to salvation through emulation of the upper classes and of paying reverence to the Protestant ethic, Andersen also showed that this path was filled with suffering, humiliation, and torture—it could even lead to crucifixion." Zipes describes Andersen's fairy tales as a representation of "the creative process of a dominated ego endeavoring to establish a unified self. . . . The fictional efforts are variations on a theme of how to achieve approbation, assimilation, and integration in a social system that does not allow for real acceptance or recognition if one comes from the lower classes."[51] Much of the same might be used to describe Walt Disney's creative vision as well.

Though the Disney Company's adaptation of Andersen's "The Little Mermaid" appears at first to significantly alter the original fairy tale, Andersen's Protestant ideology, which celebrated servile subjugation, remains intact, though it is at war with itself to some degree in Disney's version. Like Andersen's fairy tale, Disney's *The Little Mermaid* dramatizes the hegemony of adult power over the child, especially the sublimation and redirection of emotional need from conscious awareness to unconscious repression.

The Disney film associates Ariel with her collection of human artifacts. It is clear that her desire for human junk suggests her desire to be something other than she is. The manner in which animators depict her secret cave suggests that her longing is in part caught up in her ongoing transition from pubescent girl to biologically mature woman. This the film makes clear, though indirectly, for Ariel's coming of age is dramatized as her transition from mermaid to human, from a girl without legs to a woman with legs. When King Triton discovers his daughter's "secret"—that she is, in fact, on her way to becoming a woman—he explodes in a rage suggesting the violence of an angry father and at the same time, the rage of a jealous, jilted lover.

The father's rage is ostensibly in response to Ariel's interest in a "human." More importantly, however, King Triton—like Mufasa in *The Lion King*—is explicitly concerned about the fact that Ariel deliberately disobeyed his authority. After all, Triton rages, this is *my ocean* and when you live in my ocean *you will obey my rules*. Ariel is a daughter, but first and foremost she is a subject to the king. When one questions the relations of power, violence is justified. Ariel's transgression requires a lesson in terror in order to reestablish the father's authority over the daughter's body, her feelings, and her dreams. It is a lesson taught by violence and rage, and it is a scene that the film never repudiates. The final scene of the film, in which Ariel longs to go ashore and her father transforms her back into a human being, clearly and insistently reproduces the film's overarching ideological conservatism: it is the father's trident that controls the child, her body, and her future. It is his to give away.

King Triton's "correction" of Ariel with his fire-throwing trident is, in some respects, a rape scene. The child's subjugation to the adult—and the female's subjugation to the male—is made real through the violence and the ongoing threat of violence of the adult/father/king. Moreover, the violence that structures and maintains the ideological hierarchy of the relationship between the adult and the child is never questioned in the narrative. Rather, the narrative reproduces the hierarchical, violent nature of the relationship between father and child in Ariel's romanticized and idealized relationship to Prince Eric. In him she has found "true love," when in reality, the latent narrative implies, Ariel has found a man who, like her father, will use violence to maintain his domination and control over her. Prince Eric's ability to destroy the power-wielding female is, after all, the act that wins him King Triton's approval.

Animators modeled Ursula's character on the drag queen, Divine.[52] Adults may find this a subversive gesture on the part of Disney animators, for Ursula's musical number underscores her role in the narrative as an implicit site of ideological resistance to King Triton's status quo. She is a female with male ambition, male anger, and, for a time, male power. When Ursula sings and teaches Ariel how to get a man, she explicitly states that one's identity is a game and that gender is nothing more than a role dictated by the dominant culture. Ursula explicitly suggests that one might learn to manipulate oneself in order to more effectively manipulate others. Ursula is a provocative—and threatening—figure in the movie. She represents a direct challenge to King Triton's essentialist ideology, represented as a depiction of the hypermasculine male hero.

The woman who plays with gender as a tool does so at her own risk, for in challenging King Triton, Ursula implicitly threatens to dethrone the Disney patriarchy. This, finally, the narrative will not allow. When Ursula captures King Triton and his trident as her own, her monstrosity is at last completely revealed. Ursula grows obscenely large and her rage becomes all-consuming. She threatens to consume the world, and only the man from above the sea—Prince Eric—is capable of addressing her threat to the natural order of things. The message here is clear: the father's rule is the rule of the benevolent natural order, whereas the "mother's" rule is perverted, obscene, and tyrannical, a standard component of the Disney myth dating back to *Snow White*. In reestablishing the father's rule, Prince Eric wins the right to marry Ariel because he has revealed himself to be a benevolent father/king/god in his own right. And so after Ursula's death Ariel *returns* to the role of the subjugated daughter, moving from her father's castle under the sea to her husband/father's castle above the sea. This is no hierarchical climb up the ladder for Ariel; rather, her move is a lateral one. She has always been a pawn in the adult's game of power, violence, and revenge.

Ursula-as-octopus-body appears as an oil spill with flaccid, groping tentacles. She is toxic. Yet her power makes her attractive and her disregard for the patriarchal order makes her even more interesting. Her dialogue speaks a truth about the world, that identity is a fiction, that gender is merely a show put on for others, and that Ariel might find her own way by accepting these truths—and these are destabilizing truths to the ideological status quo. Yet Ursula does no favors for her "daughter." As a mother figure Ursula uses seduction as one expression of her murderous rage. She wants to consume Ariel as she has consumed all of her other victims, by tempting them each with what they consider to be the longing of their hearts. Beware, Ursula implicitly seems to say: what you long for is not what you really long for and your ignorance may be used against you.

King Triton's kingdom represents a fractal image of a world within a world, each bearing the imprint of exactly the same ideological hierarchy. The smallest world of *The Little Mermaid* is defined by the margins of King Triton's kingdom. We see this at the beginning of the film where Ariel and her fish companion, Flounder, are preyed upon by a shark, described by Ariel as a "bully" in the fish-eat-fish predatory hierarchy outside Triton's kingdom. One must accept the "civilized" hierarchy of King Triton's kingdom in order to protect oneself from the sharks. King Triton's monarchy is racially hierarchized, the Mer-folk residing at the top of the chain. Sea creatures of assorted varieties serve the Mer-folk as willing and "happy campers," singing and playing all day, as made clear by the love of music so common to the undersea world. Sebastian, the chief of the servants to the white, male Protestant God-King, has a Caribbean accent while his fellow crustaceans are drawn with stereotypical African-American features. It is clear that in King Triton's world, the white, male Protestant rules—by divine as well as contractual right—while the other fish happily support his rule.

King Triton forbids his daughter to have anything to do with the humans, for they represent a callous, consuming species that eats fish. Triton's fear of the human world at first seems to be misplaced, for when the audience meets Prince Eric, it meets a lover of the sea. Clearly Prince Eric feels no personal malice towards the crabs that his chef fricassees. In fact, Prince Eric's human world takes no account of the fish under the sea any more than the Mer-folk concern themselves with the rocks and the ocean water. For the humans, the Mer-folk do not exist, suggesting on the one hand that King Triton is wrong and that the world of Prince Eric is not so barbarous after all, though they *do* eat fish, crabs, and, perhaps the occasional *mermaid.* Yet the human disregard for the world under the sea suggests a sensibility even more sinister than King Triton's racism. The humans as upper-class denizens simply do not *need* to concern themselves about the underclass because the underclass does not exist.[53]

There is every reason to believe that Walt Disney himself would have approved of *The Little Mermaid* as a true Disney classic. In the end it appears that Ariel gets what she wished for. But, in fact, the narrative obfuscates whether or not Ariel has actually found her heart's desire. Freedom is what she initially desired, singing early on in the narrative of a life above the sea as a woman on her own. As a reactionary fairy tale, however, *The Little Mermaid* punishes the girl child for daring to dream such dreams, and uses Ariel's desires to motivate a narrative that does not grant Ariel's wish to be free, but rather, represses and redirects her desire towards a more ideologically appropriate end: the reproduction of the ideological status quo. The narrative does this by conflating Ariel's need for "true love" with her need for freedom. When King Triton finally transforms Ariel into a human female—complete with legs, reproductive organs, and a shimmering dress—he has dressed her for her future as Prince Eric's wife. The narrative transforms Ariel's desire for freedom into her unqualified acceptance of her father's unquestioned authority over her, for she has learned—and the audience has been encouraged to learn with her—that freedom is one and the same with obedience.

The rise of television and the proliferation of mass media formed an almost seamless ideological representation of what the child-consumer already experienced in the lived relations with the adult at home, at school, and elsewhere. Disney capitalized on these technological developments to further expand its market share with the long-running *Mickey Mouse Club* and *The Wonderful World of Disney* and, later, its purchase of the American Broadcasting Company. While all of this was happening, however, one artist began to explore and depict in picture books the child's emotional experience of the world the adult had made for him. Maurice Sendak's seminal picture books—*Where the Wild Things Are, In the Night Kitchen, Outside Overthere,* and *We Are All in the Dumps with Jack and Guy*—tell the child's story from the perspective of an artist who claimed as his greatest inspiration the ability to remember what it was like to be four years old.

NOTES

[1]See Thomas J. Schlereth, *Victorian America: Transformations in Everyday Life, 1876–1915* (New York: HarperPerennial, 1991).

[2]Ibid., pp. 174–75.

[3]Ibid., pp. xv.

[4]Ibid., pp. 169–70.

[5]Ibid., pp. 173.

[6]Louise J. Kaplan, *No Voice Is Ever Wholly Lost: An Exploration of Everlasting Attachment between Parent and Child* (New York: Touchstone, 1996), pp. 223–25.

[7]Ibid., p. 224.

[8]The two men were so close—and Walter Parr trusted Elias's religious judgment to such an extent—that when Reverend Parr was on vacation Elias Disney would take his place behind the pulpit. Elias helped to rebuild and add on to Reverend Parr's church. Walt Disney's older brother, Roy, was born in 1893 and so caught up in the Exposition was Elias Disney that he wanted to name him "Columbus." In a rare moment of influence, Flora Disney prevailed, and they named their second-born son Roy.

[9]The Disney corporation takes great care in preserving the image of Walt Disney. As a result, only one authorized biography of Walt Disney's life has been written, by Bob Thomas: *Walt Disney: An American Original* (New York: Hyperion, 1994). Thomas was given access to Disney archives as well as friends and family of Walt Disney. The unauthorized biography is by Marc Eliot: *Walt Disney: Hollywood's Dark Prince* (New York: Birch Lane Press, 1993). Eliot's biography purports to be a tell-all exposé. Ironically, the authorized biography, though it has more avuncular tone—compared with acidic tone of Eliot's work—tells enough. In Thomas's account are countless examples of the violence that Walt Disney suffered as a boy and then lived out in his relationships with his employees, his family, his friends, and his audiences.

[10]Ibid., p. 31.

[11]Ibid., p. 32.

[12]Eliot, p 7.

[13]Thomas, p. 35.

[14]Ibid., p. 39.

[15]Kaplan writes,

> Affect repressed in childhood does not lead to growth and vitality. The vitality of the child survives, if it survives, in spite of childhood experiences, not because of it. Childhood trauma always resurfaces in the form of adult behavior mediated by character structures—compensatory behaviors learned as a child and given a physical reality by the emotional energy

stored in the body since childhood. In other words, then, the grandiose narcissist who desires to dominate his world might, ironically, succeed, but never from his point of view, for the chronic and unending emotional need will always demand the need for more and ever greater achievements. Moreover, repressed anger and unfelt sadness often turn to depression. (*No Voice*, p. 237)

[16]Paulo Freire, *The Pedagogy of the Oppressed* (New York: Continuum, 1993), pp. 25–38.

[17]From Eliot, p. 35.

[18]Ibid., p. xviii.

[19]Ibid., p. xviii.

[20]Ibid., p. xvii.

[21]The quote and summary come from Matt Roth, "The Lion King: A Short History of Disney Fascism," *Jump Cut* 40 (1994): 15–20. Also compare what was going on in the Disney studios with what was happening in Germany at the time. When Joseph Goebbels and the Nazis took over UFA—the state-owned German film studio—they hired Riefenstahl, a young actress, as a result of a shortage of experienced talent, having lost directors and actors in mass emigrations after the Nazis came to power. Even so, *Triumph of the Will* was released in 1935 and *Olympiad,* her second propaganda epic for Hitler was released in 1938. Both are film triumphs, albeit for a decidedly ruthless cause. *Triumph of the Will* is the story of the Nazi Party at Nuremberg, famous for its images of mass rallies and torchlight processions, and undoubtedly the source for Disney's idea of Nazi "mass hysteria" that he attacked in his cartoons. Unlike Disney studios, Riefenstahl's UFA was state-owned and Hitler poured unlimited resources into it, for he understood the power of a shared story, and the power of film narrative to deliver that story to the people. As a result Riefenstahl had an almost unlimited budget for her productions along with an almost unlimited government demand for propaganda. Of the 1,300 feature films that the Nazi-controlled UFA sponsored, fully 25% were overt propaganda, often of a decidedly anti-Semitic nature. The rest were, as was Disney, caught up in the dominant ideology of the era.

Riefenstahl was born in 1902 and shared a similar parenting experience as a young child—both children experienced what Alice Miller calls "poisonous pedagogy," or what others have called the "black pedagogy." Both worked for their governments when called to do so, and both felt it their moral and political duty to stand for the "truth."

[22]Ron Rosenbaum, *Explaining Hitler: The Search for the Origins of His Evil* (New York: HarperPerennial, 1998), p. xxxix.

[23]Eliot, pp. 48–49.

[24]Ibid., p.16.

[25]Ibid., p. 50.

[26]Allen Woll, *The Latin Image in American Film,* rev. ed. (Los Angeles: UCLA Latin American Center, 1980), p. 55.

[27]Ibid., p. 55.

[28]Julianne Burton-Carvajal, "Surprise Package: Looking Southward with Disney," p. 134, in *Disney Discourse: Producing the Magic Kingdom,* ed. Eric Smooden (New York: Routledge, 1994). See also Richard Schickel, *The Disney Version: The*

Life, Times, Art and Commerce of Walt Disney (New York: Simon & Schuster, 1968), pp. 276–77.

The Three Caballeros represents Disney's most controversial feature-length propaganda piece. *The Three Caballeros* captured and represented the anxious mood of the times as well as the mind of Walt Disney. Schickel writes,

> it is fair to say that the film reflected Disney's own mood. Nothing made sense to him. He had gone, in a decade, from threatened poverty to success of the sort he had dreamed of for many years, then back to a poverty that seemed to promise very little. . . . Disney had certainly been one of the bourgeoizifiers and since he had never really known what he was doing culturally, he, particularly, could not find his roots. Between him and his past he had erected a screen on which were projected only his own old movies, the moods and styles of which he mindlessly sought to recapture cut rate in the bastard cinematic form of the half-animated, half-live action film.

[29]See Thomas, pp. 176–82.

[30]Schickel, pp. 273–74.

[31]Ibid., p. 274.

[32]Quoted in Thomas, p. 184.

[33]According to Eliot, Disney's work for the government was contentious, made difficult by the influx of military control over production. Used to sole control over production, Disney chafed at the military way of doing things even though the military pedagogy so closely matched his own. The most memorable of Disney's propaganda cartoons was, according to Eliot, *Der Fuehrer's Face,* "in which Donald Duck openly mocked Adolf Hitler." This cartoon "identified Disney as one of the nation's leading celebrity patriots" (p. 166). *Der Fuehrer's Face* won an Academy Award in 1942 as the best cartoon. According to the authorized, sanitized biography of Disney by Bob Thomas, Disney received mail accusing him of being a war profiteer. Indeed, he was.

[34]Paul Hollister, "Genius at Work: Walt Disney," *Atlantic Monthly* 166 (December 1940): 689–701.

[35]Louis Althusser, *Lenin and Philosophy and Other Essays* (New York: Monthly Review Press, 1971), p. 163.

[36]Paul De Roos, "The Magical Worlds of Walt Disney," *National Geographic* (August 1963), pp. 159–207.

[37]Susan Willis and Jane Kuenz, *Inside the Mouse: Work and Play at Disney World* (Durham, N.C.: Duke University Press, 1995).

[38]Henry Giroux, *The Mouse That Roared: Disney and the End of Innocence* (Lanham, Md.: Rowman & Littlefield, 1999) p. 13.

[39]Eliot, p. 279.

[40]The Disney Store, originally resisted by Eisner and later promoted heavily, now accounts for up to 25 percent of the company's income. Consumers, it seems, continue to have a heartfelt need to buy everything Disney.

[41]Quoted in Eliot, p. 183.

[42]Ibid., p. 184.

[43]The film remains in circulation overseas, and in Japan, and according to Walt Disney World, *The Song of the South* "is a howling success." Susan Miller and Greg Rode, "The Movie You See, The Movie You Don't: How Disney Do's That Old Time

Derision," in *"From Mouse to Mermaid: The Politics of Film, Gender, and Culture,* ed. Elizabeth Bell, Lynda Haas, and Laura Fells (Bloomington: Indiana University Press, 1995), p. 88.

[44]Miller and Rode.

[45]Ibid., p. 89.

[46]Jason Mauro, "Disney's Splash Mountain: Death Anxiety, the Tar Baby and Rituals of Violence," *Children's Literature Association Quarterly* 22 (1997): 116–17.

[47]Ibid., p. 116.

[48]Jack Zipes, *When Dreams Came True* (New York: Routledge, 1999), pp. 80–81.

[49]See *The Classic Fairy Tales: A Norton Critical Edition,* ed. Maria Tatar (New York: W. W. Norton, 1999). In it, Tatar writes about Andersen: "Cruelty and violence have often been seen as the signature of German fairy tales, but P. L. Travers, the British writer who created Mary Poppins, found the Grimms' tales downright tame by comparison to the stories composed by Hans Christian Andersen: "How much rather would I see wicked stepmothers boiled in oil—all over in half a second—than bear the protracted agony of the Little Mermaid. . . . There, if you like, is cruelty, sustained, deliberate, contrived. Hans Andersen lets no blood. But his tortures, disguised as piety, are subtle, often demoralizing. . . . Andersen promotes what many readers might perceive as a cult of suffering, death, and transcendence for children rivaled only by what passed for the spiritual edification of children in Puritan cultures" (p. 212).

[50]Zipes, *Dreams*, p. 91.

[51]See Laura Fells, "Where Do the Mermaids Stand? Voice and Body in *The Little Mermaid*," in *From Mouse to Mermaid*, p. 182.

[52]The Disney-administered town of Celebration, Florida represents one of the latest experiments in ideologically administered living of the Walt Disney Company. Touted as an expression of Walt Disney's own vision for the new world of leisure, harmony, and consumption, Celebration is also decidedly fascistic in its organization and its ideological justification. Ideological control is based on the cost of the homes in Celebration, which is considerably higher than the average price of a home in any other part of Florida. To buy into Celebration's five thousand acres of suburban living, nestled in another five thousand acres of surrounding forest, one must have money. If one has enough money, one can live as Prince Eric lives, pretending the sea creatures at your borders do not exist even as you eat them for dinner. Two books have recently come out on Disney's Celebration. For more information, see Andrew Ross, *Celebration Chronicles: Life, Liberty and the Pursuit of Property Values in Disney's New Town* (New York: Ballantine Books, 1999). And see also Douglas Frantz and Catherine Collins, *Celebration U.S.A.: Living in Disney's Brave New Town* (New York: Henry Holt, 1999).

CHAPTER 6

Maurice Sendak and the Detachment Child

You can survive a sick mother.
You can survive a weak father.

—MAURICE SENDAK,
"Conversations with Maurice Sendak"

CAT AND *MAUS*

Just as his latest picture book, *We Are All in the Dumps with Jack and Guy,* was about to hit bookstore shelves in 1993 for its short, failed run as a consumer product, Maurice Sendak was interviewed by Art Spiegelman for the *New Yorker.* For readers of Sendak, the interview covers familiar territory. "Childhood is deep and rich," he says "It's vast, mysterious, and profound" (Spiegelman, "In the Dumps," pp. 80–81). And sounding perhaps his most controversial note, Sendak defends the nature of his children's art, its intensity, and its brutal honesty: "You can't protect kids; they know everything." For Sendak this amounts to a belief that adults *should not* protect kids, but should honestly offer up the mysterious confusion of the adult world—and the sometimes horrific consequences of the adult's attempt to control and order it. Sendak makes this remark in the context of defending what was then his latest picture book, and the most political to date: *We Are All in the Dumps with Jack and Guy,* a story about the abandoned child who, for Sendak, is a Gandhi, a Christ, and a Jewish Holocaust victim all rolled into one. The picture book is uncompromising as a commentary on the many ancillary cultural consequences that detached human relations give rise to, including homelessness, greed, and predatory violence. The frankness of the story—and the starkness of the situation—undoubtedly led to its commercial failure, though not to its critical success. *Jack and Guy* failed to become a commercial favorite not just because it didn't appeal to children—though this is certainly a part of the situation—but because it disturbs adults who have a difficult time with a children's text that does not idealize and simplify the child and childhood. In short, *Jack and Guy is a very scary story.* The child, according to Sendak, already understands the story because he is living it all the time. Adults, on the other hand, have learned to forget what happened to them as a child, and *Jack and Guy* is a painful, challenging reminder.[1]

In the interview for the *New Yorker,* Art Spiegelman—a controversial artist and illustrator in his own right and a New Yorker contributor—furnished two pages of cartoon-like illustrations in which he depicts himself and Sendak strolling, chatting, and discussing Sendak's latest work, *Jack and Guy.* The two men consider the nature of childhood and how much children know about the world around them. The reader takes in their conversation by reading the dialogue bubbles that appear over them just as they do in children's comic books—and just as they do in Spiegelman's stunning, award-winning two-volume graphic novel about the Holocaust, *Maus.* The interview is vintage Spiegelman in the way it captures the two positions and sets the artists and their work against each other, not resolving anything, but simply offering the problem to the reader. The problem is this: what should children know about the adult world, and when should they know it? Does censoring the truth about the human condition protect the child? Or, on the other hand, when the adult tells the truth about violence or sex, is this tacit encouragement to the child to participate in such things at will? More problematic still, what is the truth about these matters after all? In other words, might not the adult's claim to understand the "truth about violence" be just another way to traumatize and terrorize the child?

The interview begins and the "chorus" reads, "Art Spiegelman visits Maurice Sendak at his idyllic Connecticut estate, where the celebrated illustrator recently finished *We Are All in the Dumps with Jack and Guy,* a children's book about homeless kids living in garbage" (Spiegelman, "In the Dumps," pp. 80–81). Sendak explains to Spiegelman early on, in regard to his work, that now, after sixty-five years, he has come to the "pleasure principle." He does what he likes, in other words. No more Sturm und Drang about his life, career, and work.

Sendak shocks Spiegelman when he mentions his next project—illustrating Herman Melville's *Pierre.* "You're doing a book for grown-ups?" Spiegelman asks, incredulous. Sendak responds in disgust; he is tired of just this kind of distinction, which his audience routinely makes. "Kid books . . . Grown up books . . . that's just marketing. Books are books!" Spiegelman does not back down. "I suppose. But when parents give *Maus,* my book about Auschwitz, to their little kids, I think it's child abuse . . . I wanna protect my kids!" Spiegelman tells Sendak that his six-year-old daughter thinks that

"Daddy draws mice" for a living. Spiegelman's face beams in the illustration. He is proud of how he has limited his daughter's access to his work and its horrific content. After all, what can a six-year-old do with information about the Holocaust?

Sendak responds, "Art—you can't protect kids . . . they know everything!" Sendak goes on and Spiegelman's illustrations depict a close-up of Sendak's face as he exclaims, "Childhood is cannibals and psychotics vomiting in your mouth!" Spiegelman depicts Sendak with sharp, pointed teeth; beads of sweat pour from his brow; his eyes are spirals as if he is hypnotized, or hypnotizing. Spiegelman draws Sendak as a crazy monster. He looks dangerous.

We have to consider Spiegelman's own genre-crossing text, *Maus*, to fully appreciate the images and ideas that Sendak has drawn into *Jack and Guy*. When I had the opportunity to talk with Sendak about the relationship between his work and Spiegelman's *Maus*, he stated simply, "You're right to see a connection here because there is one."[2] *Maus* is a biography of sorts. It represents in graphic form the story of the Jewish Holocaust as it devastated the Spiegelman family—among countless others—in Poland from 1935 to 1945. What makes *Maus* so compelling—apart from its surprisingly effective comic-strip presentation of the Holocaust—is the story of the relationship that occurs *after* the Holocaust between Vladek Spiegelman, the father and survivor, and his son, Art Spiegelman. The Holocaust, Spiegelman suggests, might be best understood—if at all—as a story of generational family conflict and ideological transposition. "What makes transposition so much more awesome than ordinary generational transmission is the *amount of psychological space* the parent's past occupies in the child's ongoing existence."[3] Artie the son who was born *after* Auschwitz learns that Auschwitz never ended for his father, and as a result, whether Artie likes it or not, Auschwitz never ended for him either. He struggles with the same survival trauma as his father and the story of their relationship is the story of Artie coming to terms with his own existence, determined as it was before he was even born. The work is a heroic work in its attempt to foreground his struggle—Spiegelman invites his readers to remember so that we might put behind us what we should never forget.

The comic strip format of black-and-white graphics makes up the vehicle for the narrative and frees it from any need to speak the unspeakable in realistic terms, undermines itself as an authoritative account of the Holocaust, and instead offers a tale of human relations at their most ordinary in one plot, and at their worst in another—and in the process manages to underscore the horror of genocidal violence. All at once Spiegelman suggests that the most ordinary human relations are implicitly and explicitly caught up in the most extreme cases of relational violence. This is the challenge Spiegelman's work brings to his readers.

Spiegelman depicts the Nazis as cats, the Jews as mice, the Polish as pigs, and the Americans as dogs. Once past the basic metaphors that structure the story, Spiegelman's choices make a kind of obvious sense; cats and mice have a predatory, hierarchical relationship on the food chain. The cat takes the mouse. The Nazi takes the Jew. There seems to be something essential, natural, biological, and inflexible about the cat-and-mouse metaphor, at least at first glance, because Spiegelman's depiction of the predatory nature of human relationships suggests that the German-as-cat is *always* the predator and that the Jew-as-mouse is *always* the victim. Mice never catch and eat cats. Yet Spiegelman's story is, frankly, more than a Holocaust story and because of this it constructs its metaphoric hierarchy of predatory and prey and then happily deconstructs it soon after and consciously names it for what it is: an insufficient metaphor that can only mislead, misdirect, and offer misunderstanding.

Yet because the reader cannot help but identify emotionally with the mice—and is invited to do so by Spiegleman's depiction of their humanness, their vulnerability, and their suffering—the narrative draws the reader into the essential dilemma of Cartesian dualism as it is lived out in human relationships: "I think, therefore I am" relies on the philosophic assumption that my thoughts are a product of some "me," some "self" that I have access to. As a result, I am me. It follows then that you are not me. Ideology simultaneously converts this basic split into a relationship of self and other; the need for hegemonic power further intensifies the relationship of self and other to that of predator and prey. When one remains caught up on the notion of "me" as distinct from "you," one remains caught up in a culture on the road *to* and *from* Holocaust.

WE ARE ALL IN THE DUMPS WITH JACK AND GUY

In an interview in 1993, Sendak said,

> *Dumps* does confront the outer world, but it's as internal as anything else I've done when it comes to crucial relationships. There's Max coming to grips with his mother, Ida coming to grips with her mother and baby sister, and here it's children coming to grips with each other. The boys accept the baby, the baby is fighting for a home. It's essentially the same story I've always told about children.[4]

Sendak all but requires his readers to understand Max's story in *Wild Things* as a point on the arc of his creative vision that led to the brown baby's story in *Jack and Guy*. The same story, Sendak claims, is the story of adult detachment, abandonment, and neglect as child-rearing. The narrative crisis of his seminal picture books takes place as fantasy flights of the child away from home and back again, and this structure appears in Max's story, Mickey's story, Ida's story, and finally Jack and Guy's. Each picture book depicts how the child copes with emotional isolation, which, according to Sendak, reflects his own experience of emotional isolation as a child. For Sendak, then, the role of the artist is to explore the individual's experience and offer it as a universal truth, even if the individual in question is four years old.

"You have to approach [the child] with ferocious honesty," Sendak stated in yet another interview while speaking about his work in children's theater. In fact, in almost every interview Sendak has granted, he speaks of the child's need for "ferocious honesty" in whatever the child is presented with, be it a picture book or an opera. He sees his own work as a direct challenge to the general trend in children's culture. "Most things published for children," Sendak argues, "are strictly for their parents and strictly for grandma, because kids have no money."[5] Yet Sendak resists the sometimes squeamish adult audience and writes for an audience of children that he perceives as intuitively aware of all that goes on around them, including the lies, the half-truths, and the sugar-coatings that adults apply to the world in order to "spare" children. Sendak has never spared his audience, and this is nowhere more obvious than in his opera *Hansel and Gretel,* which depicts the Witch's oven as a crematorium, or his 1993 picture book, *We Are All in the Dumps with Jack and Guy,* that depicts a children's orphanage-as-concentration camp.

In *Jack and Guy,* Sendak illustrates a Brooklyn back alley as an urban nightmare populated by human refuse, namely, children, among whom live Jack and Guy. Jack and Guy are a schizophrenic representation of Sendak's child-hero as he first appeared as Max from *Where the Wild Things Are* in 1963, then as Mickey from *In the Night Kitchen* in 1970, and then as Ida from *Outside Overthere* in 1981 Moreover, all of the children represented in *Jack and Guy* portray aspects of the one child Sendak has been writing about his whole career, which, I would argue, speaks to the position of the child in the dominant culture as the original and primal "other."

It is unclear where the story opens.[6] The cover may be the opening, though it may also be the ending of the story. The half-title page depicts a brown baby dying, alone, framed by the title, surrounded by white space. The title page, a fully-illustrated double-page spread, announces the title of the work, the author's name, and a preview of the entire story. On the far left is the brown baby saying "help." *Jack and Guy* seem uninterested. Homeless children abound. Kittens appear everywhere. The moon looks down with a dejected face. Even before the narrative proper begins, Sendak suggests, he demands that the reader see the world of Jack and Guy as all-encompassing reality, a reality that transcends the narrative frame—even the book cover itself. The story of Jack and Guy cannot be contained by the physical limits of the text itself, but rather, is always already everywhere.

The cover and the title pages portray how and where Jack and Guy live:

in boxes as homeless waifs among other homeless waifs, other cultural dis-
cards, or as Spiegleman says, "in garbage." When the nursery rhyme text
begins on the second double-page spread, the brown baby, a much smaller
and more vulnerable waif than the others, has been seized by a pair of adult-
sized rat predators who carry off the brown baby along with a sack of kittens
pitifully mewing. Jack and Guy appear distressed, along with the others, who
call out: "Look what they did! Look what they did! The rats stole the kittens
and the poor little kid!"

In the next double-page spread, Jack and Guy pursue the rats, who,
dressed as playing cards, agree to play a game of bridge for the brown baby.
Here the children are forced to play the adult's game by the adult's rules. The
implication is, of course, that the child has no way of escaping his fate. The
game is rigged from the start, and Jack and Guy are overmatched. The baby is
trussed—perhaps swaddled—and ready for export even before the game is
through. The moon looks on as a pathetic, powerless observer disturbed by
what she sees. One character on the left-hand side of the page, dressed only in
a newspaper, offers a clue regarding Sendak's intention in *Jack and Guy*. The
headline on the newspaper that clothes her reads: "AIDS EP . . ." There is,
Sendak suggests, an epidemic of homelessness, of disease, and of victimization in the margins of the dominant culture.

The rats win their game of bridge and march the brown baby and mewing
kittens away, all in the shadow a skyscraper named "Trumped Tower," an
almost heavy-handed image of the dominant culture's wealth, power, and
neglect. The high-finance world of capitalism, Sendak implies here, takes little real interest in the cultural runoff created by its insatiable greed and its
general disdain for the life of the community in its shadow. By the next double-page spread, the rats pull away in a handcart labeled "St. Paul's Bakery
and Orphanage." Above this scene, the moon weeps while Jack, Guy, and others cover themselves in newspapers with only a few headlines legible. These
include the words "AIDS" on one newspaper and "WAR" on another. The
brown baby reaches out for help with both hands, a forlorn look on its face.

In the next double-page spread the brown baby has broken free from the
handcart and stumbles towards the crowd on the left-hand side of the page.
These onlookers—strangely passive and immobile—remain dressed in newspapers, the headlines now more legible. Sendak's attack on consumerism and
its obsession with acquisition is his most angry and ironic statement yet about
the dominant culture's disregard for the child. No longer simply an attack on
high finance, this double-page spread attacks the reader with newspaper
headlines announcing that it is the time to "BUY BUY," the "DISTINCTIVE
HOMES," all for "SHORT TERM MONEY." The consumer can "PROFIT FROM OUR
LOSSES" but must remember that there are "NO KIDS ALLOWED." Near the center seam under the headline which reads "VERY SMART LIVING 70%," there is
one headline that has nothing to do with mortgage rates. It reads: "WANT A

KITTY TO CUDDLE?" The irony here is again almost heavy-handed. The rats have made off with the kittens and will again make off with the brown baby. To what fate? No one is asking, for the homeless children have now become a part of the problem; Sendak depicts them as passive, afraid, and unwilling to help. They look away and hide behind their newspapers as the rat reaches out to grab the brown baby.

The consequences of inaction are clear, for the next double-page spread reads: "The Baby is Bit." The background has changed, however, for the moon has descended and looms large, its mouth gaping wide behind the rat and the brown baby. Who bites the brown baby? Clearly the rat; however, the moon is about to do its own biting as well. The crowd of homeless continue to look away, still dressed in newspapers which now announce "LEANER TIMES MEANER TIMES." This is where the moon steps in and grabs Jack and Guy, who have up to now remained passive and unwilling to interfere in the rats' business. "The Moon's in a Fit," the text reads, and as a result, Jack and Guy become unwilling volunteers in the mission to save the brown baby from the rats.

The moon drops Jack and Guy into a field of rye located just outside "St. Paul's Bakery and Orphanage" and watches with some pleasure even as Jack enacts the violence that he and Guy are ostensibly challenging. "Come says Jack let's knock him on the head," and Jack turns on the brown baby with a ferocious expression on his face, apparently angered by fact that the brown baby kissed him. Kissing, tenderness, and affection are not allowed, at least for the moment, and Jack grows outraged. The potential violence of these pages recounts the entire narrative. The brown baby is once again meekly calling out "help," a victim of a larger, violent force. The gentler half of this schizophrenic duo remains calm and intercedes on the brown baby's behalf yet again. "No says Guy, Let's buy him some bread," and he points to the orphanage and reminds Jack of their real mission. And so, united again, Jack and Guy crawl through the rye, scooping up stray kittens along their way, brown baby in tow. Suddenly, there is no moon, but instead only a giant white cat walking along with them. All three enter the orphanage on the back of the cat and vanquish the rats. This harrowing of hell saves the prisoners—all of whom are, in fact, children illustrated as abandoned kittens—and the liberated rejoice, the kittens cuddle with the cat, and Jack, Guy and the brown baby consume the bakery's bread together. What the bread represents, however, serves to undermine the ostensible triumph of the text's end.

The smoke belching from the chimneys in *Jack and Guy* demands that the reader consider the chimney image, for Sendak repeats it on almost every page of the entire second half of the book. This is no regular orphanage and this is no ordinary bakery. After the rats have been vanquished, the liberated kittens croon and snuggle with the mother cat, while Guy's face beams with pleasure and he reaches for a loaf of bread even as the brown baby munches on another. What Guy does not see—because it is "over his head," is that the loaf he is reaching for has the shape and the face of a kitten. Though Jack and Guy seem to triumph over the rats, their triumph is complicated by the horror that frames the entire story. The rats make bread from orphans. So when Jack and Guy celebrate their victory over the rats and eat the bakery's bread they in effect—and without realizing—consume themselves.

Finally, on the penultimate double-page spread, the moon, no longer a cat, no longer a mother, is now the cross upon which the baby has been crucified. Sendak maintains that "the moon is every one's mother." With this in mind, then it, seems that the moon has saved the brown baby and that all will be well. On the other hand, no crucifixion can take place without a cross. It is against the bifurcated backdrop of the moon-as-mother and the moon-as-cross that the child's position in *Jack and Guy* hangs.

Consider the double-page spread in which Jack and Guy have rescued the brown baby and run along with him holding two large loaves of bread. The mother cat has transformed back into the moon, and the kittens are in the her mouth. The illustration image suggests the complicated nature of maternal care as an expression of the unconscious, narcissistic, oral greed of the mother. With this in mind the moon might be understood not simply as the loving maternal mother, but rather, as the all-consuming Witch/Mother of, say, "Hansel and Gretel," who loves children so much that she wants to eat them. When Jack and Guy take the "crucified" brown baby down from the moon, they take it off of the cross and at the same time out of the mouth of the mother.

Some critics find hope at the end of *Jack and Guy*, yet indulging in hope is a complicated ideological affair. The optimist, for instance, sees in the moon an image of maternal care as it transforms itself into the cat and rescues the kittens and the brown baby. Yet this implies the same complicated dualistic hierarchy that *Maus* involves the reader in, for if the reader celebrates the cat's triumph over the rats, he or she at the same time celebrates a return to the "natural" order of predation. Rather than giant rats preying on tiny kittens, a giant cat preys on the relatively smaller rats. The optimistic reader is forced, by his or her optimism, into the philosophical dualism that engenders hierarchy, predation, and violence in the first place, all in the name of "hope." Predation threatens to consume the brown baby, and it is predation "rightly" ordered that saves him. The term "rightly"—only implicitly suggested by *Jack and Guy* and *Maus*—represents the primary site of ideological contestation, for it is in this term, among others, that the destabilizing effects of ideology might be seen at work. The dominant ideology has offered "rightly ordered" human hierarchies for thousands of years while leaving unexamined the predatory nature of the relationship between the adult and the child. The result is a dominant culture that remains blind to the root and source of its predatory human hierarchy, and, by extension, of the ongoing threat of genocidal violence. How did we get here?

THE CHILD ACCORDING TO CRITICAL THEORY

In *Capitalism, The Family, and Personal Life,* Eli Zaretsky argues that psychoanalysis posits the family as a stable, transhistorical phenomenon and, as such, tacitly requires the reification of history, or the invention what Adorno calls "universal history."[7] From this perspective, the family of Freudian psychoanalysis remains largely unaffected by historical conditions, modes of production, and so on. This assumption, according to Zaretsky, undermines the usefulness of psychoanalysis as a tool for understanding either the child's life or the life of the community in terms of history, and as such leads to cultural amnesia.

Erich Fromm and the Frankfurt School took up the problem of pychoanalysis and history[8] and Fromm observed that, when Marx and Freud meet, Freud suddenly becomes "exquisitely historical." Fromm sketches the basic outline of his project in his 1932 article, "The Method and Function of an Analytic Social Psychology," reprinted in *The Crisis of Psycho-Analysis.* For Fromm, psychoanalysis represents a materialist psychology that reveals and attempts to demonstrate how instinctual drives represent primary forces for human behavior. Most importantly, Fromm argues that psychoanalysis analyzes the influence of specific life experiences on the inherited instinctual constitution. Thus, in Fromm's view, Freud's theory is "exquisitely historical: it seeks to understand the drive structure through the understanding of life history" (p. 139). Fromm offers us a way of seeing the child's life as a story of psychological, economic, political, intellectual, historical, and emotional contestation. Further, the individual's life history represents not only the production of the individual's consciousness, but also the site of the production of cultural consciousness. The process of individual and social contestations might be understood as a hermenuetical one in which the individual lives out the culture and, in so doing, reinscribes it in all of its contradictions, confusions, and tensions. Thus the key conception of psychoanalysis for Fromm is the "active and passive adaptation of the biological apparatus, the instincts, to social reality" (p. 107). Psychoanalysis is especially valuable for social psychology in that it seeks "to discover the hidden sources of the obviously irrational behavior patterns in societal life—in religion, custom, politics, and education" (p. 141).

The psychoanalytic emphasis on the primacy of the family in human development can also be given an historical materialist twist, Fromm believes. Since "the family is the medium through which the society or the social class stamps its specific structure on the child," analysis of the family and socialization processes can indicate how society reproduces its class structure and imposes its ideologies and practices on individuals. Fromm suggests that psychoanalytic theories that abstract from study of the ways that a given society socialized its members into accepting and reproducing a specific social structure tend to take bourgeois society as a norm and illicitly universalize its findings. Historical materialism provides a corrective to these errors by stressing the intrinsically historical nature of all social formations, institutions, practices, and human life. Fromm writes,

> In certain fundamental respects, the instinctual apparatus itself is a biological given; but it is highly modifiable. The role of primary formative factors goes to the economic conditions. The family is the essential medium through which the economic situation exerts its formative influence on the individual's psyche. The task of social psychology is to explain the shared, socially relevant, psychic attitudes and ideologies—and their unconscious roots in particular—in terms of the influence of economic conditions on libido strivings. (p. 149)

The Frankfurt School and others who have explored the history of the family and Western society suggest a perspective from which we might see the family and its "highly modifiable" psychological condition as a result of history and cultural conditions, while at the same time suggesting that the family helps to create the wider culture that sustains it. Zaretsky writes, "If we can simultaneously view [the family] as part of the "economy," a step would be taken toward understanding the connection between our inner emotional lives and capitalist development."[9] Edward Shorter's *The Making of the Modern Family* does just this and argues that, in fact, the rise of capitalism in the eighteenth and nineteenth centuries had a profound impact on the family, and by extension, the definition of "the child." Once the family was a communal affair in which extended families merged with the wider community. The nineteenth century saw the rise of the "family as nest," and the idealization of motherhood and the invention of childhood. Gone was the permeable barrier of the fifteenth- and sixteenth-century families, in which an extended family, (a stem) including servants, friends, and other community members, freely moved across the boundaries of family life. In the family-as-nest, or nuclear family, the raising of the child became a chief concern of the biological mother. The community continued to exert considerable force, but less as community festivals and rituals decreased.

The rise of the nuclear family made the barriers between the outer world and the inner world of the family less permeable, more private. The rise of the nuclear family saw breast-feeding of one's own infant return as a dominant cultural value. Influencing this ideological shift were the ideas of Jean-Jacques Rousseau and the "naturalness" of the family; the family was idealized as a place of spirituality, as an enclave safe from the brutalities of competitive society. From the middle to the late nineteenth century the mother was idealized, and by extension, the importance of "childhood" grew. Still, according to Zaretsky (and later explored by Freud), filial relations were intensified and charged with unsuspected emotions by the sexual repression and prudery characteristic of the period of capital accumulation. As Freud soon demonstrated, the Victorian bourgeois family-as-nest was a cauldron of anger, jealousy, fear and guilt—not to mention sexuality.[10]

According to Shorter, this tension might be understood as the result of market forces permeating the family. The individual's sense of individuated "selfhood" blossomed during the Industrial Revolution as a result of increasing living standards and the cultural codification of "one's self interest" as a legitimate and even central concern. This resulted in a polar tension between, on the one hand, the notion of the family as a private escape from the pressures of the external world, and on the other, the individual's physical and emotional desire to be free. Shorter argues that the values concomitant with the capitalist marketplace represent the most significant contributing factor in the eighteenth- and nineteenth-century realignment of the family-as-nest, and at the same time the family-as-prison.[11]

Freud's psychoanalysis grew directly out of the ideology of the family and the child during the latter half of the nineteenth century in Europe, propelled as it was by the rise of the Industrial Revolution and market capitalism. As a result, Freud's contributions to the understanding of the development of the child in many ways supported the Victorian status quo in regards to power, authority, and sexuality in the family system. For Freud, the family develops as the result of instinctual "drives," and these drives are unaffected by historical and social conditions. As mysterious as Freud's drives are, psychoanalysis implicitly reifies them, and psychoanalysis "tends to project the family of developed capitalist society onto all previous history."[12]

Not only the family, but history itself undergoes a process of reification which, in many ways, guarantees history's existence, and (for Adorno) history-as-a-history-of-totalitarianism. On the reification of history as a "universal history," Adorno states:

> universal history must be construed and denied. After the catastrophes that have happened, and in view of the catastrophes to come, it would be cynical to say that a plan for a better world is manifested in history and unites it. Not to be denied for that reason, however, is the unity that cements the discontinuous, chaotically splintered moments and phases of history—the unity of the control of nature, progressing to rule over men, and finally to that over men's inner nature. No universal history leads from savagery to humanitarianism, but there is one leading from the slingshot to the megaton bomb. (p. 320)

Maurice Sendak's work—from *Where the Wild Things Are* to *We Are All in the Dumps with Jack and Guy*—suggests that the story of childhood in the dominant culture is one and the same with the story of the genocidal move from "the slingshot to the megaton bomb." Fascism, for Horkheimer and Adorno, is the "final historical stage of a cultural process of decay"—rather than progress. Fascism cannot be explained solely as the outcome of the conflict between forces of production and relations of production but rather, from the "internal dynamic of the formation of human consciousness . . . the process of civilization took the form of a spiral of increasing reification that was set in motion by the original acts of subjugating nature and reached its logical conclusion in fascism." One conclusion that Horkheimer and Adorno draw is the denial of any dimension of progress in civilization other than that which is manifested in an intensification of the forces of production.[13]

The concept of universal history is an ideological concept always already assuming that human history—and the dominant culture that it celebrates—tells the story of humankind's triumph over barbarism. Ideology conflates humankind with human culture, thereby justifying a flawed and violent culture as a result of a flawed and violent human nature. *The dominant culture* is flawed, however, in the way that it reproduces itself through relations of power and oppression, namely, through its children. Universal history, then, is not real so much as an ideological reality that results from a narcissistic projection of the dominant culture looking for, and finding, itself in the waters of time.

The narcissistic character structure is one and the same with totalitarian consciousness. It should not come as a surprise, then, that sociologists have described American culture in particular as narcissistic to the core. What this means, broadly, is this: the dominant culture teaches that in perfecting and enacting its story of "progress" we perfect and enact what it is to be human. This is ideology at work. Consider the dominant cultures' child-rearing practices as a representative example of how the "myth" of progress blinds the dominant culture to the logic of decay that informs the relationship between the adult and the child.

Parenting ideologies—all of which *as ideologies* grow directly out of a culture's ideologies—shape and give rise to a "split" in the child's consciousness. The child is born first into the physical world and is, in this sense, alive and aware—exquisitely aware. The child is simultaneously born into a world of ideology from her first moments and for the rest of her life. In her newborn state, the child is her body. Immediately, however, the ideological world around her teaches her that she is to ignore her body and to place her attention externally on the parent / ideological figure of authority, for it is from here that her well-being or her suffering will come. To the extent the mother or father uses the child's needs to gain control over the child, the adult might be said to be "abusing" the child. Given the dominant culture's child-rearing practices and its predominant hierarchical ideologies of wealth and power, it seems difficult for the parent to parent in such a way that is not abusive to children. And this is true, given the limits of our ideological assumptions about the child; it is our parenting ideologies and not our children that need fixing.

Twentieth-century child-rearing practices include the seemingly innocuous and innocent hospital birth, the bottle-fed infant, the crib-raised child, the day-care child, and more. These common child-rearing pedagogies lead to a split in the child's consciousness in which the child's biological and emotional needs (the body) take a back seat to the adult's needs as they are defined not by the body, but rather by ideology as it overwhelms the body's internal dialogue. Quickly the child learns that there is a sometimes an unbridgeable gap between her basic needs and the needs of the culture as they are represented by the parents. And so it follows that from an adult-centered, ideological perspective we can call a baby "good" or "bad" based on her biological needs.

Still, the tendency to label a baby who makes adult life easy as "good" and one who makes adult life more difficult as "bad" shapes an infant's exquisitely aware consciousness. No longer is life just what it is: life has become split into "good" and "bad," and the child quickly learns when he is "good" and when he is "bad." The result is the child who learns to ignore his body, his biological needs, and his emotional needs in favor of behavior that might be labeled as "good," that is, easy on the adult. Ironically, the child sells his sense of wholeness for the split in the name of "wholeness," that is, in the name of getting her basic attachment needs met. The end result of this devil's bargain, however, is a split in the child's consciousness out of which the psychoses and neuroses so common to twentieth-century culture will grow. The intensity of the individual's later psychoses or neuroses depends, among other factors, on the degree to which the child's emotional needs were found acceptable by the parent as the child navigates the internal split between his physical needs and the external ideological "reality." It must be noted, however, that the "external" reality of the parent is quickly internalized by the child as a kind of superego who watches over, or shadows, the child's body, judging it and its needs as either "good" or "bad."

As a result, the child's physical sense of itself—its intuition—remains cut off and buried under years of repressed biological need and the attending affect that has, perhaps, also been repressed as a result of parental and institutional pedagogies of obedience and "good behavior." Ironically, though not surprisingly, detachment culture—our consumer culture—then offers itself as a solution to the problems it has helped to establish in the child. An addiction to culture results in which we attempt to rediscover our humanity through inhuman means—and so teach our children to do the same. In short, we do not know what we feel or what we need, and so we *consume*. This equation might have been similar in Nazi Germany, but it would read like this: we do not know what we feel or what we need, and so we *obey*.

WHERE THE WILD THINGS ARE

Consider Sendak's breakthrough and now classic children's picture book: *Where the Wild Things Are* (1963). Most readings of this picture book concentrate on Max's imaginative power, his ability to cope with his "normal" situation, his exuberance, and his "relief" at returning home. In a recent article, Jennifer Shaddock reads Max's journey as a colonialist romp in which he "tames" the savage beast within himself. Still, like the colonized know so well, Max's only hope in the "domestic" world is to learn and master the lessons of the oppressor. Sendak depicts this inculcation of hierarchical, monarchical values as Max relates to the wild things as a king to his subjects. He rules the wild things as he has been ruled by his mother, and then and only then is he fit to return to his place in the "real" world, perhaps wild still, but nominally tamed; Max has been domesticated a bit through the process of child-rearing enacted from the margins of the text by the disembodied voice of the mother. Read "mother" as "mother culture."

In *Where the Wild Things Are*, Sendak shows us how a child is interpolated into a culture that sees as its first job the suppression of the exuberance of the child. Max's exuberance, or his "wildness," is not the whole story, though. At least as important as Max's exuberance is how Max relates to it. And how he relates to it (like a kind of colonialist lion tamer) tells the story of Western culture in a nutshell.[14] "Taming" his emotional needs is paramount. They mean nothing other than the threat wildness represents to the adult, domestic order. Max does not question the antecedents of his behavior or his "wildness," but rather learns through punishment in the form of isolation that "wildness" must be tamed. Adults, it seems, have no wildness and Max will be declawed as well, and so made defenseless to the further encroachment of the colonizer.

In Max's hierarchical world, negotiation does not take place, for negotiation requires two parties who recognize each other's needs as legitimate. Words are not used to make sense of the situation, for it is implied and inferred that Max is beyond words. He is a savage beast. In other words, Max's mother does not speak with Max to help him read his own behavior, his emotional needs, or his "wildness." Rather, Max's mother transmits a central adult-centered value implicit in almost all that adults do: big people have the power to interpolate the child in their own image. How? Through unconscious ideological transposition that takes the child through child-rearing practices.

Max's home—like so many homes for children—is a kind of prison. Max's door has a lock on it, carefully drawn under the doorknob of Max's bedroom door. Max's bedroom—when not a jungle—is as spare as any prison cell. Max, however, does have a window, and he has the moon. For Sendak, as we have seen, the moon is often a mother figure, but his inconsistent handling of the phases of the moon in *Wild Things* suggests to me that Sendak understands on some level that the moon is just not enough for lonely children.

When Max enters his dream world, he works out his rage with the wild things, but he does it in an ideologically bifurcated way. On the one hand, Max is a child with the power to dream dreams that send him "in and out of weeks and almost over a year to where the wild things are." When Max gets there via the power of his emotional inferiority, he then draws on adult ideologies—modeled by his parents, no doubt—about how to handle fear and anxiety. You command it to "BE STILL!" The result of this command is, in a way, every child's dream: the wild things that scare you ultimately recognize your true nature, your true authority as a human being, and they make Max king. In other words, Max's therapeutic vision includes a large dose of adult-centered notions of monarchy, history, economics, hierarchy, and power.

To function in the world Max has been born into, one must exercise one's sense of power, yet as a child one rarely if ever has a chance to do this, except with a sibling. I think Sendak explores this option in *Outside Overthere.* In *Wild Things,* however, Max has only the family dog, his dolls, and his parent's tools to abuse. When these forms of expression do not satisfy, Max attempts to take power from his mother. "I'll eat you up!" he screams, echoing his own fears of being consumed by the adult order, and as a result, he is "punished" for speaking this truth, and sent to bed without the one thing his mother, apparently, does provide him with when he behaves according to her desires: food.

When Max returns from his fantastic voyage, Sendak signals in the last pages of the story just what Max has returned to. The glaring double-page spread of white that ends the book does not represent the warmth and safety Molly Bang suggests it does, but rather, this last double-page spread suggests that Max's show is over and the lights have come up. He will return to his life—one in which he has, for all intents and purposes, been abandoned. His mother has—like some kind of ghost-jailer—brought him his food, "and it was still hot." These last lines are printed across a glaring spread of white. Max has had a respite from reality in his dreams, yet the relationship he has returned to after his journey is "still hot," still glaring, still the same. The tension, anxiety, and, yes, rage are still there between Max and his mother, but now they have been sublimated in a way, turned into something that seems innocent enough: the mother's need to physically nourish her child. Food mediates the relationship between Max and his mother, flowing downhill from the punisher who has the power to grant pardons. For this the prisoner should be grateful.

THE CHILD ACCORDING TO ATTACHMENT THEORY

From *Wild Things* to *Jack and Guy,* Sendak's work might best be understood as the child's emotional landscape as it internalizes and then attempts to cope with a relational world of adult detachment. In *Jack and Guy,* the illustrations make it plain that the consequences of detachment parenting are common, too common. Sendak depicts homelessness, the abandonment of children, poverty, and the possibility of cultural collapse in the illustrations of the first half of *Jack and Guy.* Images of playing cards, games, and puns on the word "trump" make the point about the child's chances in an adult world especially clear. What chance does the child have to win at this card game? Who understands the rules? The rats, it seems, understand the rules, and so does the moon.

What might be described as "detachment parenting" derives from John Bowlby's "attachment theory" of human development. In *The Making and Breaking of Affectional Bonds,* Bowlby explains that attachment theory is "a way of conceptualizing the propensity of human beings to make strong affectional bonds to a particular other and of explaining the many forms of emotional distress and personality disturbance, including anxiety, anger, depression, and emotional detachment, to which unwilling separation and loss give rise."[15] Attachment theory looks at the primary relationships of childhood and takes childhood memories as a necessary starting point for understanding later emotional and psychological problems in the adult. So, though attachment theory owes a lot to Freud's discoveries, it breaks with Freudian—and Freudian-derived—theories of human development. In Freudian models, food and sex are primary drives. The child's first relationships—with mother and father—take their shape as a result of the primal human drives, like sex and food. Attachment theory, on the other hand, takes the emotional and physical relationship between child and parent as primary rather than secondary. Attachment theory maintains that the child's emotional needs are primary, and all other drives derive from this fact. Bowlby and other attachment theories argue that "attachment behavior is conceived as a class of behavior distinct from feeding behavior and sexual behavior and of at least an equal significance in human life." Bowlby explains,

> the key point of my thesis is that there is a strong causal relationship between an individual's experiences with his parents and his later capacity to make affectional bonds, and that certain common variations in that capacity, manifesting themselves in marital problems and trouble with children as well as in neurotic symptoms and personality disorders, can be attributed to certain common variations in the ways that parents perform their roles.[16]

"Detachment parenting," then, is a style of child-rearing common to the dominant culture reproduced ideologically even as the lived relation between the adult and child enacts the ideology. "Detachment parenting" encourages the child to repress his own emotional needs in favor of the adult who "knows better," and so believes that whatever the child experiences emotionally need not be a real concern to the adult. Rather, detachment parenting ignores the rich tapestry of the child's emotional life, seeing in it instead something chaotic that cannot be understood. It simply makes no sense and therefore need not be addressed, or if the child's emotional life is addressed it is addressed negatively, as a command to silence, swallow, or otherwise hold in feeling. "Detachment parenting" is chronically concerned about "spoiling" the child and believes that the child who can "hold it in" is learning how to operate in the "real world."

Attachment theory, on the other hand, argues that there is no such thing as spoiling. "Spoiling" is a misnomer of an *adult* condition. That is, when a child has emotional needs that have not been met—or even acknowledged—by the adult, the child will chronically *need*. If emotional need as a primary condition is denied by the parent, the child will then transfer her insatiable need to things, food, and so on. Thus, the child will appear to be "spoiled," never having enough. This is true in one sense. The child will never have her emotional needs met by things, only by the parent. If the parent of the "spoiled" child has been raised according to detachment ideals, the parent will simply be mystified by the child's insatiable desire for things. In this way, frustration, exasperation, and chronic anxiety are handed down from parent to child.

Detachment parenting encourages the adult to remain unaware of the child's anxiety because, in detachment parenting, the child has no subjective inferiority that feels trauma the way adults do. Children simply "go off," or "melt down," for no apparent reason, because the *emotional reasons* behind the child's behavior are invisible to the parent who is blind to his or her own emotional condition. Attachment parenting, on the other hand, assumes there is a reason for the child's emotional condition, and when the parents discover their own emotional reality, they can then bear witness to the child's emotional reality. Both parent and child can experience their shared sense of rejection, abandonment, and isolation. The family will then find an emotional balance again. On the other hand, detachment parenting encourages forgetting, which often comes in the form of repression of the child's emotion. Repression of the child's emotion is, oddly, made possible by parental threats of further detachment. "Detachment parenting" celebrates the child's independence, even *in infancy,* so children sleep alone, often from the earliest days of their lives. "Detachment parenting" also, though not always, avoids breastfeeding infants and instead favors science and technology in the form of the laboratory's "formula."

The world of detachment parenting is the world Sendak writes about. The attachment anxiety that the adult suffers from is handed on as an unconscious repetition of relational practices to the child. That is, as adults try to work out their anxiety through their children, they often, quite unintentionally, pass on the very belief systems that were handed down to them by their parents. Therefore, this is not an argument blaming anyone; rather, it is a plea to look behind our deepest, most unconscious conceptions of the child, and bring them into the light of critical scrutiny. Why? Because many of the adult's deepest, most unconscious conceptions of the child grow directly from what the adult has been taught about his or her own emotional needs when a child. In short, obedience is one of the most common lessons a child is forced to learn; only later (say, during adolescence) do we realize that the child's obedience has little or nothing to do with his or her respect for the authority figure. In other words, the child might obey me (and thus show respect for my force, my power, my ability to punish), but the child does not necessarily respect my humanity, because the child has been taught to ignore his or her own humanity. And in so doing, we teach the child to dominate the "other" rather than negotiate, for the "other" must be seduced, subdued, conquered, and put in her place, even if the "other" is the child herself. Or, as in *Wild Things,* Max dominates himself just as his mother has taught him.

"Attachment anxiety" represents the normative result of "detachment parenting" and it is difficult to describe because its symptoms are the exact descriptors of what it means to live in the late twentieth century as an American adult. Symptoms include chronic anxiety, acute self-consciousness, and confusion about consumption, especially food and other material goods. Addictions of all kinds proliferate, especially concerning sexuality; relationships, drugs, media, and any and all practices that represent a momentary distraction from the confusion. Chronic anxiety is so chronic that we have mistaken it for the conditions of life itself. We parent our children not into the subjective interiority of their lives, but rather, into an *ideology* that encourages them to deny that they have a significant subjective interiority at all.

Sendak's work introduces children (and adults) to a literary code foreign to the world children are introduced to via popular culture, television, and children's programming. Sendak's literary code is sophisticated enough that adults struggle with his picture books—especially his later ones—perhaps more than children do. To the child that has just begun to be confused by the adult world, by the adult's obfuscation, by the befuddling ideologies of adults, by the lies of adults—Sendak sends a message in code: life is a confusing nightmare under the conditions that most children live it. But the child does live, Sendak tells his readers; the child does have a life inside of him or her that, while it lasts, is as big and mysterious as the universe itself.

Sendak takes as a prevailing assumption in his work that children have an emotional, subjective interiority even though they are "just children." Second, Sendak *celebrates* the child's subjective interiority and maps its devastating and devastated landscape as no other author, for children or adults, has done.

John Cech writes something similar about Sendak in his thoughtful book, *Angels and Wild Things*. "Sendak," Cech explains, "has created a kind of map of the emotional and visionary terrain of childhood. . . . Sendak has given these feelings shape, form, and place in our collective geography of the psyche; they are to be found 'where the Wild Things are,' dreamed 'in the night kitchen,' located 'outside over there.' "[17]

Sendak's vision of childhood is a world filled with rage, power, abandonment, and loneliness. Along with this overarching world, Sendak depicts the child's incredible ability to use fantasy within it as a light that forestalls the darkness for a while. Still, Sendak dramatizes what children always already know to be true and only adults find difficult to remember: childhood is often a terrible, confusing time, made more so by an adult-centered ideology that implicitly requires the child to ignore his felt experience of this truth. *Wild Things* dramatizes this most clearly. Max is punished—and pardoned—by the disembodied, detached voice of his mother.

Like *Wild Things, In the Night Kitchen* dramatizes the fantasy that takes place as a result of the distance between the adult and the child and the anxiety produced in the child by that distance. Mickey's anxious attachment to his parents and the noises they make serve as the narrative background against which his dream journey through the world of the night kitchen takes place. In it, three bakers desire to bake Mickey and consume him. Mickey escapes the three obese Hitlers and their "Mickey oven" for the moment through the power of his fantasy-filled dream-flight. "Cockadoodle doo!" Mickey cries at the end of the narrative, alive and well, celebrating his nakedness, his boyhood, his burgeoning sexuality, and his humanity. Yet throughout the text we are reminded of the world Mickey skims over: the baker's oven behind him and the urban landscape under him. It is this cityscape that reappears in the pages of *Jack and Guy,* stripped of Sendak's optimistic fantasy about the child's ability to persevere and sustain himself through the power of his imagination. Sendak's optimism in *Night Kitchen* is not so much an observation as a prayer about the child. *Jack and Guy* lacks the optimism of *Night Kitchen,* and for good reason. The margins of the dominant culture are as full as ever as it appears in *Jack and Guy,* replete with the refuse of a dominant culture grown cold to its weak, its poor, its diseased, and its children. Even so, Mickey's more optimistic night kitchen wants to devour him. Mickey's cartoon world is yet filled with images of the predator and of the prey, of the Nazi and of the Jew, of the adult and of the child in a mysterious fantasy land inhabited by strange bakers who stay up all night and who would gladly bake Mickey and serve him for breakfast. Mickey transforms his anxiety and his confusion into something life-affirming—like Max on his journey—and he saves himself from the oven.

Max, Mickey, and Ida of *Outside Overthere* triumph over their condition as children of detachment, but only for the moment. Sendak reminds us that, even though children live in a world invented by the adult, the child has a powerful, dynamic interior life whether the adult believes in it or not. The child's ability to have a relationship with himself in his dreams, in his fantastic voyages, offers the adult reader a glimpse into the inner world of the child *as Sendak remembers it* and perhaps reminds the adult of his or her own interior life as an adult and as a child. That the child has an inner world as profound and emotionally complicated as an adult's inner world, Sendak believes, is news for many of his adult readers.

Ida's journey in *Outside Overthere* brings her back to a mother who might best be described as clinically depressed. Here it is clear what Sendak means when he says that the child can survive a "sick mother and a weak father." Sendak depicts Ida's mother, abandoned by her husband and depressed, as a static figure who, it appears, can barely move, let alone raise two daughters. Ida must step into this void to claim her mother's mantle and rescue the baby sister. Ida returns to her family having saved her little sister from the goblins and from the icy, catatonic state of abandonment, which is a real victory. At the same time, however, Ida returns as a mother to her sister. She saves herself, her little sister, and perhaps opens the door to some kind of relationship with her mother, though Sendak does not promise this by the end of Ida's fantastic journey. What we do know is this: children like Ida often willingly take on the role of the mother though they are still children themselves. In short, Ida achieves motherhood before she has been mothered completely herself. This is heroic and tragic, and this is Sendak's central story.

When I had the opportunity to speak with Sendak, he made clear his "outrage" at this culture and its self-serving definitions of childhood; which exploit, ignore, and otherwise chronically abuse the child. The stories of Max, Mickey, and Ida depict a normative childhood experience in an adult culture that practices detachment. These picture books represent, in other words, Sendak's vision of what the child experiences emotionally while the adult world rolls on around and over him. *Jack and Guy,* then, is the story of the manifold consequences of an adult world that detaches from the child and so detaches from its own humanity. *Jack and Guy* is a terrifying story, for it evokes the nightmare world of the Nazi death camp—and the predatory world of Spiegelman's *Maus*—in order to make an astonishing claim: the child's ideological position in American culture is one and the same with the Jew in Nazi Germany.

In *Jack and Guy,* Sendak depicts the consequences of detachment ideology as obvious and far-reaching. Homelessness abounds in *Jack and Guy.* Children suffer; children are preyed upon; children are eaten by rats just as mice are eaten by cats. Sendak's allusions to Spiegelman's *Maus,* a graphic novel of the Holocaust, suggests an even darker truth about the plight of the child. At the end of *Jack and Guy,* the cultural indifference to the child turns to something far more sinister: Sendak picks up on a recurring image of an

Auschwitz chimney in Spiegelman's *Maus* and employs it in *Jack and Guy*. Sendak depicts St. Paul's Bakery and Orphanage as concentration camp of sorts to which the brown baby and the kittens have been taken by the rats. Orphans are cremated and consumed there. Even as the mother cat vanquishes the rats, we're reminded of where we are: the kittens look on from the background, neatly lined up in concentration camp bunks stacked one on another. When I had the opportunity to speak with Sendak about this, he said that he and Spiegelman were just "two traumatized Jews trying to make sense of the twentieth century. You're right to see a connection, because, as I've said before, there is one."[18]

In Spiegelman's Holocaust story the Jews / mice are entirely the victims of Nazi genocide. Yet, near the end of *Maus: A Survivor's Tale,* Spiegelman honestly and courageously shows that the poison of predatory thinking—racism in this case—is alive and well in Vladek Spiegelman, a survivor of Auschwitz. When Francoise, Vladek's daughter-in-law, stops to pick up a hitch-hiker (a black dog, that is, an African American) Vladek goes crazy. "Oh my God! What's happened to his wife," Vladek explodes in Polish. "She's lost her head . . . I just can't believe it! There's a Shvarster sitting in here! I had the whole time to watch out that this shvartser doesn't steal us the groceries from the back seat!" Later, after dropping off their passenger, Artie and Francoise confront Vladek's racism with anger and disbelief. "That's outrageous! How can you of all people, be such a racist! You talk about blacks the way the Nazis talked about the Jews!" "Ach! I thought really you are more smart than this, Francoise," Vladek responds. "It's not even to compare the Shvarsters and the Jews!" (99).

Spiegelman's brutally honest depiction of his father's racism reveals a fundamental logic which, I suspect, underlies all racist ideologies. Racism allows us—even encourages us—to rank the human species into hierarchies based on a value system propagated by the "ranking" race—that is, the race doing the "ranking." We are then left with ideological hierarchies of racial ranking that, ultimately, lead to the rhetoric of oppression, including central concepts like, inferior-and-superior; first-world-and-third world; master-race-and-degenerate-race, and I would have to include, adult-and-child.

When an adult invites and makes room for a child's emotional response—whatever the traumatic event—a child will not have to resort to repression, denial, or play-acting in an attempt to fulfill poisonous adult pedagogy. As an "adult," Sendak makes room for the emotional lives of his child-heroes, Max, Mickey, and Ida. Unfortunately, the adult world of Max, Ida, Mickey, and the brown baby does not share Sendak's perspective, which is the reason-for-being of these picture books. Sendak says: "Look here, you detached parents! Look here and see what's going on inside your child! You may learn something!" Unfortunately, we were not always invited to experience our own emotional lives when we were children and, as a result, fail to observe and successfully deal with our own complex emotional lives as adults. Thus, we struggle—and sometimes refuse—to recognize the emotional complexity of children. Further, because we remain locked in our own coping mechanisms learned in our own childhood, we pass these on as well. This often takes the form of child abuse. Miller's observations offer us a way to understand the individual as a process of recovering—remembering— one's own personal history, even if those memories take the form of forgotten emotions and later present themselves as conscious or unconscious ideological leanings.

What I am suggesting here is something obvious though often overlooked. Our emotional lives—our attachment histories—play as large a role in our belief systems as our intellectual epistemologies, philosophies, ontologies, and teleologies. The discourse of the affective has been overlooked because, I think, academics develop and exercise their intellects while downplaying or even ignoring their emotional lives. Yet this begs the question. Why do academics so routinely develop their intellects and neglect their emotional lives? The answer is simple, though not simplistic: because of their traumatic experiences as children. I think it is safe to say that successful scholars, writers, and critics draw upon skills that once were childhood coping mechanisms: we saved ourselves when we withdrew into books, study, thought, and our own intellects. The cognitive life begins when the "life of the heart" becomes too full with shame of its own "wildness."

The abandoned baby in the detached, predatory world of *Jack and Guy* speaks after the fact to how we could have arrived at the atrocities of the Holocaust at all, and, having witnessed them, go on to invent an even more terrifying, horrifying future: the constant threat of nuclear annihilation, overpopulation, environmental collapse, and so on. At the heart of this terrifying mystery of our genocidal impulse rests the child and our cultural invention of it. Sendak reminds us of this conception by depicting on the cover of *We Are All in the Dumps with Jack and Guy* a homeless child draped in a newspaper. The headline of the newspaper reads "Kid Elected President." The irony is clear, especially in the broader context of the picture book. That we would elect a child as president is an absurd, almost unthinkable notion—almost as unthinkable for some as electing a woman or an African-American as president. That a child-president strikes us as an ideological impossibility—an outlandish absurdity—speaks without speaking of the child's position in the ideological hierarchy of the dominant culture.

THE CHILD ACCORDING TO BARNEY

Consider the television and cultural phenomenon *Barney and Friends* in terms of this brief sketch of attachment theory and as one of the many ambient relational stories fed to children that teach them about the nature of human relationship, power, violence and obedience. Barney's world is a world of detachment, or what Bowlby calls "anxious attachment," like Max's in *Wild Things*. Attachment behavior, according to Bowlby, is "any form of behavior that results in a person attaining or retaining proximity to some other differentiated and preferred individual, who is usually conceived as stronger and or wiser" (p. 129). The constant fear of losing one's attachment figure produces "attachment anxiety."

The Barney phenomenon exemplifies how adults create the stories children consume and, by extension, how the televised enactment of these stories encourages a split between "true" self and "false" self in the child.[19] Barney has been wildly successful; his status as pop icon includes the television show, *Barney and Friends*, live road shows, a burgeoning book trade, a Barney fan club, a Barney magazine, Barney videos, an official Barney web site, and, of course, a feature-length Barney movie. The official web site touts a picture of the purple dinosaur shaking hands with Nelson Mandela as evidence of Barney's staggering popularity. Barney is an ambassador of goodwill—goofy, badly choreographed goodwill—to all the world. Barney's goodwill disturbs me, though, probably because it is, well, relentless. In some of the newest Barney books for children, like *Barney and Baby Bop Go to the Doctor,* or *Bedtime for Baby Bop,* or *Barney's Treasure Hunt,* the Barney pedagogy of the television show crosses over to book form perfectly. In Barney's world, "love" is not really love at all. Barney peddles a fantasy of emotional mystification meant to shape children into docile, obedient consumers.

John Bradshaw writes about mystification in his book *Creating Love.* The child experiences mystification when adults implicitly teach the child that "I only matter to my [parent] when I'm not being myself. This is confusing. In this state of confusion, the child inevitably has another thought: The only time I am lovable is when I'm not being myself. . . . Once we come to believe that we are this false self, *we do not know that we do not know who we are*" (pp. 6–7).

Barney's world is a world of mystifying ideology. Quality fantasy invites us into our own internal sensibilities even as it invites us to come to a deeper awareness of our own psychic world. Barney's world, on the other hand, does not invite the child into his or her own interiority, but rather, encourages the child to ignore his or her own interiority in favor of the group value system, which is, of course, Barney's value system. Barney's children look to and rely on his unctuous approbation, for without it they are nothing.

Barney's pedagogy persuades precisely to the degree that it seems invisible and appears to be common sense. The values implicit in Barney's world are directed at both parents and children, and they include the following:

1. Obedience is the quickest way to happiness.
2. Obedience will be rewarded by group approval.

3. Group approval is absolutely imperative for your survival.
4. Questioning Barney's authority is never an option for you in Barney's world.
5. Authority is directly related to physical size.
6. Barney is the biggest—he knows the most. He teaches, you learn.
7. The adult never really learns from the child.
8. Children should trust large people; they have authority over small people simply because they are physically large.
9. If we are not feeling giddy joy, something's wrong with you. Fake it if you have to.
10. Sing, and your conflict will disappear no matter how you really feel.
11. If the group disapproves of your choices, you know you are making bad choices.
12. If Barney disapproves of your choices, you know you are making bad choices.

Most parenting pedagogies go unannounced and seem to be self-evident and obvious. To question the pedagogies of mystification so prevalent in the dominant culture's child-rearing ideology is to elicit incredulous reactions, as if one is questioning the right of grass to grow. How unnecessary! What a silly question! Get a life! This not uncommon response to the investigation of Barney and what the Barney story means says something about the shame we experienced when we first began to think for ourselves. Rather than experience shame or abandonment, as children we learn quickly to obey, and to stop thinking for ourselves. When we think for ourselves, however, we make something out of "nothing." That is, we diverge from the group and often challenge the authority figure; we feel our own power and authority; we become creative; we self-activate rather than wait for permission from the parent. This is what visionaries and leaders are remembered for—ironically, it's also how young children get labeled with attention deficit disorder (ADD). Yet we resist this obvious truth because, like Barney's friends, our notions of love are as deeply mystified and confused as Barney's.

Still, parents and children are hungry for the kind of clarity, authority, and sense that Barney's world models. In Barney's world, everything has its place, especially the child. When there is order between the adult and the child, the child will—as if by magic—behave, sleep well, and not be bothered by strong emotions, doubts, or worries. The ideal child in Barney's world is a child free from any of the nagging problems that go along with being human, like worry, rage, feelings of abandonment, confusion, and incessant, almost unnamable need. Above all, Barney's children stay in their place. Barney's children do not question authority. Barney's children do not scream "No," and Barney's children never question their lack of authority or power. After all, as

Barney so sweetly models episode after episode, children have no other wish than to be trained like puppies.

Barney notwithstanding, for any love relationship to function, negotiation between or among individuals is essential.[20] Negotiation happens among equals and negotiation is *never choreographed*. When it is, negotiation is not true negotiation, but rather, manipulation. Barney's world is so peaceful not because authority is shared, but rather, because his children know their place in the hierarchy. Starved for love and attachment, Barney's children accept the approval and harmony that flows as a result of their obedience. However, this Pax Barnica—this choreographed harmony of Barney's world—exacts a real price from the child: to fit in, the child separates from his or her own subjective emotional reality in favor of the authority figure's reality, and not long after, "we do not know that we do not know who we are."[21]

Some might say I am reading too much into Barney, that it is "just TV," and that the child does not pick up on any of the hierarchical ideology latent in the relationship between Barney and his children. This question underestimates children to an almost tragic degree and represents ideology at its most intense. Is ideology just for adults? Is ideology just for professionals? Is ideology just for critical theorists? Does ideology begin to have an impact on one's life only after one can drive a car? Or drink alcohol? I think the point is obvious. So why do we as a rule underestimate our children? Claiming that children do not pick up on everything around them masks adult resistance to their own history as children. My students resist the idea that children pick up on everything, and no one resists this idea more than those who work with or parent small children. We get defensive because we love our children and are invested in seeing ourselves as efficient and effective rulers of our petty kingdoms. To give up on this fiction means that I have to give up on much of what culture teaches me about my identity as an individual, as a parent, as a child. It means that I have to give up my culturally bound, ego-driven claims to power over them, and moreover, that I must give up my ideological belief that I do, indeed own my life, and by extension, that I own my children.

I provide a reading of *Barney and Friends* at length to show how we begin to beguile children with value-laden ideologies that inadvertently encourage them to detach from their internal reality and focus on external authority figures. *Barney and Friends* relies on a detachment approach to child-rearing which identifies the child's developmental drives as the determining developmental issue and, as a result, produces television narratives that aim at socializing the wild animal into a tame "human being." Ironically, the child needs "taming" because her emotional, attachment needs have not been met and she does not know how to explain this to her parents. What is the answer to this riddle? Even more training for the child in manifold forms. The upshot of all of this is, of course, that the child is tamed by an adult-sized

Tyrannosaurus rex, a cartoon version of what paleontologists describe as the most ferocious of all meat-eating dinosaurs. As such, Barney is a simulacrum—a purple, cartoonish simulacrum if you will—of an imagined adult reality of the T-rex, itself a simulacrum of some ancient, "pre-historical" creature. What is real here? In fact, nothing is really real other than the chain of ideological signifiers that Barney rings across and uses to evoke, even obliquely and seemingly in an innocent fashion, a predatory relationship to children in the most invisible way imaginable. Consider how Barney's authority over his children is maintained by a magical morphing from small toy to large authority figure. Does anything prevent Barney from morphing into a sharp-toothed meat eater at any given moment? In fact, no. As a dinosaur, even as a cartoonish caricature of the dominant culture's shared idea of the killer T-rex, he is, nonetheless, enough of a T-rex that the audience recognizes the imaginary reality that informs his meaning. In other words, he is a nice T-rex because he is not a mean T-rex. But what stops Barney from magically morphing into a meat-eating T-rex? The children, of course, for their good behavior makes it unnecessary for Barney to display his true nature. Yet, even at work here is a caricature that remains firmly a part of the predatory, ideological hierarchy that justifies the adult's authority over the child. Barney the cartoon dinosaur is a reflection of a real dinosaur precisely in proportion to the degree to which his children are a reflection of real children. As a cartoon, Barney reproduces the predatory, ideological hierarchy in a safe, "lovable" form. The *Barney* show is a caricature of violence; it dramatizes a cartoon T-rex eating cartoon children. The hierarchy between predator and prey is all that remains when the cartoons are dismissed as "just kid's stuff."

A child's willingness to obey and follow orders—and reject her own spontaneous feelings, responses and needs—is still somehow equated with a child's goodness even when it means her emotional death. Sendak's *Jack and Guy* suggests that the results of how we have been conceiving and enacting the child-adult relationship are catastrophic. The Jewish Holocaust represents only one tragic story, and other human tragedies are ongoing—as in the former Yugoslavia—or threaten to erupt at any moment, as in the continuing threat of a nuclear holocaust, chemical holocaust, or environmental collapse. Clifford Geertz offers another way of thinking about our Western predilection for genocide when he describes cultural habits as a "metaphor" or a kind of "meta-social commentary upon the whole matter of assorting human beings into fixed hierarchical ranks and then organizing the major part of collective existence around that assortment. Its function, if you want to call it that, is interpretive" (p. 46). So, for example, the threat of a nuclear holocaust, then, is a Western reading of the Western experience, that of the already real history of the Jewish Holocaust; genocide, it seems, is a story we tell ourselves about ourselves.

NOTES

[1]Though *Jack and Guy* fared poorly as a commercial product, the commentary and criticism suggest that it is, indeed, a fine example of Sendak's work and is his most overt political statement about children. Lawrence R. Sipes's "The Private and Public Worlds of *We Are All in the Dumps with Jack and Guy*," *Children's Literature in Education* 27 (1996): 87–108, Peter Neumeyer's work, and Jane Doonan's "Into the Dangerous World: *We Are All in the Dumps with Jack and Guy*," *Signal* 75 (1994): 155–71, are just a few of the first-rate scholarly articles that take *Jack and Guy* as their subject matter.

[2]From a series of phone conversations I had with Sendak in February 1997.

[3]See Louise J. Kaplan, *No Voice Is Wholly Ever Lost: An Exploration of the Everlasting Attachment between Parent and Child* (New York: Simon and Schuster, 1995), pp. 222–24. For other readings on *Maus,* many of which deal with cultural memory, history, family history, metahistory, and the production of autobiography, see Michael E. Staub, Michael Rothberg, Angelika Bammer, Miles Orvell, Marianne Hirsch, Edward Shannon, Joan Gordon, Rick Iadonisi, and Richard Martin.

[4]Promotional pamphlet from HarperCollins.

[5]Jamie Driver, "Conversations with Maurice Sendak," *Opera America Newsline* 7 (1998):15.

[6]Peter Neumeyer, *"We Are All in the Dumps with Jack and Guy: Two Nursery Rhymes with Pictures by Maurice Sendak,"* in *Celebrating Children's Literature in Education,* ed. Geoff Fox (New York: Teachers College Press, 1995), 139–50. Neumeyer writes that though *Jack and Guy* is Sendak's angriest work yet, it remains a "document of reconciliation and of hope" because, for him, the cover of *Jack and Guy* represents Sendak's final narrative statement even as it introduces the reader to the book. On the cover, the story of the brown baby, having been first "taken down from the moon and resting at the end in sleep-death in Jack's arms, comes full circle. He appears, open-eyed, before the amazed lookers-on. . . . That is, technically, the book's beginning. In fact, it was the book's end. But the end—rescue, salvation, resurrection—simply marks a beginning for us children; for the triumphant book, itself. Because the little Black Baby is come again, announcing, curiously even in the book's design, that 'in my end is my beginning' " (149–50). Neumeyer's final word on *Jack and Guy* speaks not so much to the indomitable spirit of the child as to the indomitable spirit of the adult writing about the child.

[7]Eli Zaretsky, *Capitalism, the Family, and Personal Life* (New York: Harper Colophon, 1976).

[8]The Frankfurt School was a group of scholars who, between the two world wars, attempted to develop a way of seeing that borrowed heavily from Marxist thought, psychoanalysis, and the empirical sciences. Max Horkheimer, Theodore Adorno, Herbert Marcuse, Leo Lowenthal, and Erich Fromm were prominent figures and helped to focus the groups' intellectual work. "Their works were permeated by an awareness of the fact that, owing to the increasing integration of the working class into the late capitalist system, a theory based on Marx had lost is social target group. . . . The Institute's research activity was the question of 'how the psychic mechanisms come about which make it possible for tensions between social classes, which are forced to

become conflicts because of the economic situation, to remain latent.'" Nowhere is this more apparent than the ongoing, though latent, conflict between adults and children and the hegemony that exists between them. This codification of this ideological hegemony is so complete that it represents one of the few unquestioned and largely unrecognized scenes of human oppression. The Frankfurt School "explored a *sociopsychological investigation* of the integration of individuals through socialization (by Fromm) and a *cultural analysis* of the effects of mass culture, which came to concentrate on the newly emerging culture industry." Jay Martin, *The Dialectical Imagination: A History of the Frankfort School and the Instititute of Social Research* (Boston: Little, Brown, 1973).

[9]Zaretsky, p. 35.

[10]Ibid., pp. 52–53.

[11]Cf. Edward Shorter, *The Making of the Modern Family* (New York: Basic Books, 1975).

[12]Ibid., p. 128.

[13]Honneth, p. 233.

[14]For a fuller reading of Sendak's *Wild Things* as colonialist romp, see the article by Jennifer Shaddock "Where the Wild Things Are: Sendak's Journey into the Heart of Darkness," *Children's Literature Association Quarterly* 22/4 (1997–98): 155–59.

[15]John Bowlby, *The Making and Breaking of Affectional Bonds* (London: Routledge, 1979), p. 127.

[16]Ibid., p. 135.

[17]John Cech, *Angels and Wild Things: The Archetypal Poetics of Maurice Sendak* (University Park: Pennsylvania State University Press, 1995). Cech's *Angels* and Selma G. Lanes's *The Art of Maurice Sendak* (New York: Harry N. Abrams, 1980) contain a wealth of biographical commentary by Sendak about himself, his childhood, and his art.

[18]Sendak shared with me his interpretation of the Moon in *Jack and Guy* in a series of conversations I had with him in 1996.

[19]Criticizing television might be considered too easy. Certainly, it's not very original. Yet, even the most avid TV watchers—say, television programmers—suggest we take only a little at a time. This implies a game of double-think that goes on by watchers and creators. The creators create TV as if it were to be taken in an hour at a time, or perhaps two. This is nonsense, of course, because the average television is watched by children for 7 or more hours a day. Given this fact, most people agree that seven hours a day is too much TV, but we're not sure why, and we can't turn it off, and so it stays on. It is a poison of the first order.

[20]Perry Nodelman makes a similar argument "negotiation" in chapter 7 of *The Pleasures of Children's Literature* (White Plains, N.Y.: Longman, 1996).

[21]In *For Your Own Good: Hidden Cruelty in Child-rearing and the Roots of Violence,* trans. Hildegarde and Hunter Hannum (New York: Farrar, Straus, & Giroux, 1983), Alice Miller describes totalitarian methods of child-rearing as "poisonous pedagogy," a phrase she develops from her analysis of German child-rearing manuals that championed the "black pedagogy" discussed in chapter 2. Miller describes "poisonous pedagogy" this way:

Adults are the masters of the dependent child. They determine in godlike fashion what is right and what is wrong. The child is held responsible for their anger. The parents must always be shielded. The child's life-affirming feelings pose a threat to the autocratic adult. All this must happen at a very early age, so the child "won't notice" and will therefore not be able to expose the adults. The methods that can be used to suppress vital spontaneity in the child are: laying traps, lying, duplicity, subterfuge, manipulation, "scare" tactics, withdrawal of love, isolation, distrust, humiliating and disgracing the child, scorn, ridicule, and coercion even to the point of torture.

It is also a part of "poisonous pedagogy" to impart to the child from the beginning false information and beliefs that have been passed on from generation to generation . . . though they are demonstrably false: e.g. a feeling of duty produces love. Hatred can be done away with by forbidding it. Parents deserve respect simply because they are parents. Children are undeserving of respect simply because they are children. Obedience makes a child strong. A high degree of self-esteem is harmful. A low degree of self-esteem makes a person altruistic. Tenderness (doting) is harmful. Responding to a child's needs is wrong. Severity and coldness are a good preparation for life. A pretense of gratitude is better than honest ingratitude. The way you behave is more important than the way you really are. Neither parents nor God would survive being offended. The body is something dirty and disgusting. Strong feelings are harmful. Parents are creatures free of drives and guilt. Parents are always right. (pp. 57–60)

CHAPTER 7

Conclusion
The Etiology of Consumerism

> *The central problem is this: How can the oppressed, as*
> *divided, unauthentic beings, participate in developing the*
> *pedagogy of their liberation? Only as they discover them-*
> *selves to be "hosts" of the oppressor can they contribute*
> *to the midwifery of their liberating pedagogy.*

> —PAULO FREIRE, *The Pedagogy of the Oppressed*

EXPLAINING HITLER

In 1998 Ron Rosenbaum published the much-acclaimed *Explaining Hitler*. In it, Rosenbaum explores the competing, often conflicting versions of Hitler that have been written over the past sixty years, from the earliest German journalists of the 1930s who wrote disparaging criticism of Hitler and the "Hitler party"; to post-war psychological and metaphysical explanations that describe Hitler as an "evil genius" largely responsible for German militarism, German fascism, and the Jewish Holocaust; to contemporary "functionalist" scholarship that explains Hitler as the product of "deeper forces of history and society . . . rather than as a singular '(im)moral agent.' "[1]

All attempts to explain Hitler necessarily fall short, according to Rosenbaum, for Hitler represents a site of inexplicability—an intellectual abyss— into which scholars cannot help but project their own concerns, their own anxieties, and, as it turns out, their own theories of human motivation. Attempts to bridge the abyss and discover the inner workings of Hitler's "thought world" inevitably fail due to a lack of evidence. An enormous amount has been written about Hitler, Rosenbaum states, "but little has been settled." Rosenbaum holds up to special scrutiny Alice Miller's analysis of Hitler's childhood experiences in her study of German child-rearing pedagogies in *For Your Own Good*. To explain Hitler as a product of his child-rearing experiences is, according to one critic whom Rosenbaum cites, "an obscenity as such" (p. xxxi). Those critical of Miller's analysis of Hitler's childhood contend that understanding Hitler's experiences with his mother and father—and the dominant culture of Germany at the turn of the twentieth century—might lead to a kind of recognition of his status as a victim in his own right, which in turn might lead to a broader understanding of Hitler's experience, and this, according to one explainer, Claude Lanzmann, represents an "enterprise of understanding" that, in his view, is "obscene."[2] There can be no understanding, for understanding leads to forgiveness, and forgiveness, for Lanzmann, leads not to healing, but rather, to the danger of forgetting and repeating. Yet in Lanzmann's bitter refusal to understand Hitler lies his bitter rejection of understanding in general, for in rejecting an understanding of Hitler, he rejects the ten thousand years of human culture that have produced fascistic, genocidal leaders similar to—though none exactly like—Hitler. Lanzmann's perspective is not an uncommon one, for he believes that Hitler represents a freakish cultural aberration, and any other understanding of Hitler's historical presence risks belittling the massive suffering of the Jews—and others—during Hitler's reign. Lanzmann's perspective suggests that rather than a product of his times, his culture, and his childhood, Hitler was a breakthrough of some wicked force outside humanity, which is too ghastly to comprehend. Unfortunately, essentializing Hitler and his role in the Holocaust as a kind of extrahuman event leaves untouched the cultural and ideological pedagogies that produced Hitler's character, as well as the characters of his henchmen and his countless willing accomplices in Germany and throughout Europe.

Rosenbaum is too quick to dismiss Miller's analysis of Hitler's childhood experiences. He claims that stories of Hitler's childhood remain historically unreliable, for Hitler is the only eyewitness to the abuse he experienced as a child. When he claims to have been beaten by his father, Rosenbaum argues, we must doubt his sincerity. Even so, Rosenbaum admits that the corporal punishment of children was widespread in Germany at the time, conceding Miller's argument that Hitler, like so many of the children who grew up in Germany at the turn of the twentieth century, suffered under the "black pedagogy" of the German child-rearing tradition. However, the familiar argument against locating childhood abuse as the primary antecedent for adult neurosis and psychosis goes something like this: many children are beaten and turn out "fine," and yet there is only one Hitler. So, the logic presses us forward: there must be something other than child-rearing experiences that make up the individual's character structure, especially a character structure like Adolf Hitler's. As familiar and reassuring as this argument is, it nevertheless remains inaccurate and is driven by the need to deny the obvious. Hitler did not kill six million Jews all by himself. In fact, it is difficult to find any documents that claim Hitler killed anyone with his own hands. Others did it for him. Others followed his monstrous, indirect orders. Others interpreted his vague and bizarre commands. These others included his chief assistants, men such as Göring, Goebbels, Heydrich, Himmler, Eichmann, Reinhard, Kietel, von Ribbentrop, Borman, and Höss; the SS, the Gestapo, the Stormtroopers, and the *Einsatzgruppen* were conceived and led by Hitler's men. The *Einsatzgruppen*—Hitler's "mobile killing squads"—sought out enemies of the state after the German army moved through conquered territories, including Poland and the Soviet Russia. The *Einsatzgruppen* accounted for the deaths of nearly 600,000 Jews, aristocrats, intellectuals, priests, women, and children in Poland. After the *Wehrmacht*—the regular German army—had done its job, the *Einsatzgruppen* came after and followed its orders: to systematically kill all Jews and political enemies of Germany. German soldiers were promised that no action undertaken during this war of annihilation would be prosecuted, for Hitler's war of annihilation was sold to the Germans as a new kind of holy war in which the will to power justified any and all action undertaken.

The *Wehrmacht* participated in the slaughter as well, and, sadly, civilians hunted down and murdered Jews, Gypsies, homosexuals, and any others deemed unworthy of life in the Third Reich.[3] In short, there was more than one Hitler, vastly more. To claim otherwise is to ignore the culpability and guilt of hundreds of thousands of others, for there were many Hitlers in Nazi Germany—and elsewhere—waiting for an opportunity to express explicitly or implicitly their fear, anxiety, sense of shame, and murderous rage. European anti-Semitism offered itself as a long-standing site of projection, and from *Mein Kampf* until the closing days of the war, Hitler made it clear that the Jews would bear the brunt of his rage. Not all chose to become murderers. Enough, however, did choose this path, not simply because they were forced to, but voluntarily. Violence against the Jew became for Nazi Germany an act of patriotism. It is unlikely that genocide was on the minds of all those who murdered Jews. Rather, unquestioned obedience to the Führer, to the Fatherland, and to fascist ideology offered the ordinary German—whether in uniform or out—a way of seeing murder and destruction as a culturally, ideologically, and politically sanctioned way of participating in the creation and self-preservation of a "new" Germany. The ordinary German's willingness to kill Jews surprised even Hitler.

In Hitler studies, the question remains, from where did his world-shattering anti-Semitism come? Of the Hitler explainers of this century, the ones that Ron Rosenbaum gives particularly short attention to—the psychohistorians—argue that murderous rage comes from the unconscious, and the unconscious, according to psychohistorians such as Miller, is not filled up with the violence of human nature, but rather with the rage left over from the violence of human nurture. Human nurture corresponds directly with the dominant ideology, the dominant culture, and the child-rearing pedagogies that express and reproduce the dominant culture, which, in the case of Nazi Germany, was a culture of the will. Hitler presided over a psychopathic state, producing and reproducing his own psychopathic state in and through a population vulnerable to the external authority figure; for the German, the child-rearing tradition of the "black pedagogy" produced a preponderance of psychopathic characters, and Hitler exploited it mercilessly. The will enacts the ideology and reproduces itself with no physical, biological, compassionate intuition to check its progress. The Nazi "self" was intellectualized ideology. The individual identified with the ideology external to the body rather than the feelings and motivations of the body, just as the child was taught to do.

Though Hitler has been seen only as the enraged madman in contemporary film footage, his aides and even ordinary German civilians have described the hypnotic effect of Hitler's eyes. He was a seducer, and he seduced his audience even as he terrified them into submission. The psychopath practices control in every relationship and in every contact with another individual—relationships are always already opportunities to gain control and so fill the unconscious need for power. The psychopath knows little of sorrow or fear and is often restricted to feelings of exultant triumph or enraged frustration. The etiology of the psychopathic character structure develops as a defense and a pattern of holding the adult out, for the child feels invaded and, at the same time, powerless to stop the invasion. The adult rationalizes this invasion as "my will be done," and so the child learns that this ideological defense is the way those in authority deal with subordinates. Invasion is inevitable and necessary in order to bring up the child as a proper citizen. Like the Victorian period, the black pedagogy advocated frequent and harsh corporal admonition, for according to the black pedagogy, the child must *fear power* in order to obey and live "right." The child imagined here is "wicked" and "sinful"—born broken—and only through adult correction might the child be fixed. Yet the adult's repair work was in fact merely the passing on of the adult's own unconscious childhood experiences.

The adult seduction of the child represents the primary trauma that leads to a psychopathic character and invents the child with a character structure built on the child's betrayal by the adult compounded by the repression of affect that occurs as a result of adult demands. The child attempts to hold up against the adult threat of punishment, abandonment, or humiliation, and so he or she holds in the affect that seems to offend the adult—be it mother, father, au pair, nanny, day-care provider, or any adult authority figure. Holding in feelings incompletely and imperfectly results in the felt sense that the individual has a fragile and tenuous hold on reality or sanity, and that at any moment the mind might fly apart except for the force of will that holds it together. Hence, the psychopath is often hostile and insecure and sees in others a threat to his control.

Child-rearing offers itself as the primary site of historical and sociological inquiry because ideology and propaganda alone do not sufficiently explain how so many ordinary Germans embraced genocidal ideology. Germans were reared as children in such a way as to make them vulnerable to beguiling, violent, racist ideologies. In part out of blind obedience, in part to vent unconscious rage, and in part out of unidentified need, ordinary Germans participated in genocide, or, out of fear, allowed it to go unchallenged in their own towns, even as those towns were made "Jew free" by the Nazis. The child-rearing traditions of German "black pedagogy" offer an important explanation of why so many embraced the genocidal policies of the Nazi party. Yet Nazi war crimes are one thing, it seems, and child-rearing is something else entirely. Even this, however, is an ideological assumption bearing the stamp of the dominant ideology, an ideology that sees the child as essentially "childish." Adult matters grow from adult concerns, or so the argument against psychohistory suggests. In *For Your Own Good*, Miller questions these objections: "Those who have never experienced the power of the unconscious may find it naive to try to explain Hitler's deeds as an outgrowth of his childhood experiences. There are still many men and women who are of the opinion that 'childhood matters are merely childish matters' and that politics is something serious, something for adults, and not child's play. These people think connections between childhood and later life farfetched or ridiculous, since they would like, for good reason, to forget completely the reality of those early years (p. 175).

Yet the reality of those early years is written across individual human relations as well as relations between communities and nation-states. Adult culture—especially as it manifests itself in the pedagogy of human relationships—represents the unconscious and "forgotten" experiences of the child. In other words, the child *never forgets* what happens. It is the dominant ideology of the adult that teaches the child that expressions of resistance to the conditions of the child's existence is a sign of the child's need for further adult indoctrination. This takes on all forms, from the most physically abusive to the most subtle and manipulative. All in all, the adult attempts to train the child into behaving in accordance with adult demands, and so ignores the system feedback the child's behavior represents.

More importantly, an infant raised according to the strictures of the black pedagogy, which include putting the infant child on an adult-centered schedule, communicates to the child a suffocating reality: the human "self" in the child does not exist, and so, quite early, that self atrophies, and in its place is unconscious, unnamed need, longing, anger, confusion, shame, and fear. To unconsciously address the physical realities of early child-rearing experiences of the black pedagogy, the child develops a character structure, a structure identified by some as the basis of the "fascistic personality" or the "authoritarian personality." The most primary elements of the fascistic personality lie in the adult's rejection of the child's emotional and physical reality in favor of the external authority's, be it the schedule the clock keeps for feeding, sleeping, and toileting, or the more violent ministrations of the adult's "training" of the child to suit the dominant culture's projected delusion of what makes a child a "good" citizen.[4]

Misbehavior is an adult description of what is more accurately perfect behavior given the conditions of the child's existence. The myth of the "spoiled" child is the adult's unconscious admission of having forgotten how to address his or her own emotional needs, and as a result, the child's as well. When the adult then labels the child's behavior with a description of criminality, as in the child is a "spoiled brat" because nothing is good enough to make her happy, the adult enacts a relational scene in which the dominant culture is produced and reproduced. First, the child learns that she is congenitally needy and nothing the adult can do will be enough. This is a fault for which the child can do nothing, yet she will be punished for her condition nonetheless. Understanding that her condition is not her nature, but rather a reaction to the nurturing she has received, is unavailable to the child except through adult intervention, and yet the adult does not understand the child's feedback except as misbehavior, defiance, and more evidence that the child is simply "rotten." The adult misinterprets the child's behavior because this is how the adult's behavior was interpreted as a child.

Second, because the adult's emotional and unconscious life remains hidden under years of repression and psychic defense against pain and humiliation, the child's emotional expression of neediness is incomprehensible to the adult except as a threat to adult authority. As a result, the child learns early and often that the feelings associated with the adult's narcissistic labels should be hidden away. After months or years of effort, the child quite often succeeds and takes the shape intended by the adult, though this is often tenuous. The child fears flying apart and losing control, and so the adult must always stand close by as the child's "loving" judge to help the child "control" herself. Ultimately, the child will become fused to the adult "judge" and carry the ideological and emotional content of adult judgment, at war with herself whenever her own needs and intuition lead her away from the constraints imposed by the ideological judgment of the fused adult. Anxiety and chronic tension in the body result. When anxiety and chronic tension become extreme, a release is sought or occurs spontaneously when conditions are right. In any event, the sought-after release is often confused and murderous, as the gun violence of American culture demonstrates on an increasingly regular basis, for the anxious individual does not know whom to strike out against. All he knows is that someone is to blame and someone must pay.

CATCH-22

In *The Book: Or, on the Taboo against Knowing Who You Are*, Alan Watts suggests that the adult invents the "other" through a process of invisible, chronic emotional obfuscation experienced early and often by the child. Though falling far short of traditional definitions of child abuse, the process of indoctrination is effective because of its chronic and horizonless quality in the child's experience. Watts writes that the child's experience of the adult world is chronically confusing, for it is a state of affairs

> known technically as the "double-bind." A person is put in a double-bind by a command or request which contains a concealed contradiction. "Stop being self-conscious!" "Try to relax". . . . Society, as we now have it, pulls this trick on every child from earliest infancy. In the first place, the child is taught that he is responsible, that he is a free agent, an independent origin of thoughts and actions—a sort of miniature First Cause. He accepts this make-believe for the very reason that it is not true. He can't help accepting it, just as he can't help accepting membership in the community where he was born. He has no way of resisting this kind of social indoctrination. It is constantly reinforced with reward and punishments. It is built into the basic structure of the language he is learning. . . . we befuddle them hopelessly because we—as adults—were once so befuddled, and, remaining so, do not understand the game we are playing. (p. 56)

Adolf Hitler understood this game and played it out with the German people, for the story of Nazi Germany is the story of befuddling relationships in which the psychopathic character dominates, drowning out or shouting down the voice of an intuitive self that suffers along with the victims of the psychopath. The psychopathic voice of Hitler corresponded perfectly with the psychopathic voice of the adult bent on practicing the black pedagogy on the child. Without Hitler, the latent rage of the German people may have lain dormant, and perhaps have exorcised itself without wholesale slaughter of "the other." The fascistic child-rearing traditions of the black pedagogy become of central concern here, for Hitler could *not* have risen in an adult culture that espoused and practiced compassion, tolerance, and understanding toward the child, toward the "other."

The "exceptional" Hitler who spontaneously produces himself and thrusts himself on an unsuspecting German people is popular among many scholars, for it expunges the possibility of societal complicity. From this perspective Hitler is "off the charts" of human evil and cannot be understood.

Though this may in part be accurate, the argument fails to consider the vast numbers of accomplices, for it is not simply Hitler's "evil" that is "off the charts." Rather, Hitler's relationship to the German people—like the moon's reflection in the water—represents a spontaneous reciprocal event that could not happen without the proper cultural and ideological conditions. Nazi Germany is an expression of individual, cultural, and ideological conditions coming to fruition. Nazi Germany as fruit of the "black pedagogy" of nineteenth- and twentieth-century child-rearing tradition in Germany suggests that the relationship between the adult-conceiver and the child-creation is one of subject and object, of oppressor and victim, a commentary on the sociological origins of "self" and "other," suggesting that our tendency towards sociological and cultural bifurcation is not only the relationship between white and black, male and female, Nazi and Jew, or cat and mouse, but rather, the history of the child in Western culture is a history marked by what can only be described as a genocidal, predatory relationship.

Nazi Germany remains the most obvious example of how child-rearing and ideology and the reproduction of the dominant culture come together. Miller quotes Rudolf Höss, commandant at Auschwitz and member of the Death's Head faction of Himmler's SS, as writing, "It was constantly impressed upon me in forceful terms that I must obey promptly the wishes and commands of my parents, teachers, and priests, and indeed of all grown-up people, including servants, and that nothing must distract me from this duty. Whatever they said was always right. These basic principles by which I was brought up became second nature to me" (p. xx). She notes that most Germans, like Höss, "were trained to be obedient so successfully and at such an early age that the training never lost its effectiveness; the structure never displayed any fissures . . . nor did feelings of any kind ever jar it. To the end of their lives, these people carried out the orders they were given without ever questioning the content" (p. 65). When on trial at Nuremberg after the war, Hitler's foreign minister, von Ribbentrop, exemplified the power of the relationship Hitler had with his subordinates. Von Ribbentrop confessed that had Hitler walked through the door of the Nuremberg court room, he would have unquestioningly obeyed any order of the Führer, regardless of the consequences.[5]

Hitler's fascism unsettles in part because of his ability to harness latent, unconscious energy and draw it out and intensify it through a process of ideological refraction, including media propaganda, mass rallies, terror, and, of course, the indoctrination of the young through the "Hitler Youth" programs that targeted boys and girls from the age of ten. Hitler understood that when the dominant culture invents the child, the dominant culture invents itself. Education—Nazi content and Nazi pedagogy that delivered that content— became a key component of Hitler's goal to produce and reproduce the Third Reich and make it last for "a thousand years." Miller quotes Hitler as writing,

My pedagogy is hard. What is weak must be hammered away. In my fortresses of the Teutonic Order a young generation will grow up before which the world will tremble. I want the young to be violent, domineering, undismayed, cruel. The young must be all these things. They must be able to bear pain. There must be nothing weak or gentle about them. The free, splendid beast of prey must once again flash from their eyes. I want my young people strong and beautiful. That way I can create something new. (p. 142)

When Hitler came to power he appointed Bernard Rust as the Minister of Education in Prussia, a man who ultimately gained control over all education in Germany. "It is less important that a professor make discoveries," Rust wrote, "than that he train assistants and students in the proper views of the world."[6] As one historian notes, however, it was not only the mob that acquiesced to Nazism. Professor Ernst Krieck, a newly appointed rector of the University of Frankfurt, asserted during his investiture that German universities could never have struggled from what he considered their cultural and intellectual paralysis without what Krieck called a "folk renascence." Krieck stated that "the chief characteristic of this renascence is the replacement of the humanistic ideal by the national and political. Nowadays the task of the universities is not to cultivate objective science but soldier-like militant science, and their foremost task is to form the will and character of their students."[7] Krieck's celebratory acceptance of Nazi ideology was *common* among the masses as well as among the intellectuals. In fact, the failure of the intelligentsia to resist Hitler stunned Albert Einstein. His close colleagues watched him leave the country as a disenfranchised Jew, his theories of special and general relativity denied by Nazi Germany thirty years after they rocked the scientific world because the discoveries came from a Jew and were, therefore, nonsense and lies. Many of Einstein's colleagues accepted Hitler's government and agreed to "cooperate joyously in the reconstruction of the new national state." "In general," Einstein wrote, "the lack of courage on the part of the educated class in Germany [was] catastrophic."[8]

The shift from the humanistic ideal to the national and political was not as great as Krieck and others believed it to be. Nazism represented not a shift, but rather, an intensification of already existing ideologies of power, domination, and subjugation. Hitler's Nazism represented a moment in which the dominant ideology of European civilization intensified from the invisible and unconscious *background* to the cultural and material *foreground*. Cultural propaganda, education, and terror that encouraged an entire nation to celebrate power and its use to dominate, subjugate, or exterminate so-called inferior cultures and inferior races, all of which struck a familiar chord in Germany, in Europe, and in America, for Western ideology had been advocating Hitler's brand of cultural subjugation based on specious racist doctrines for hundreds of years, including even *the passive and active practice of geno-cide* if it served the dominant culture.

For Aimé Césaire, Hitler came as no surprise. Hitler was nothing more and nothing less than an example of a barbarous civilization turned against itself and seeing itself for the first time. In *Discourse on Colonialism*, he writes, "Whether one likes it or not, at the end of the blind alley that is Europe . . . there is Hitler. At the end of capitalism, which is eager to outlive its day, there is Hitler. At the end of formal humanism and philosophic renunciation, there is Hitler" (p. 15). Moreover, Césaire observes that Hitler's brand of fascism, racism, and violence had been long anticipated by the "humanists" of Europe and the ideology and pedagogy of European colonialization. According to French "humanism," a racist ideology that lurks in the pages of Jean de Brunhoff's *Story of Babar*, "the regeneration of the inferior or degenerate races by the superior races is part of the providential order of things for humanity" (Ernest Renan quoted by Césaire, p. 16). European colonialism asserts its right to dominate others so that significant natural resources would not "live forever idle in the hands of incompetents" (M. Albert Sarrant quoted by Césaire, p. 17). It is only a short step from European ideologies of colonialism to the Nazi death-slogan, "*arbeit macht frei.*"

Yet for many historians and scholars, explaining Hitler and Nazism as a psychodrama and as a product of the dominant culture is an "obscenity."[9] To place Hitler on a continuum of cultural and historical events diminishes his crimes and suggests that he is hardly different from other dictators and despots, when it seems clear how different he is. As difficult as it is to acknowledge, Hitler's dominance of the German people—and almost total extermination of the European Jewish population—could not have been possible except through the chronic and willful inattention and inaction of other nations, including France, England, Switzerland, Italy, the Soviet Union, and the United States.[10]

Hitler was above all else a product of German child-rearing traditions, traditions made popular by the black pedagogy of the Grimms' fairy tales, of Dr. Schreber's child-rearing manuals, of German Protestantism, of Victorian colonialist ideologies, of rampant anti-Semitism, and of a brutal father who used violence and humiliation as a way of "beating the impudence out of his son," *in exactly the way the child-rearing manuals of the day indicated the father should.*[11] Hitler's Nazi Party intensified, recycled, and returned his version of the dominant cultural mind—as familiar and familial as it was—to the German people, and, ultimately, the vast majority of the population acquiesced to Hitler's Nazism *without realizing what they were acquiescing to,* for they had been reared as children to accept and respect authority, *especially when they were afraid of it.* It bears repeating the power and the appeal of Hitler as an "*über*-father," for this is what Hitler was to his subordinates and to the majority of the German people. As imperfect and painful as the child's experience was under the black pedagogy, Hitler was a living embodiment of the "rightness" of this cultural tradition. The ordinary soldier and the ordinary citizen recognized in Hitler a version of their own unconscious needs for an idealized "super father" come to life. Hitler offered the ordinary German a way to idealize and defend the abusive, violent childhood so common in Germany and elsewhere. At the same time Hitler offered the German people a place to project unconscious murderous rage left over from their subjugation to the adult hegemony. Germans had been betrayed, Hitler agreed, but not by themselves, or by their parents, or by their leaders, but rather, by the shadowy "other" among them, the Jews. Hitler's seduction of his German "children"—and the consequences for the Jews of Europe—was an event (at least) two thousand years in the making.[12]

AN ONGOING TRADITION

The nature of the adult's relationship to the child from the Germany of the Brothers Grimm, to the Victorian period of England and America, to the post-Freud era of the twentieth century has changed only inasmuch as the existing ideological and cultural pedagogies of child-rearing have implicitly and explicitly encouraged an intensification of the use of the child as a site of cultural and ideological production and reproduction. The child has always been a resource for adult culture. The last four hundred years have witnessed an intensification of the emotional exploitation of the child, all "for the child's own good." The Germans did not invent the "black pedagogy," rather, they refined the child-rearing practice and codified it. Shakespeare's mind and culture, as it presents itself in *Hamlet,* reveals what appears to be a distinctly "modern" relationship between adult and child, suggesting that the psychodynamic preconditions for the fascistic state existed long before the emergence of socioeconomic conditions associated with the rise of modern conceptions of childhood. At the same time, however, contemporary revisions of *Hamlet* for children, especially Disney's *The Lion King,* manifest the degree to which adult culture has intensified the production and reproduction of adult culture through the invention of the child-as-masochistic servant to the adult, psychopath-leader.

Consider once again how Disney film circulates this story. In 1994 Disney released what would become its most economically successful animated movie, *The Lion King.* Like the Grimms' fairy tales, the movie represents a conscious and unconscious site of ideological production, but not for the reasons that motivated the Brothers Grimm. Rather, Disney's fairy tale, *The Lion King,* is a product of and about cultural and ideological hegemony and cultural homogenization for the sake of economic power. Consider the relationship of the adult to the child in *The Lion King,* and the depiction of the world in which the adult and child live and move; it suggests that the reactionary political environment that dominated the relationship between Hamlet and Claudius—and which Shakespeare depicted as a corrupt cultural condition—has, in the hands of Disney, become a cultural ideal not to be challenged, but rather, to be celebrated, emulated, and disseminated to a mass market.

The Lion King's popularity speaks directly to the character structures that dominate the consumer market that comprises its audience. It is a story of a father, a son, a deceitful uncle, and of passive females who cannot do for themselves without the mystical power of the "leader" to focus and guide them. It is a story of racism and the desperate necessity to keep the cultural hierarchy stable in its proper order, for in the pride lands of *The Lion King,* the social and cultural order is not, in fact, cultural or social, and the dominance of one species over another is biologically ordained.

The monarchy—Disney's favorite political model—must be maintained, for as in *Hamlet* or *Julius Caesar,* when the rightful leader is ousted, the entire order of things is destabilized. The rain will not fall. There will be no food to eat. The dead walk the streets. This state of affairs is terrifying, to say the least, especially when jack-booted hyenas, complete with "black" and "Hispanic" gangland voices, threaten to invade your neighborhood. Only the father—the rightful leader—can make things right, yet he is dead. In *Hamlet,* the demands of the dead father are a burden that Young Hamlet must overthrow when he accepts his role not as king, or even prince, but of moral human. *The Lion King* pays lip service to the mortality of all living things as Mufasa explains the "circle of life" to his son, but this is superficial compared to the ideological production and reproduction the film engages in.

Like the "circle of life" philosophy, the jack-booted hyenas are a kind of distraction from the dominant concerns of *The Lion King.* Uncle Scar is depicted as fascist leader in his one song-and-dance number, complete with inferno-like flames and jack-booted hyenas marching under his watchful eye. This scene serves as an overdetermined indication of how the adults and children should view Uncle Scar: he's the bad guy who adults and children can unquestionably rally *against.* And to rally against the totalitarian schemes of Scar is, by default, to rally behind Mufasa, the dead father.

Simba has fled to the cool and sumptuous forest where he cavorts in relationships that are endearing and subtly coded as "unnatural," for the lion lies down with the lamb, and this is *not* how Mufasa's kingdom works. Every day that Simba does not participate in the endless cycle of predator and prey, he fails his father, and he fails the natural order of things as it has been presented to him by his father. For his father returns from the dead to remind him of, well, of Mufasa and of their relationship. "Remember who you are," Mufasa intones from the clouds, echoing Old Hamlet's words to Young Hamlet, "remember me." By the end of Shakespeare's play, Old Hamlet's words are, in effect, a kind of curse on Young Hamlet. In *The Lion King,* Mufasa's words are nothing short of Simba's salvation. To forget the father, according to Disney, is to bring on the death of culture, the death of ideology, depicted by the death of the pride lands. Nothing could be worse. In spite of this reactionary position, Disney artists depict Simba's second home in the jungle world as idyllic, easy, and with "no worries" except for the latent guilt Simba brings with him. But this, along with timely reminders about Simba's duty— brought by his one-time girlfriend, Nala—is enough to drive Simba from his unnatural state in the jungle back to the pride lands. The rightful order of things is restored when Simba obeys his father and drives the usurper, Scar, from his throne and takes his rightful place as the leader. The rains come. The music swells. The rightful king is on his throne. All is right with the world.

"But pure spectacle," Matt Roth writes, "does not suffice to get the message across to Disney's satisfaction. Mufasa, the king, spends half the movie impressing on his son, Simba, the duties and indispensability of the king, on whom the *entire natural order* seems to rest: in bland eco-speak, he explains that the king maintains "the delicate balance of nature." The king's significance extends both to the natural order of the pride lands as well as the "natural" order of the relationships within the pride lands. "The lionesses, witnessing the devastation all about them, are strangely passive"—even though they do all of the hunting and are collectively strong enough to defeat Scar and his hyenas. "Instead, they abandon all hope until they rediscover Simba, the rightful heir, whom they had thought dead. By this time, Simba is utterly useless by any [military] standard, having spent his youth doing nothing but dancing around eating bugs. But no matter: he functions as the Leader—and without a Leader, even groups who possess *all of the apparent power* are in reality helpless."[13]

In Scar's destruction and Simba's resurrection, the rightful order of things is restored, and all under the father's watchful eye, for Mufasa-the-father watches from heaven, the home of dead monarchs; Disney's heaven, like Mufasa's pride lands, is organized as a monarchy, complete with a Father-as-Leader who rewards those who defend and reproduce the status quo. That Scar is no fascist is clear. He is indolent, lazy, and, in his own way ends the class system of Mufasa's kingdom and creates an uneasy culture that mixes hyenas and lions. The devastation and disorder that this brings can only mean one thing, however, for when the hyenas—the blacks and Hispanics— are returned to their dark ghetto beyond the pride lands (where the sun does not shine) all is made right again. The culture war is over and the fires are quenched by the heavens.

Simba as a latter-day Mufasa represents the authoritarian leader who champions the conservative sexist and racist hierarchies that made his father's kingdom great, and from the restoration of this "natural" order, the pride lands become once again green and "stuffed with prey." The ostensible threat of the hyenas and of Uncle Scar make Simba's—and Mufasa's—return to the throne appear to be necessary, inevitable, and emotionally desirable. Like fascistic propaganda, *The Lion King* appeals to the audience in much the same way that Hitler appealed to his audience: propaganda harnesses the language of the dominant culture and speaks it fluently. Propaganda draws on ideology that is always imbedded within the dominant culture so as to make the ideological appeal invisible, innocent, obvious, and *emotionally satisfying,* but only temporarily, as all successful propaganda is transient. In its successful appeal to unconscious need, propaganda embraces its own failure, thereby assuring the individual's need for more stimulation in order to sustain the delusional reality the propaganda depicts. In short, the best propaganda is addictive.

Consider *The Lion King* not simply as fascistic propaganda—though it employs familiar fascistic themes—but as emotional propaganda that appeals to the unconscious needs of the victim, and so drives consumer markets as a result of the narrative's failure to meet the unconscious needs it stirs up while supplying the audience with immediate substitutes for these needs in the form of merchandise. Disney exploits the ongoing need of its audience through state-of-the art merchandizing programs which, like all advertising, promise to deliver *The Lion King* all over again, but this time as a stuffed toy, a necktie, a lunch box, a coloring book, bubble bath, or, in the perfect marriage between consumer need and ideological reproduction, a merchandizing alliance between the Disney Company and the McDonald's Corporation. Still hungry for more after watching *The Lion King*? Go to McDonald's. It's more—or less—than food there. It's a carnival, it's a theme park, it's a lunch, and it's a way to try and recapture the emotional incompleteness revealed by the experience of watching the latest Disney animated feature. All the while the alliance between Disney and McDonald's, and the consumer's participation in that alliance, represents a primary economic force in the production and reproduction of the dominant culture's ideology of consumerism, all innocently packaged as lunch and a movie. That Disney movies so often reproduce fascistic or colonialist themes, and that a McDonald's lunch requires a bedroom-sized chunk of Amazonian rain forest to produce it, is simply not an issue for a culture bent on ignoring—yet at the same time, unconsciously feeding—its emotional needs.

Late-twentieth-century consumer culture, like fascism, exploits the emotional needs of the child by offering a seeming plethora of culturally sanctioned substitutes for the child's basic physical and emotional needs while at the same time suggesting to the child that happiness and satisfaction lie in the acceptance of adult culture and adult ideology. This is the ideology born of the "black pedagogy" made new. In fascist culture, the seeming plethora of culturally sanctioned substitutes boils down to one: obedience to the general will as it manifests itself through the "super father." In consumer culture, ide-

ologically and culturally sanctioned substitutes for the biological needs of the
child and young adult promise satisfaction if the child obeys his or her need to
consume. Unlike overt fascism, consumer culture fragments the voice of culture so that it seems to come from every quarter, and so, the voice of the dominant culture's ubiquitous presence implicitly represents its obvious and
inevitable reality.

CONSCIOUSNESS

The adult's conscious desire to dismiss childhood as a time of innocence and
insubstantiality when attempting to understand adult life is an enactment of
the dominant ideology, and therefore a significant ideological moment in the
production and reproduction of the dominant culture. In forgetting the significance of their childhood personally, adults fail to recognize the relationship
between their own child-rearing experiences, their own body, and the political and ideological environment of the dominant culture, and thereby unconsciously become a willing participant in the dominant culture without willing
it at all.[14] The contents of human consciousness, then, are always already ideological. Ideology *feels* real because the ideologically determined conscious
mind, paradoxically, cannot feel itself as it lives in the body, but rather, can
only think itself thinking. In other words, the conscious mind remains fused
to its idea of itself by the energy of repressed, unconscious affect. Letting go
of affect stored since childhood is what Freud indirectly understood to be an
abreaction. More directly, D. T. Suzuki, the Japanese Zen master, calls this a
whole-body experience that precedes awakening, or an opening. Gestalt psy-
chotherapy names the experience the "death layer."[15] By any name, however,
letting go of one's self and the emotional energy that gives rise to one's
attachment to self is a central part of the process by which one can let go of
one's ideologically determined conflict with the "other." This process has
been called the work of mystics, of gurus, and of students of Zen. The child
understands this process intuitively. Ideology inflicted through adult pedagogy interrupts the child's intuitive understanding.

Consciousness when filled is always already filled with relative cultural
material that is passed on to children by adults in their child-rearing years, not
as relative cultural material, but rather, as information essential for life and
being. The child needs contact, emotional attachment, and understanding,
and what he receives are lessons in obedience and the cultural history that
stands as "proof" of the necessity for the child's lessons to be learned. In that
consciousness is neither true nor false, but functions as a container for the
cultural material—or ideology—circulating at a given time, consciousness
makes no distinction between the relative meaning of liberal humanism,

fascism, representative democracy, or bourgeois wealth and leisure. That consciousness works best when it does not identify itself with any fixed mode of thought has been argued by Western existentialists like Kierkegaard and Sartre as well as students of Zen, Catholic mysticism, Hindu yoga, and Gestalt approaches to human awareness. Consciousness filled is always a burdened, self-conscious, fragmented, intellectualized, anxiety-ridden mind, and this mind is the mind of the dominant culture of the West, and of Nazi Germany as well. The empty consciousness is the spontaneous consciousness, acting spontaneously not according to plan, but according to the compassionate heart that is always already available when not bound by iron bands of ideological indoctrination and emotional repression. This "no-mind," as Zen Buddhism calls it, is not an "empty mind" so much as a mind always available, not stuck on any one thing, but rather, like a tool, it moves freely to the point at which it sets itself to work. Consciousness is a tool of the heart, of the intuition, and of the body. When severed from a relationship with the intuitive and affective information the body provides, consciousness can only consider itself and so become self-conscious and remain caught up in its own split while obsessively trying to master itself. Video games, for example, are a prime example of the mind externalizing its war with itself while the body grows ever more numb to the violence that surrounds it. The body that can no longer feel is subjugated to the rationalizations of the self-conscious mind. The tragedy that took place at Columbine High School remains the signal example of the degree to which murderous violence is justified by the self-conscious mind as a legitimate—if perverted and indirect—expression of one's rage at having been neglected, dominated, and forgotten as a child. Ideology offers the enraged young adult a culturally sanctioned hierarchy of human relations among children and between children and adults, maintained by power, and compounded and intensified by the dominance of adult culture that, to preserve itself, "forbids" the young adult's rage, or ignores it, all the while offering contradictory stories of all kinds that celebrate the effectiveness and beauty of murderous violence.

The mind structured by the dominant ideology is not a mind of "false consciousness," for there is no "true consciousness" to which one might compare the contents of the conscious mind. The contents of the conscious mind are neither true nor false, but rather, consciousness functions as a container, and it can hold anything. When it holds particularly violent ideologies it does so because: (1) the dominant culture holds them as well, (2) the child learns what he lives in his relationships with the adult, and (3) an ideology of power and violence offers an explanation for the unconscious, pent-up affect that informs the body while at the same time offering an ostensible outlet and solution. That the ostensible outlet and solution frequently result in death and destruction should come as no surprise because enactments of violence and destruction reproduce the dominant ideology of the dominant culture that the child has grown up with in his lived relationship with the adult, and in his ideologically informed education. From all quarters, in other words, the child is made to understand that genocide means peace. How can a child learn anything but the beauty and utility of violence in a culture so determined to wield violence as a creative expression of love?

Consciousness in its most effective form lies in its potential, like a cup valued for the empty space it delimits and the potential the emptiness represents. A cup always filled no longer serves its purpose, for its purpose is to contain different things when called upon to do so. When the contents of consciousness become more significant than the container itself—or when acquisitiveness becomes more important than emptiness—fascism lurks close by, for the individual convinced of his own rectitude when dominating others, acts with conviction precisely because he has seen the contents of his conscious mind as "right" and "true" and "necessary" for life and being. Marking the relative difference between compassion and murder comes from somewhere other than the conscious mind; it comes from the body's intuitive center, and it is the intuitive, emotional center from which the child learns early and often to dismiss and to disassociate. The intuition of the body, when working in concert with the relative emptiness of the conscious mind, serves as a powerful conduit for action and compassion. Western child-rearing pedagogies sever the body from the conscious mind and so initiate a series of splits and fragmentations that leaves the adult anxious, insecure, and under the impression that life must be waged as a war of the will.

CONCLUSIONS

Violence and suffering represent a form of feedback that provides indicators as to the relative health and well-being of a community. When the entire community of life—and not simply the human community—is considered as one large feedback system, the story of Western culture has grown increasingly clearer in spite of the dominant culture's implicit promises of progress-through-destruction. The destruction of rain forest habitat, the loss of ozone, the effects of global warming, the increasingly rapid destruction of animal species, the poisoning of the oceans, and the mountains of radioactive waste and other industrial pollution, represent only a handful of the myriad consequences of a dominant culture whose desire to dominate the planet has left an environmental legacy that future generations will, no doubt, recognize as criminal. Moreover, the human community continues to suffer as well, as the dominant culture exports an ideology of rapacious greed called a "standard of living" by Western nations.

Multinational consumer capitalism represents an intensification and reiteration of Victorian colonialism. Late-twentieth-century militarism championed by the dominant culture and its arsenals of terror, including stockpiles of nuclear, chemical, and biological weapons of mass destruction, is justified by the dominant ideology in precisely the same way that Hitler defended his war of annihilation: self-preservation against a perceived Bolshevik threat. Moreover, the logic of the dominant ideology equates the threat of extermination with the preservation of peace, and from this, children are implicitly and explicitly taught, comes the world's security. One might just as easily suggest that Western culture enjoys its dominance not because it is more civilized but rather, because it practices a reign of implicit terror, made silent, invisible, but no less deadly through the intensification of technological production. And children are taught every day to accept—and to embody—the dominant ideology that justifies the threat of *genocidal violence* as a legitimate way to "keep the peace."

Though experts forecast a leveling off of the human population in the Western world, population is expected to double yet again sometime in the twenty-first century, all because of rising populations in India, Brazil, China, Indonesia, and other so-called developing nations.[16] As staggering as the problem of rising population is, there is an equally if not more pressing population threat: Western consumption. According to conservative estimates, an American consumes approximately thirty times more in energy in all of its manifold forms than an individual from a developing nation. Even so, the dominant culture has been selling the notion of American-style prosperity—which means American-style consumption—as the way to continued prosperity at home and security abroad.

There is a double-bind embedded here in the logic of population control and consumption that needs to be unknotted and foregrounded. With an American population fast approaching three hundred million, and with a world population somewhere just over six billion, simple multiplication makes the problem clear. If three hundred million Americans consume thirty times as much as the individual in a developing nation, then three hundred million American consumers amount to a population that has the environmental effect of *nine billion people*. Population growth oversimplifies the problem facing the global habitat. *Consumption*—and the reproduction of an ideology of consumption—exacerbates problems associated with population growth exponentially, for if two billion individuals in developing nations demanded the right to consume global resources as Americans consume them, what then? Exporting the so-called American Dream abroad is not the way to peace and security, but rather, to international tension, habitat destruction, and ongoing famine in developing nations—and it amounts to latter-day economic colonialism of the most insidious kind. For instance, India's and

Pakistan's appetite for nuclear weapons strongly suggests that any "right" a nation claims for itself will be, as always, justified by its "might," which in the nuclear era has been routinely equated with the ability to lay waste to entire cities with one bomb.

To promote and reproduce American consumption habits abroad while encouraging the intensification of consumption at home is nothing short of alarming. And it all comes back to child-rearing. Because child-rearing traditions of Western culture remain firmly entrenched in an ideology of domination and subjugation, the child becomes firmly attached to an idea of his or her developing self as a "me" always in sharp contrast to an "other." The "other" for the child is, of course, defined by relations of power. Who has it, who does not, and who can one exercise it against. Detachment and unconscious emotional neglect in late-twentieth-century child-rearing pedagogies exacerbate the consequences of relations of power, for in a culture that celebrates violence and consumption, the child learns early and often that to reclaim lost power, to secure an insecure identity, the use of power in all of its manifold forms is not only necessary but sexy, glossy, and a real sign of "maturity." Even so, the child raised in such a way will inevitably become an adult blind to his or her unconscious emotional needs, firmly attached to the idea of "selfhood" ideologically determined by the dominant culture, and as a result the individual will seek substitutes that reproduce the ongoing imaginary relationship the individual has to the body—and to the actual conditions of existence. The dominant culture raises children according to institutional values that have become so obviously real that they are seldom questioned: obedience, passivity, hierarchy, competition, and the domination of the child by the adult institution—all, ostensibly, for the child's own good—leave the child vulnerable to the dominant culture's ideology of power and consumption as it circulates in narratives of all kinds, and especially in lived relations. The child is vulnerable to beguiling ideologies because the child in emotional need can do nothing but cling to—and later perhaps violently reject—the dominant culture's institutions. Either way, adult culture confirms itself, and the status quo is reproduced, for the obedient child proves the benefits of adult hegemony even as the violent, disobedient child proves the need for adult hegemony all the more clearly. For the adult culture dedicated to the domination of the child, there will always be ample evidence to justify relations of power. Ideology makes the misuse of power necessary, inevitable, obvious. According to adult culture, in other words, violence engenders the need for more violence, and this guarantees security. Security, however, cannot be guaranteed. The need for secure security only assures the need for more relations of power, domination, and control. Life is essentially insecure. Peace, on the other hand is another matter. There can be peace in accepting the insecure nature of life. Unfortunately, peace has little chance in a culture that routinely and ritualistically interprets its relations of power and violence as signs of its civilizing progress.

NOTES

[1]Ron Rosenbaum, *Explaining Hitler: The Search for the Origins of His Evil* (New York: HarperPerennial, 1998), p. xiii.

[2]Ibid., p. xvi.

[3]There continues to be a heated debate about the degree to which ordinary civilians participated in genocide, as well as the causes. See Scott Abbot, ed., *The German Army and Genocide: Crimes against War Prisoners, Jews, and Other Civilians in the East, 1939–1945*, trans. Omor Bartov (Hamburg: Hamburg Institute, 1999). Also see Christopher R. Browning, *Ordinary Men: Reserve Police Battalion 101 and the Final Solution in Poland* (New York: HarperPerennial, 1993). The most debated study about the level of civilian participation in German genocide is Daniel Jonah Goldhagen, *Hitler's Willing Executioners: Ordinary Germans and the Holocaust* (New York: Knopf, 1996). Goldhagen posits that widespread and chronic anti-Semitism came to fruition during Nazi Germany, which prompted so many to join Hitler's cause, perhaps not consciously but unconsciously, as an expression of their own personal rage and sense of powerlessness. Norman G. Finkelstein and Ruth Bettina Birn take on Goldhagen in their essays from *A Nation on Trial: The Goldhagen Thesis and Historical Truth* (New York: Henry Holt, 1998). They argue that Goldhagen exaggerates or misinterprets evidence in order to make his sweeping attack against German civilians. Goldhagen answers these charges in the preface to the German edition of his book.

[4]See the German psychoanalytic literature about the fascistic personality. Also see Theodor Adorno, *The Authoritarian Personality* (New York: Norton, 1969), p. 120.

[5]For a fascinating exploration of the mind of a technocrat–cum-mass murderer, see Rudolf Höss, *Death Dealer: The Memoirs of the SS Kommandant at Auschwitz*, trans. Andrew Pollinger (Buffalo, N.Y.: Prometheus Books, 1992).

[6]Quoted in Ronald W. Clark, *Einstein: The Life and Times* (New York: Avon, 1984), p. 571.

[7]Quoted in ibid., p. 572.

[8]Ibid.

[9]See Rosenbaum's first chapter in *Explaining Hitler.*

[10]See Eli Weisel, *All Rivers Run to the Sea: Memoirs* (New York: Knopf, 1995). He recounts his discussions with world leaders in which he asks them directly about their inaction during the darkest years of the "final solution," from 1939 to 1945. Why did the Americans not bomb the tracks running in and out of Auschwitz—and any other of the three hundred concentration camps run by the Nazis? This would have definitely saved lives—thousands, perhaps a great deal more. Weisel documents persuasively that Allied leaders understood in principle Hitler's "final solution" for the Jews, yet any attempt to deal with it even indirectly was inexpedient to the wartime effort.

Another recent study demonstrates persuasively that killing squads were frequently made up of German volunteers who were *civilians,* laying to rest the notion that only Hitler's elite SS made up the killing squads that hunted Jews in Europe.

[11]These are Hitler's own recollections of his father's abuse (Helm Stierlin, *Adolf Hitler: Familien Perspektiven* [Frankfurt: Suhrkamp, 1978]). Still, Hitler's sister confirms his story. In *Adolf Hitler: A Family Perspective,* Paula Hitler says, "It was my brother Adolf who especially provoked my father to extreme harshness and who got his due measure of beatings every day. He was rather a nasty little fellow, and all his father's attempts to beat the impudence out of him and make him choose the career of a civil servant were in vain." Others, like Franz Jetzinger in his book *Hitler's Youth* (London: Hutchinson, 1958) dispute the story of beatings, though only indirectly and without conviction, for Jetzinger sees Hitler as an "exceptional" figure of demonic proportions and cannot implicate Hitler's father or German child-rearing culture.

[12]Explanations that attempt to explain why Hitler chose the Jews as his primary target include the long-held suspicion that Hitler had Jewish blood in his family, and that perhaps Hitler was one-quarter Jewish on his father's side. Or, perhaps a Jew had cheated Hitler's family; or, perhaps a Jew had seduced a family member; or, perhaps a Jew had given Hitler syphilis as a young man. In all cases, as Rosenbaum argues in *Explaining Hitler,* there is an implicit attempt in the explainers of Hitler to unintentionally recycle the anti-Semitism they seek to understand in that the explanations of Hitler consistently appeal to theories that lay the blame, however light, on the Jewish people for some action that may have instigated Hitler's rage. That the Jews were responsible for Hitler's anti-Semitism is a tragic missing of the point. Anti-Semitism was common in Hitler's Europe—and still is.

[13]Matt Roth, *"The Lion King:* A Short History of Disney Fascism," *Jump Cut* 40 (1994): 18.

[14]This is what I take Alice Miller to mean when, in *The Drama of the Gifted Child: The Search for the True Self,* trans. Ruth Ward (New York: HarperCollins, 1997), she writes that "we are all prisoners of our childhood" (p. 25).

[15]In *Zen and Japanese Culture* (Princeton, N.J.: Princeton University Press, 1973), D. T. Suzuki characterizes what I am describing here as an experience in which the whole body, not just the mind, works out a problem. The end result is a release, a "kufu" that precedes or accompanies satori. It is a supercharged emotional release made significant precisely to the extent the individual has been holding against it.

[16]Malthussian projections of a world gone haywire as a result of overpopulation, once thought to be overstated, now seem to be coming true. World population is expected to hit twelve billion in the first quarter of the twenty-first century and shows no signs of stopping, at least while the food holds out. See Nicholas Eberstadt, *The Tyranny of Numbers: Mismeasurement and Misrule* (Washington, D.C.: American Enterprise Institute Press, 1995) as one recent analysis of global population expectations. He argues that in the twenty-first century, "developed" nations will continue to experience population stabilization while "undeveloped" nations will continue to grow until they *vastly* outnumber American and European populations. Hitler had a name for "peace and prosperity." He called it *lebensraum*—living space for German people. On the basis of this ideal, he proceeded to invade the Soviet Union and slaughter Jews in the process.

Bibliography

Adorno, Theodor. *The Authoritarian Personality*. New York: Norton, 1969.

――――. *Negative Dialectics*. Translated by E. B. Ashton. New York: Seabury Press, 1973.

Althusser, Louis. *Lenin and Philosophy and Other Essays*. New York: Monthly Review Press, 1971.

Aries, Philippe. *Centuries of Childhood: A Social History of Family Life*. New York: Random House, 1962.

Axtell, James L. *The Educational Writings of John Locke*. Cambridge: Cambridge University Press, 1968.

Bammer, Angelika. "Mother Tongues and Other Strangers." In *Displacements: Cultural Identities in Question*, edited by Angelika Bammer, 90–109. Bloomington: Indiana University Press, 1994.

Barker, Ernest. *Social Contract: Essays by Locke, Hume and Rousseau*. Oxford: Oxford University Press, 1960.

Baudrillard, Jean. *Simulations*. Translated by Paul Foss, Paul Patton, and Philip Beitchman. New York: Semiotext(e), 1983.

Bercovitch, Sacvan, and Myra Jehlen, eds. *Ideology and Classic American Literature*. Cambridge: Cambridge University Press, 1986.

Berger, John. *Ways of Seeing*. New York: Penguin, 1977.

Boswell, John. *The Kindness of Strangers: The Abandonment of Children in Western Europe from Late Antiquity to the Renaissance*. New York: Pantheon, 1988.

Bowlby, John. *The Making and Breaking of Affectional Bonds*. London: Routledge, 1979.

Bradshaw, John. *Creating Love: The Next Great Stage of Growth*. New York: Bantam, 1992.

Bronner, Simon J. *Following Tradition: Folklore in the Discourse of American Culture*. Logan: Utah State University Press, 1998.

Browning, Christopher R. *Ordinary Men: Reserve Police Battalion 101 and the Final Solution in Poland*. New York: HarperPerennial, 1993.

Brunhoff, Jean de. *Babar the King*. New York: Random House, 1935.

———. *The Story of Babar.* New York: Random House, 1933.

———. *The Travels of Babar.* New York: Random House, 1934.

Calvert, Karin. Children in the House: *The Material Culture of Early Childhood, 1600–1900.* Boston: Northeastern University Press, 1992.

Carpenter, Humphrey. *Secret Gardens: A Study of the Golden Age of Children's Literature.* Boston: Houghton Mifflin, 1985.

Carroll, Lewis. *Alice in Wonderland.* Norton Critical Edition. Edited by Donald J. Gray. New York: W. W. Norton, 1998.

Cech, John. *Angels and Wild Things: The Archetypal Poetics of Maurice Sendak.* University Park: Pennsylvania State University Press, 1995.

Césaire, Aimé. *Discourse on Colonialism.* Translated by Joan Pinkham. New York: Monthly Review Press, 1972.

Clark, Ronald W. *Einstein: The Life and Times.* New York: Avon, 1984.

———. *Freud: The Man and the Cause.* London: Jonathan Cape and Weidenfeld & Nicolson, 1980.

Cunningham, Hugh. *Children and Childhood in Western Society Since 1500.* New York: Longman, 1995.

DeMause, Lloyd, ed. *The History of Childhood.* Northvale, N.J.: Jason Aronson, 1995.

Demers, Patricia, and Gordon Moyles, eds. *From Instruction to Delight: An Anthology of Children's Literature to 1850.* New York: Oxford University Press, 1982.

Dewees, William. *A Practice of Physic.* Philadelphia: Carey & Lea, 1830.

Doonan, Jane. "Into the Dangerous World: *We Are All in the Dumps with Jack and Guy.*" *Signal* 75 (1994): 155–71.

Driver, Jamie. "Conversations with Maurice Sendak." *Opera America Newsline* 7 (1998): 15–24.

Dundes, Alan. *Little Red Riding Hood: A Casebook.* Madison: University of Wisconsin Press, 1989.

Eagleton, Terry. *Criticism and Ideology: A Study in Marxist Literary Theory.* New York: Schocken, 1978.

———. *Ideology: An Introduction.* London: New Left Books, 1991.

Earle, Alice Morse. *Child Life in Colonial Days.* Stockbridge, Mass.: Berkshire House, 1993.

Eliot, Marc. *Walt Disney: Hollywood's Dark Prince.* New York: Birch Lane Press, 1993.

Ellis, John M. *One Fairy Story Too Many: The Brothers Grimm and Their Tales.* Chicago: University of Chicago Press, 1983.

Fanon, Frantz. *The Wretched of the Earth.* Translated by Constance Farrington. New York: Grove Weidenfeld, 1963.

Finkelstein, Norman G., and Ruth Betinna Birn. *A Nation on Trial: The Goldhagen Thesis and Historical Truth.* New York: Henry Holt, 1998.

Freire, Paulo. *The Pedagogy of the Oppressed.* New York: Continuum, 1995.

Freud, Sigmund. *The Complete Letters of Sigmund Freud to Wilhelm Fliess: 1887–1904.* Translated and edited by Jeffrey Moussaieff Masson. Cambridge, Mass.: Harvard University Press, 1985.

Fromm, Erich. *The Crisis of Psycho-Analysis: Essays on Freud, Marx, and Social Psychology.* New York: Holt, 1991.

Geertz, Clifford. "Ideology as a Cultural System." In *Interpretations of Cultures: Selected Essays*, 193–223. New York: Basic, 1973.

Giroux, Henry A. *The Mouse that Roared: Disney and the End of Innocence*. Lanham, Md.: Rowman & Littlefield, 1999.

Goldhagen, Daniel Jonah. *Hitler's Willing Executioners: Ordinary Germans and the Holocaust*. New York: Knopf, 1996.

Gordon, Joan. "Surviving the Survivor: Art Spiegleman's *Maus*." *Journal of the Fantastic in the Arts* 5, no. 2 (1993): 81–89.

Grahame, Kenneth. *The Wind in the Willows*. New York: Macmillan, 1950.

Gramsci, Antonio. *Selections from the Prison Notebooks*. Translated by Quentin Hoare and Geoffrey N. Smith. New York: International Publishers, 1972.

Greenblatt, Stephen. *Renaissance Self-Fashioning*. Chicago: University of Chicago Press, 1980.

Griswold, Jerry. *Audacious Kids: Coming of Age in America's Classic Children's Books*. New York: Oxford University Press, 1992.

Haase, Donald, ed. *The Reception of Grimms' Fairy Tales: Responses, Reactions, Revisions*. Detroit: Wayne State University Press, 1993.

Heilbroner, Robert L. *The Worldly Philosophers: The Lives and Times and Ideas of the Great Economic Thinkers*. New York: Simon & Schuster, 1980.

Herorard, Jean. *Journal sur l'enfance et la jeunesse de Louis XIII*. Edited by Eud. Soulié and E. de Barthélemy. Paris: 1868.

Hildebrand, Ann Meinzen. *Jean and Laurent de Brunhoff: The Legacy of Babar*. New York: Twayne, 1991.

Hirsch, Marianne. "Family Pictures: *Maus*, Mourning, and Post-Memory." *Discourse: Journal for Theoretical Studies in Media and Culture* 15, no. 2 (1992–93): 3–29.

Hollan, Norman N. *Psychoanalysis and Shakespeare*. New York: McGraw-Hill, 1964.

Hoole, Charles. *A New Discovery of the Old Art of Teaching School*. Menston: Scolar Press, 1960.

Horkheimer, Max, and Theodor W. Adorno. *Dialect of Enlightenment*. Translated by John Cumming. New York: Herder, 1972.

Hutt, Marucie, ed. *Napoleon*. Englewood Cliffs, N.J.: Prentice-Hall, 1972.

Iadonisi, Rick. "Bleeding History and Owning His (Father's) Story: *Maus* and Collaborative Autobiography." *CEA Critic* 57, no. 1 (1994): 23–39.

Jameson, Fredric. *The Political Unconscious: Narrative as a Socially Symbolic Act*. Ithaca, N.Y.: Cornell University Press, 1981.

Johnson, Stephen. *Humanizing the Narcissistic Style*. New York: W. W. Norton, 1987.

Kamenetsky, Christa. *The Brothers Grimm and Their Critics: Folktales and the Quest for Meaning*. Athens: Ohio University Press, 1992.

Kaplan, Louise J. *No Voice Is Wholly Ever Lost: An Exploration of the Everlasting Attachment between Parent and Child*. New York: Simon & Schuster, 1995.

———. *Oneness and Separateness: From Infant to Individual*. New York: Simon & Schuster, 1978.

Kincaid, James R. *Child-Loving: The Erotic Child and Victorian Culture*. New York: Routledge, 1992.

Kohl, Herbert. *Should We Burn Babar? Essays on Children's Literature and the Power of Stories*. New York: New Press, 1995.

Lanes, Selma. *The Art of Maurice Sendak*. New York: Harry N. Abrams, 1980.

Liedloff, Jean. *The Continuum Concept: In Search of Happiness Lost.* Reading: Perseus Books, 1977.

Locke, John. *Some Thoughts Concerning Education.* Oxford: Clarendon Press, 1693.

Lowen, Alexander. *Bioenergetics.* New York: Coward, McCann and Geogehan, 1975.

———. *Depression and the Body.* New York: Coward, McCann and Geogehan, 1971.

———. *Fear of Life.* New York: Macmillan, 1980.

———. *The Language of the Body.* New York: Collier, 1958.

MacDonald, Ruth K. *Beatrix Potter.* Boston: Twayne, 1986.

Mannheim, Karl. *Ideology and Utopia: An Introduction to the Sociology of Knowledge.* Translated by Louis Wirth and Edward Shils. New York: Harcourt Brace, 1936.

Markham, Felix. *Napoleon.* New York: Signet, 1963.

Marton, Jay. *The Dialetical Imagination: A History of the Frankfurt School and the Institute of Social Research.* Boston: Little, Brown, 1973.

Masson, Jeffrey. M. *Assault on the Truth: Freud's Suppression of the Seduction Theory.* New York: Farrar, Straus & Giroux, 1984.

Mauro, Jason. "Disney's Splash Mountain: Death Anxiety, the Tar Baby and Rituals of Violence." *Children's Literature Association Quarterly* 22 (1997): 113–17.

Meltzer, Milton. "A Common Humanity." *Teaching and Learning Literature* 5 (spring 1996): 67–72.

Miller, Alice. *The Drama of the Gifted Child: The Search for the True Self.* Translated by Ruth Ward. New York: HarperCollins, 1997.

———. *For Your Own Good: Hidden Cruelty in Child-rearing and the Roots of Violence.* Translated by Hildegarde and Hunter Hannum. New York: Farrar, Straus & Giroux, 1983.

———. *Thou Shalt Not Be Aware: Society's Betrayal of the Child.* Translated by Hildegarde and Hunter Hannum. New York: Meridian, 1984.

Miller, Susan, and Greg Rode. "The Movie You See, The Movie You Don't: How Disney Do's That Old Time Derision." In *From Mouse to Mermaid: The Politics of Film, Gender, and Culture,* edited by Elizabeth Bell, Lynda Haas, and Laura Sells. Bloomington: Indiana University Press, 1995.

Mitchell, Stephen. *Relational Concepts in Psychoanalysis: An Integration.* Cambridge, Mass.: Harvard University Press, 1988.

Mulcaster, Richard. *The Training Up of Children.* London: Da Capo Press, 1581.

Murray, Gail S. *American Children's Literature and the Construction of Childhood.* New York: Simon & Schuster Macmillan, 1998.

Neumeyer, Peter. *"We Are All in the Dumps with Jack and Guy: Two Nursery Rhymes with Pictures by Maurice Sendak."* In *Celebrating Children's Literature in Education,* edited by Geoff Fox, 139–50. New York: Teachers College Press, 1995.

Nodelman, Perry. *The Pleasures of Children's Literature.* White Plains, N.Y.: Longmann, 1996.

Opie, Iona, and Peter Opie. *The Classic Fairy Tales.* New York and Toronto: Oxford University Press, 1980.

Perls, Frederick S. *Gestalt Therapy Verbatim.* New York: Bantam, 1971.

Pecora, Norma Odom. *The Business of Children's Entertainment.* New York: Guilford Press, 1998.

Peppard, Murray B. *Paths Through the Forest: A Biography of the Brothers Grimm.* New York: Holt, Rinehart and Winston, 1971.

Pollock, Linda A. *Forgotten Children: Parent-Child Relations from 1500–1900.* Cambridge: Cambridge University Press, 1983.

Pool, James. *Hitler and His Secret Partners: Contributions, Loot and Rewards, 1933–1945.* New York: Pocket, 1999.

Postman, Neil. *The Disappearance of Childhood.* New York: Delacorte Press, 1982.

Potter, Beatrix. *The Tale of Peter Rabbit.* London: Frederick Warne, 1992.

Quinn, Daniel. *Ishmael: An Adventure of Mind and Spirit.* New York: Bantam, 1992.

Rosenbaum, Ron. *Explaining Hitler: The Search for the Origins of His Evil.* New York: HarperPerennial, 1998.

Roth, Matt. "*The Lion King:* A Short History of Disney Fascism." *Jump Cut 40* (1994): 15–20.

Rothberg, Michael. "We Were Talking Jewish": Art Spiegelman's *Maus* as "Holocaust" Production. *Contemporary Literature* 35 (1994): 661–87.

Rowse, A. L. *Shakespeare the Man.* New York: Harper & Row, 1973.

Said, Edward W. *Culture and Imperialism.* New York: Knopf, 1993.

———. *Orientalism.* New York: Random House, 1978.

Schapiro, Barbara. *Literature and the Relational Self.* New York: New York University Press, 1994.

Schickel, Richard. *The Disney Version: The Life, Times, Art and Commerce of Walt Disney.* New York: Simon & Schuster, 1968.

Schlereth, Thomas J. *Victorian America: Transformations in Everyday Life, 1876–1915.* New York: HarperPerennial, 1991.

Schoenbaum, S. *William Shakespeare: A Compact Documentary Life.* New York: Oxford University Press, 1977.

Sells, Laura. "Where Do the Mermaids Stand? Voice and Body in *The Little Mermaid.*" In *From Mouse to Mermaid: The Politics of Film, Gender, and Culture,* edited by Elibabeth Bell, Lynda Haas, and Laura Sells. Bloomington: Indiana University Press, 1995.

Sendak, Maurice. *In the Night Kitchen.* New York: HarperCollins, 1970.

———. "Maurice Sendak Talks About *We Are All in the Dumps with Jack and Guy.*" Promotional Literature for *We Are All in the Dumps.* New York: HarperCollins, 1993.

———. *Outside Overthere.* New York: HarperCollins, 1981.

———. Phone interview with author, January and February 1997.

———. "Preface." In *I Dream of Peace: Images of Way by Children of the Former Yugoslavia.* New York: HarperCollins, 1994.

———. *We Are All in the Dumps with Jack and Guy.* New York: HarperCollins, 1993.

———. *Where the Wild Things Are.* New York: HarperCollins, 1963.

Sergeant, Philip W. B. A. *The Burlesque Napoleon: Being the Story of the Life and the Kingship of Jerome Napoleon Bonaparte, Youngest Brother of Napoleon the Great.* London: T. Werner Laurie Clifford's Inn, 1905.

Shaddock, Jennifer. "*Where the Wild Things Are:* Sendak's Journey into the Heart of Darkness." *Children's Literature Association Quarterly* 22 (1997–98): 155–59.

Shakespeare, William. *The Tragedy of Hamlet.* The Arden Edition of the Works of William Shakespeare. Edited by Harold Jenkins. London: Methuen, 1982.

Shorter, Edward. *The Making of the Modern Family.* New York: Basic Books, 1975.

Sipes, Lawerence, R. "The Private and Public Worlds of *We Are All in the Dumps With Jack and Guy. Children's Literature in Education* 27 (1996): 87–108.

Sommervill, C. John. *The Rise and Fall of Childhood.* New York: Random House, 1990.

Spiegelman, Art. "In the Dumps with Maurice Sendak," the *New Yorker,* 27 September 1993, pp. 80–81.

———. *Maus: A Survivor's Tale.* Vol. 1. New York: Pantheon Books, 1986.

———. *Maus: A Survivor's Tale.* Vol. 2. New York: Pantheon Books, 1991.

Spitz, Ellen Handler. *Inside Picture Books.* New Haven, Conn.: Yale University Press, 1999.

Stamp, Kenneth M. *The Peculiar Institution: Slavery in the Ante-Bellum South.* New York: Random House, 1956.

Staub, Michael E. "The Shoah Goes on and On: Remembrance and Representaton in Art Spiegelman's *Maus. MELUS* 20, no. 3 (1995): 32–46.

Sutton, Nina. *Bettelheim: A Life and a Legacy.* Translated by David Sharp and Nina Sutton. Boulder, Colo: Westview Press, 1977.

Suzuki, D. T. *Zen and Japanese Culture.* Princeton, N.J.: Princeton University Press, 1973.

———. *Zen Buddhism: Selected Writings.* Edited by William Barrett. New York: Doubleday, 1996.

Tatar, Maria, ed. *The Classic Fairy Tales: A Norton Critical Edition.* New York: W. W. Norton, 1999.

Taylor, Judy. *Beatrix Potter: Artist, Storyteller and Countrywoman.* New York: Viking Penguin, 1986.

Turner, Graeme. *Film as Social Practice.* New York: Routledge, 1993.

Tzu, Lao. *Tao te Ching.* Translated by John C. H. Wu. Boston: Shambhala, 1989.

Wallace, Richard. *The Agony of Lewis Carroll.* Melrose: Gemini Press, 1990.

Watts, Alan. *The Book: Or, On the Taboo against Knowing Who You Are.* New York: Random House, 1972.

———. *The Way of Zen.* New York: Random House, 1989.

Watts, Steven. *The Magic Kingdom: Walt Disney and the American Way of Life.* New York: Houghton Mifflin, 1997.

Wiener, Martin J. *English Culture and the Decline of the Industrial Spirit: 1850–1980.* Cambridge: Cambridge University Press, 1981.

Williams, Raymond. *Culture and Society: 1780–1950.* New York: Penguin, 1963.

———. *Marxism and Literature.* New York: Oxford University Press, 1977.

Willis, Susan, and Kuenz, Jane. *Inside the Mouse: Work and Play at Disney World.* The Project on Disney. Durham, N.C.: Duke University Press, 1995.

Zaretsky, Eli. *Capitalism, the Family, and Personal Life.* New York: HarperColophon, 1976.

Zinn, Howard. *A People's History of the United States.* New York: HarperPerennial, 1980.

Zipes, Jack. *The Brothers Grimm: From Enchanted Forests to the Modern World.* New York: Routledge, 1988.

————. *The Trials and Tribulations of Little Red Riding Hood: Versions of the Tale in Sociocultural Context.* South Hadley, Mass.: Begin & Garvey, 1983.

————. *When Dreams Came True.* New York: Routledge, 1999.

Zornado, Joseph. "Free Play: Christian Hierarchies, the Child and a Negative Way." *Christianity and Literature* 47 (1998): 133–66.

————. "Swaddling the Child in Children's Literature." *Children's Literature Association Quarterly* 22 (1997): 105–12.

Index

Abbot, Jacob, 102
Adorno, Theodor, xv, 77, 181–182
Alexander I, 71
Alice's Adventures in Wonderland
  (Lewis Carroll), 4, 104, 107–118
Althusser, Louis, xvii, 4, 8, 140
A Model of Christian Charity (John
  Winthrop), 14–17
Andersen, Hans Christian, 159, 162
Aries, Phillippe, 12, 30n–32n, 90–91
A Treatise of Melancholly, (Timothy
  Bright), 50–51, 68n–69n
attachment of anxiety, 187–188. *See
  also* attachment theory
attachment theory, 11–12, 186–188. *See
  also* attachment anxiety, black
  pedagogy,
  Calvinism, child-rearing, detachment
  parenting, poisonous pedagogy,
  slavery, swaddling
Auschwitz, 173, 208
Authoritarian Personality, The, 77

Babbitt, Arthur, 146, 153
Bambi (Walt Disney), 145
Barney and Friends, 4, 192–196
Bettleheim, Bruno, 84–85
black pedagogy, 65, 77–96, 103, 205.
  See also attachment theory, attach-
  ment anxiety,

Calvinism, child-rearing, detachment
  parenting, poisonous pedagogy,
  slavery, swaddling
Bonaparte, Jerome, 72–73, 80–81, 97n
Bonaparte, Napoleon. *See* Napoleon
Book, The (Alan Watts), 207
Bowlby, John, 186. *See also* attachment
  theory
Bradford, William, 2
Brothers Grimm, 4, 71–97, 211. *See
  also* Jacob Grimm, Wilhelm
  Grimm

Calvin, John 15
Calvinism as child-rearing pedagogy,
  14–23. *See also* child-rearing
*Capitalism, The Family, and Personal
  Life* (Eli Zaretsky), 179
Carroll, Lewis, 104, 109, 118. *See also*
  Charles Dodgson
Cech, John, 189
Celebration, Florida, 169n
Césaire, Aimé 96–97, 210
character structure, 11–13, 29n–30n
*Child-loving: The Erotic Child and
  Victorian Culture* (James Kincaid),
  40–41
child-rearing, xviii, 5–9, 106, 205. *See
  also* attachment theory, attachment
  anxiety, black

child-rearing *(continued)*
  pedagogy, Calvinism, detachment
  parenting, poisonous pedagogy,
  slavery, swaddling
Children and Household Tales (Broth-
  ers Grimm), 65, 73–74, 83, 89, 96
Children and Their Education (John
  Robinson), 20
Clement VII, 46
Columbine High School, xiii–xviii
consciousness, 61–62, 215–217
Continuum Concept, The (Jean
  Liedloff), 5
Copernicus, 15
Critical Theory, 179
Culture and Imperialism (Edward
  Said), 102
Curious George (H. R. Rey) 127–129

Day of Doom, The (Michael
  Wigglesworth), 5, 17–20, 27
DeBrunhoff, Jean, 126, 133n, 210
Delarue, Paul 99n
DeMause, Lloyd, 13, 30n–32n, 90
detachment parenting, 5–9, 29,
      182–183, 186–187. *See also Bar-
      ney and Friends,*
  child-rearing
Discourse on Colonialism (Aimé
  Césaire), 210

Eberstadt, Nicholas, 221n
Einstein, Albert, 28, 209
Eisener, Michael, 158–159
Eliot Marc, 146, 166n, 168n
Elizabeth I, 44–45, 49
Ellis, John 85–87, 98n
Emerson, Ralph Waldo, 23
Explaining Hitler (Ron Rosenbaum),
  201–203

Fitzhugh, George, 25
Ford, Henry, 148
*Forgotten Children: Parent-Child
  Relations from 1500–1900* (Linda
  Pollock), 31n

For Your Own Good (Alice Miller), 77,
  105–106, 198n, 202, 205
Foucault, Michel, 101, 117
Frankfort School, The 179–180,
  197n–198n
Franklin, Benjamin, 2
Frederick III, 71
Freire, Paulo, 144, 201
Freud, Anna, 39
Freud, Jacob, 35–38
Freud, Sigmund, 27–28, 33–41, 53,
      63–66, 86, 181, 186, 215
Fromm, Erich, 179–180

Genesis, 5–6
Grahame, Kenneth, 118–121, 126
Greenblatt, Stephen, 44
Grimm, Jacob, 80–83, 96
Grimm, Philip, 79–81
Grimm, Wilhelm, 80, 96

Hamlet, (Shakespeare), xv, 211–212
  as family psychodrama, 41–64,
"Hansel and Gretal" (Brothers Grimm),
  86–89
Hansel and Gretal (Maurice Sendak),
  175
Harmand, Jules, 101–102
Henry VIII, 45–46
Herorard, Jean, 53
Hitler Adolf, 72, 96–97, 201–202,
      207–208, 214, 218
Holocaust, 8, 171, 173–174, 196
Horkheimer, Max, xv, 77

ideological transposition, 138–140,
  145
infant mortality, 13
Interpretation of Dreams, The (Sigmund Freud), 36–37, 67n
In the Night Kitchen (Maurice Sendak),
  166, 189
Iwerks, Ub, 153

Julius Caesar (William Shakespeare),
  212

Kaplan, Louise, 11, 139, 166n
Keats, John, 55
Kincaid, James 40–41, 66n, 108, 117–118
Krieck, Ernst, 209

Liedloff, Jean, 5
Lion King, The (Walt Disney), xv, 158, 163, 211–214
"Little Mermaid, The" (Hans Christian Andersen), 162
Little Mermaid, The (Walt Disney) 159, 161–165
"Little Red Cap." See "Little Red Riding Hood"
"Little Red Riding Hood," 90–96, 99n–100n
Locke, John, 23, 28, 32n
Louis XIII, 53–55
Lowen, Alexander, 29n–30n
Luther, Martin, 15

Making and Breaking of Affectional Bonds, The (John Bowlby), 186
Making of the Modern Family, The (Edward Shorter), 47, 180
Maus (Art Spiegelman), 171–173, 190–191
McDonald's 157, 214
Mein Kampf (Adolf Hitler), 147, 203
Miller, Alice. xix, 13, 66n–67n, 77, 89–90

Napoleon, 71–75, 97n
Neumeyer, Peter, 197n
New England Primer, The, 14–17, 27. *See also* Calvinism
Newton, Issac, 15
New Yorker, The, 172

Oedipal theory, 28, 36–39, 53, 64
Oedipus the King (Sophocles), 37, 41, 67n–68n
"On the Aetiology of Hysteria" (Sigmund Freud), 33–41

One Fairy Tale Too Many (John Ellis), 85–86
Oneness and Separateness (Louise Kaplan), 11
Outside Overthere (Maurice Sendak), 166, 185, 189–190

Peculiar Institution, The (Kenneth Stamp), 23–26
Pedagogy of the Oppressed, The (Paulo Freire), 144, 201
Perrault, Charles, 91–92, 99n–100n
Pierre (Herman Melville), 172
Pinocchio (Walt Disney), 4, 145–150, 1152
poisonous pedagogy, 20 *See also* attachment anxiety, childrearing, detachment parenting, poisonous pedagogy, slavery, swaddling as defined by Alice Miller, 198n–199n.
Pollack, Linda, 31n–32n

Quinn, Daniel, 5

Ramsey, Jon Benet, 93
relational model of the developing self, 42–44
Robinson, John, 20
Rosenbaum, Ron, 148, 201–202
Rousseau, Jacques, 23, 28, 180

Said, Edward, 97n, 102
Schapiro, Barbara, 41–42
Schickel, Richard, 151
Schreber, Dr., 65, 78
seduction theory, 33–41
self-psychology. *See* rational model of the developing self
Sendak, Maurice, 4, 166, 171–192
Shakespeare, John, 46, 51–52
Shakespeare, Mary, 46–52
Shakespeare, William, 41–64
Shorter, Edward, 47, 180–181
slavery, 23–27. *See also* childrearing

Song of the South, The (Walt Disney),
    159–162
Spiegelman, Art, 171–172, 190–192
Splash Mountain, 159–161
Stamp, Kenneth, 23
Story of Babar, The (Jean DeBrunhoff),
    126–131, 210
Suzuki, D. T. , 215, 221n
swaddling, 13, 47–49. *See also* child-
    rearing

Thomas, Bob, 166n
Thoreau, Henry David, 9
Thou Shall Not Be Aware (Alice
    Miller), 6
transposition, 139

Uses of Enchantment, The (Bruno
    Bettelheim), 84–85

Victory through Air Power (Walt Dis-
    ney), 151–152

Wallace Richard, 105, 110–111
Watts, Alan, 207
*We Are All in the Dumps with Jack and
    Guy* (Maurice Sendak), 166,
    171–192
Weisel, Eli, 220n
wet-nursing, 13, 48. *See also* child-
    rearing
Where the Wild Things Are (Maurice
    Sendak), 166, 174, 184–189
Wigglesworth, Michael, 14–20
Wilhelm IX, 72-73
Wind in the Willows, The (Kenneth
    Grahame), 118–126
Winthrop, John, 2, 14–15, 26
Wordsworth, William, 23
World's Columbian Exposition, 135–138

Zaretsky, Eli, 179–180
Zen, 215
Zen Buddhism, 216
Zipes, Jack, 73-76, 90–91